"The massive post-evangelical community around the world includes many millions who remain open to a path of following Jesus that is morally credible and intellectually honest. Keith Mascord offers a path forward that is both. One does not have to agree with all of his proposals—I do not—to deeply appreciate the contribution he makes here towards a post-evangelical Christian future."

—DAVID P. GUSHEE
Vice president, American Academy of Religion

"We understand life through images—art, music, poetry, mythology, film, architecture, photography, the touch of another's presence. Each offers a pathway into the transcendent. Keith's challenging book explores biblical stories and the biblical storyline through such imagery. Nothing there is static, past tense, finished or formal. Bible stories are less history, more images of our human endurance and possibility. *An Honest Faith* presses the reader to discover this beyond the limitations imposed by dogma and definition."

—BILL LAWTON
Historian, researcher, and former colleague

"This book is a highly readable attempt to reconcile two basically different ways to resolve moral dilemmas in our lives. The first, like the philosophers of ancient Athens, invokes human rationality, knowledge, and experience. The second, like all the religions derived from Jerusalem, relies on religious instruction expressed in the 'revealed' Word of God. For decades, the author, an Anglican priest, has struggled with this dilemma, searching for ways to reconcile the two systems. Billions of human beings find pure human reasoning unsatisfying. They search for the peace and love that spirituality, which passes all understanding, can bring. On the other hand, close encounters with God and His worldly ministers can sometimes appear so unscientific and irrational that we keep searching for different ways of reasoning. The author instances religious cruelty and irrationality on subjects like race, indigeneity, gender, sexuality, and politics which cast doubt on religion's legitimacy. Census returns in many Western societies show a large and growing drift away from organized religion. The resulting controversy is tackled with honesty, humility, persistence, and courage. Many readers will recognize their own feelings in the author's ultimately stated conclusions."

—MICHAEL KIRBY, AC CMG
Australia

"Finding honest faith means deconstructing Church, illuminating the cowardice of those who have sufficient scholarship to know what is true, yet teach publicly based on perceived institutional interests. Keith Mascord's forthright recovery of Christianity from the midst of his own church authorities' evacuation of its meaning includes an ally's welcome glimpse at how LGBTQ+ witness to faith is a key element challenging self-righteous omertà. Honest faith, unafraid of learning, is a rich journey of discovery."
—JAMES ALISON
Catholic priest, theologian, and author

"Thoughtful faith is often hard to hear in the din of culture wars today. This book makes a vital contribution to another way forward, sharing light rather than adding heat. Grounded in considered reflection, and bearing the fruits of walking with others whose faith, gifts, and insights are often ignored, it encourages us all to a more generous hospitality and a renewing pursuit of truth."
—JOSEPHINE INKPIN
Theologian and minister

"*An Honest Faith* takes the reader on a personal journey into some of the most important, challenging, and controversial issues for contemporary believers. Mascord offers a clear, cogent and inviting reflection on the plausibility of Christian faith in today's world. Whether it is faith and reason, scripture and ethics, uncertainty and doubt, or contested moral issues; all are tackled with humility, honesty and joy. A must read for the inquiring pilgrim unafraid to ask the hard questions."
—STEPHEN PICKARD
Adjunct professor, Charles Sturt University, Australia

An Honest Faith

An Honest Faith

The Possible Friendship of Athens & Jerusalem

KEITH MASCORD

Foreword by Scott Cowdell

WIPF & STOCK · Eugene, Oregon

AN HONEST FAITH
The possible friendship of Athens & Jerusalem

Copyright © 2025 Keith Mascord. All rights reserved. Except for brief quotations in critical publications or reviews, no part of this book may be reproduced in any manner without prior written permission from the publisher. Write: Permissions, Wipf and Stock Publishers, 199 W. 8th Ave., Suite 3, Eugene, OR 97401.

Wipf & Stock
An Imprint of Wipf and Stock Publishers
199 W. 8th Ave., Suite 3
Eugene, OR 97401

www.wipfandstock.com

PAPERBACK ISBN: 979-8-3852-3537-7
HARDCOVER ISBN: 979-8-3852-3538-4
EBOOK ISBN: 979-8-3852-3539-1

VERSION NUMBER 050725

Scripture quotations are from the New Revised Standard Version Bible: Anglicized Edition, copyright © 1989, 1995 National Council of the Churches of Christ in the United States of America. Used by permission. All rights reserved.

The author gratefully acknowledges permission to reprint the following:

Noel Davis, "I Am Willing. Lead Thou Me On." and "Satisfying Our Deepest Longing," in *The Joy of Living: Our Heart's Knowing and Imagining* (Narooma, Aus.: Lifeflow Education, 2022); "Playing at the Edge," in *Together at the Edge—Trust Me* (Narooma, Aus.: Lifeflow Education, 2011); "Sacred Time," in *The Heart Waking and Breaking into Dance* (Narooma, Aus.: Lifeflow Education, 2007)

Brandon Flanery, "Initial Reason for Leaving" and "What's Gained with New Framework," graphs, 2022

William J. Gaither and Gloria Gaither, "Because He Lives," copyright © 1971 Hanna Street Music (BMI) (adm. at CapitolCMGPublishing.com). All rights reserved. Used by permission.

Les Murray, "Poetry and Religion," in *Collected Poems* (N.p.: Black, 2019)
John O'Donohue, "For a New Beginning," "For Light," and "For the Interim Time," in *To Bless the Space Between Us: A Book of Blessing* (New York: Convergent, 2008)

This book is dedicated to Judy, my wife, best friend,
most valued friendly critic and fellow faith journey traveller.

Contents

Foreword Scott Cowdell | ix
Acknowledgments | xi

HONEST ATHENS

Chapter 1
Athens and/or Jerusalem | 3

Chapter 2
Inquisitive Faith | 15

Chapter 3
Humble Faith | 34

Chapter 4
Persistent Faith | 48

Chapter 5
Courageous Faith | 61

REFORMING JERUSALEM

Chapter 6
Imaginative Faith | 77

Chapter 7
Loving Faith | 102

Chapter 8
Liberating Faith | 128

Chapter 9
Hopeful Faith | 148

Chapter 10
Being a Dual Citizen of Athens and Jerusalem | 171

Coda | 193

Bibliography | 195
Index | 203

Foreword

THIS IS A BOOK that has come out of an evangelical context and now speaks back into it. It is written as an invitation to rethink or reimagine Christian faith. Its author has been helping, clarifying, encouraging, and giving permission for this across a series of books. *An Honest Faith*, which sets out to broaden, deepen, and inclusivize evangelical Christianity, will be a breath of fresh air to many.

Keith Mascord offers a different sort of deliverance ministry—not freeing those afflicted by the world, the flesh, and the devil, but those suffering under certain distortions of Christian faith. These include an oppressive biblicism with a narrow and loveless hermeneutic; a rationalistic approach to believing that is suspicious of imagination; a fear of the feminine that fuels opposition to women's ordination; and an obsession with same-sex orientation and gender fluidity, which for many represent the sum of all fears.

The way out of this intellectually and spiritually damaging form of Christian belief involves learning to read the Bible with more generous eyes, but also with some critical acumen. We are introduced to enough insights from modern critical biblical studies to appreciate that taking it entirely literally is not necessarily to read Scripture faithfully. We are also shown how to approach key doctrines so that they sound less like law and more like gospel.

Any suggestion that this is a faithless undertaking is dispelled by the biographical passages that help illuminate Keith Mascord's argument. As well as ideas that will challenge many, we are let into the personal struggles of the author and some of his friends whose palpable faith, perseverance, and devotion will inspire others. I am reassured to see that although Keith Mascord has suffered for his honesty at the hands of evangelical authorities in his own former church, he remains open and generous minded without descending into unattractive contrarianism.

The case he makes is that Scripture and belief should embrace reason and welcome philosophical critique. Indeed, there is a sense here that worldly wisdom, along with faithful imagination, will play a key role in redeeming evangelical belief and practice. The general direction here is away from Evangelicalism towards a more liberal Protestantism, and away from a more authoritarian theism to a more holistic conception of the divine (pan*en*theism, not pantheism), also offering a less doctrinally regulated encounter with Jesus and his teaching.

Keith Mascord admits that his philosophical training and preferences do not include the alternative thought world of continental philosophy, and hence he misses out on a lot that is valuable in more recent Catholic theology and practice. Though within the liberal Protestant world, and deeply rooted in recent continental thought, there is a book on the church by American philosopher John D. Caputo that covers similar ground in a different philosophical register. Indeed, I read Caputo's *What Would Jesus Deconstruct?* just before reading *An Honest Faith*, and found a lot in common. Caputo calls his a radical postmodern faith, though Mascord might fit better under the banner of so-called post-Evangelicalism. He describes the first half of his book as an exercise in deconstruction.

In any event, Keith Mascord is on the side of the angels, offering a way back to Christian faith and confidence for troubled, perhaps disenchanted Evangelicals by opening a philosophical window onto a larger, more welcoming world. While some will find themselves well outside their comfort zone with this book, I am confident that such stepping out is precisely what mature faith requires of us.

Scott Cowdell
Research Professor in Theology, Charles Sturt University, Canberra, Australia;
author of *René Girard and the Nonviolent God*
and *Why Church? Christianity as It Was Meant to Be*

Acknowledgments

I am indebted to a host of people for the encouragement, inspiration, and suggestions that have helped to bring this book to birth. Like me, it is a work in progress, a snapshot of where I currently am in my lifelong journey of faith.

As I have done previously, and will do again in this book, I gratefully acknowledge the profound and lasting contribution of my now-deceased father and mother, Douglas and Audrey Mascord. It was they who provided early inspiration and encouragement to walk my own journey of thought and faith. They then tag-teamed beautifully with my wife Judy and later with my sons and their partners as they have provided further encouragement and helpful challenge.

I've been blessed over the years with many friends and fellow travellers, too many to mention. Among these are some who read and provided valuable feedback to earlier drafts of *An Honest Faith*, including Sarah Bachelard, John Barrett, Vic Branson, Steff Fenton, Geoff Kearns, Bill Lawton, Steph Lentz, Giselle Mawer, Graeme Sanders, and Margaret Wesley. I am also indebted to Natalie and Jay Quince, Helen Holliday, and Nathan Killick, who, along with Judy and me, brainstormed our way through an early draft of *An Honest Faith*, generating many honest and helpful suggestions.

HONEST ATHENS

THE EARLY CHRISTIAN THEOLOGIAN Tertullian (c. 155–240 CE) is famous for his combative questions: "What has Athens to do with Jerusalem? What concord is there between the Academy and the Church? What between heretics and Christians?"[1] Tertullian believed there could be no concord, that philosophy, as an essentially human activity, corrupts and misleads faith. It is therefore dangerous and to be avoided. There are many today who agree with him. I do not. I will argue against Tertullian to the conclusion that concord between Athens and Jerusalem is not only possible but urgently needed.

In the first half of this book, the essential honesty of the philosophical enterprise, as exemplified by Socrates, will be set loose to raise serious questions and challenges to Christian faith. These can be considered an exercise in deconstruction.

The second half of the book suggests a way forward towards a careful reconstruction or reformation of the faith, and considers whether Athens and Jerusalem can and should be friends.

---

1. Tertullian, "*De praescriptione haereticorum* [On the proscription of heretics]," quoted in Bettenson and Maunder, *Documents of the Christian Church*, 6–7.

Chapter 1

Athens and/or Jerusalem

JUST BEFORE SUNSET ON our first visit to Athens, in early 2023, my wife Judy and I headed for the Acropolis. Like so many before us, we were in awe of the faded splendor of this ancient temple mount. Rather than climb it, which we did the following day, we circumnavigated it. We hadn't walked far before we were climbing the slippery marble slope of the Areopagus (or Mars Hill) from which the apostle Paul had tried to persuade the mostly skeptical philosophers of Athens that his gospel was for them. Centuries earlier, the equally famous Athenian philosopher, Socrates (c. 470–388 BCE), had faced his accusers at this exact spot prior to being found guilty by the city's citizens of denying the gods and leading the youth astray.

Being in Athens was special for me. Two of the great loves of my life, theology and philosophy, coincided there. From the vantage point of the Areopagus, we could not only view the Acropolis but could also catch a glimpse of the Agora (marketplace) where Paul had engaged in conversation and debate with passersby, as Socrates had done. When, on our second day in Athens, Judy and I walked through the ruins of the Agora, I couldn't help but think of these two great men who have been so influential in my life and in the life of the world—a theologian and a philosopher—walking these same now ancient streets.

Going to Athens was special in all sorts of ways. Not long before arriving there, I had begun research for this book, which is a sequel to *A Restless Faith* and *Faith Without Fear*. It had been eleven years since *A Restless Faith* was published and seven years since the publication of *Faith Without Fear*, and my thinking had progressed a little since then. As has always been the case, new or reconsidered knowledge and experience occasion further thinking.

It was therefore time to write again, this time about the relationship between these two great loves of mine. As with the previous two books, this one will be somewhat autobiographical.

The question to be considered in this book is: Is the thinking and practice of Socrates (or of Plato or Aristotle or any of the world's great philosophers) compatible with my Christian faith? Not everyone thinks they are or can be. As for me, this question has become increasingly important.

Early Interest in Philosophy and Theology

My knowledge and love of Christian theology reaches all the way back to early childhood when I was warmly and beautifully welcomed into the life of God and of Jesus. I grew to love both Jesus and Paul.

My knowledge and love of philosophy reaches back to my teenage years. When I was preparing to go to the University of New England, in Armidale, New South Wales, I shared with my parents my intention to study philosophy. I had decided that in philosophy I would find the best possible tool to test the veracity of the Christian faith I'd grown up with. If I was deluded in believing as I did, I'd give myself the best chance to discover this. Moreover, if, as I believed more likely, I was not deluded, but rather rational and fully justified in my strongly held Christian beliefs, I could then demonstrate this for the benefit of others.

My memory is that my parents weren't overly concerned. They did however gently forewarn me that the study of philosophy could end up undermining my faith—as it had others'—and that I'd need to be alert to that danger. As a keen young Christian, I definitely took this to heart.

There is a long tradition of suspicion towards philosophy, which arguably goes all the way back to Paul. The post-apostolic Christian theologian Tertullian argued that a fertile and highly dangerous source of Christian heresy was philosophy, which he dismissed as a product of foolish worldly thinking.

> For [philosophy] is the material of the world's wisdom, the rash interpreter of the nature and the dispensation of God. Indeed, heresies are themselves instigated by philosophy.[1]

---

1. Tertullian, "*De praescriptione haereticorum* [On the proscription of heretics]," quoted in Bettenson and Maunder, *Documents of the Christian Church*, 6.

Tertullian is dismissive, to the point of sarcasm, of the conjectures of the Greek philosophers, describing them as far fetched, embarrassing, unprofitable, and cancerous. Tertullian quotes Paul in support:

> From all these, when the apostle would restrain us, he expressly names philosophy as that which he would have us be on our guard against. Writing to the Colossians, he says, "See that no one beguile you through philosophy and vain deceit, after the tradition of men, and contrary to the wisdom of the Holy Ghost." [Paul] had been at Athens, and had in his interviews (with its philosophers) become acquainted with that human wisdom which pretends to know the truth, whilst it only corrupts it, and is itself divided into its own manifold heresies, by the variety of its mutually repugnant sects. What indeed has Athens to do with Jerusalem? What concord is there between the Academy and the Church? What between heretics and Christians? Our instruction comes from "the porch of Solomon," who had himself taught that "the Lord should be sought with simplicity of heart." . . . Away with all projects for a Stoic, a Platonic or a dialectic Christianity! After Christ Jesus we desire no subtle theories, no acute enquiries after the gospel?[2]

My parents could well have drawn my attention to Tertullian and to the voices of many others who, to the present day, have contended that Athens and Jerusalem, philosophy and Christian faith, are incompatible.

They could have directed me to the Protestant Reformer Martin Luther (1483–1546 CE), who variously described human reason as a "beast," an "enemy of God," a "source of mischief," and the "devil's whore." Luther didn't believe that reason was incompetent in temporal affairs such as building houses, making clothes, marrying, waging war, and navigating, but he saw human reason as totally misleading, blind, and dangerous in matters to do with the gospel and divine revelation.

Luther is famous for prioritizing Scripture in all matters of Christian faith (*sola scriptura*—Scripture alone), and for arguing that the meaning of Scripture is clear enough in its literal or most natural sense, which even the simplest of persons can rely upon. "A simple layman armed with the Scripture is to be believed above a pope or a council without it."[3]

---

2. Tertullian, "*De praescriptione haereticorum* [On the proscription of heretics]," quoted in Bettenson and Maunder, *Documents of the Christian Church*, 6–7.

3. Bainton, *Here I Stand*, 90.

There have been many since Luther who, like Tertullian, have sidelined human reasoning/philosophy, in favor of what they believe to be the plain sense of scriptural descriptions and prescriptions.

Again, my parents could well have said to me, "Son, just go with what the Bible says. That is all you will need." That wasn't their counsel. Looking back, and with the wisdom of hindsight, I am grateful to my parents, both for their cautious advice and for their apparent confidence that I would be able to meet whatever challenges philosophy might throw at me. As mentioned in *A Restless Faith*, one of my first projects on arrival at university was to read Bertrand Russell's essay "Why I Am Not a Christian." I was disappointed. My faith wasn't given even the slightest of knocks. I also felt somewhat vindicated in my choice to study philosophy. This slight encouragement to faith paved the way for further study and, in time, to teaching philosophy and Christian apologetics.

What I discovered along the way appeared to further vindicate my decision to embark on this form of study. I became aware that not every theologian or Christian thinker had so negative an evaluation of philosophy as Tertullian or Luther. Justin Martyr (c. 100–c. 165 CE), for example, who lived before Tertullian, had almost the opposite view. He described the Christian faith as the "only reliable and profitable philosophy" and, in fact, as the culmination of all true philosophies.[4] Replying to the fair accusation that God was neglectful of those who lived before Jesus, he countered by arguing,

> Christ is the first born of God, and as [shown earlier] the reason (Word) of whom the whole human race partake, and those who live according to reason are Christians, even though they are accounted atheists. Such were Socrates and Heraclitus among the Greeks, and those like them.[5]

(I rather like the reference to Socrates, whom we will hear more about in this book.) Justin goes on to claim,

> Whatever has been uttered aright by any men in any place belongs to us Christians, for next to God, we worship and love the reason (Word) which is from the unbegotten and ineffable God.[6]

---

4. See further Justin, *Dialogue with Trypho*.

5. Justin, *Apology* 1.46.1–4, quoted in Bettenson and Maunder, *Documents of the Christian Church*, 5.

6. Justin, *Apology* 2.13, quoted in Bettenson and Maunder, *Documents of the Christian Church*, 5–6. Origen (c. 185–254 CE) argued similarly that "whatever men have rightly said, no matter who or where, is the property of us Christians" (quoted in

Clement of Alexandria (150–c. 211 CE) understood philosophy to be a preparation for the gospel:

> Thus philosophy was necessary to the Greeks for righteousness, until the coming of the Lord. And now it assists towards true religion as a kind of preparatory training for those who arrive at the faith by way of demonstration. . . . For philosophy was a "schoolmaster" to bring the Greek mind to Christ, as the Law brought the Hebrews. Thus philosophy was a preparation, paving the way towards perfection in Christ.[7]

St. Augustine of Hippo (354–430 CE) drew heavily on Plato (c. 427–348 BCE) in forging his understanding of Christian faith, effectively disregarding the advice of Tertullian, as did Thomas Aquinas (c. 1225–74 CE), who favored the thinking of the other great Greek philosopher, Aristotle. The truth is that all Christian theologians and thinkers (including Tertullian and Luther) have inevitably been influenced by ancient and contemporaneous philosophical currents and ideas. It is unavoidable.

An understanding of philosophy, both the ideas and the methodology, is helpful for people of faith, particularly for those engaged in theological studies, as I seem to have been for all of my life. I had the privilege of teaching philosophy at Moore Theological College, the Anglican seminary in Sydney, from 1992 to 2006. It was considered an important part of the curriculum. Over the years, former students have been quick to comment about how helpful it was to learn about the history of philosophy and its impact upon theology, and of efforts by Christian philosophers to meet some of the big challenges to faith. Not a few former students described philosophy as their favorite, or among their favorite, subjects.

What I would often say to students, particularly those who were new to the subject, was that philosophy as an activity is simply a concerted attempt to think clearly about matters of great importance. As Christian philosopher (the late) Marilyn McCord Adams put it, "Philosophy is thinking really hard about the most important questions and trying to bring analytic clarity both to the questions and the answers."[8] Philosophy, if understood in these terms, can hardly be an enemy to faith. Or can it?

Holland, *Dominion*, 122).

7. Clement of Alexandria, *Stomateis* 1.5.28, quoted in Bettenson and Maunder, *Documents of the Christian Church*, 7.

8. An oft-quoted description, with the source not acknowledged nor found by me.

The Spirit of Philosophy

After my days of teaching philosophy, I continued to mull over matters of faith and philosophy. I spent a few years as national chaplain with Mission Australia, providing chaplaincy support to multi-faith or no-religious-faith staff and clientele. After that, I worked for almost ten years as a parole officer, encountering an amazing array of human lives and ideological and religious convictions. I had some freedom to think outside the box, with my previous two books written during this time. I still believed that philosophy and the ideas generated by it could be a friend of Christianity, but I also increasingly came to see tensions. I began to think about the spirit of philosophy, the spirit that animated Socrates and all of the early Greek philosophers, a spirit of inquiry; a spirit of questioning; a spirit that played into my choice of philosophy and to my parents' relatively mild reaction to this plan. Looking back, I've come to see that my dad was himself something of a philosopher, or, at least, had been profoundly influenced by the spirit of Western philosophy.

I think it doubtful that Dad would have read any of the works of Immanuel Kant (1724–1804), the German philosopher, including his influential essay "What Is Enlightenment?" But he had imbibed something of the spirit of Kant's essay, a translation of some of which I've included here:

> Enlightenment is man's release from his self-incurred tutelage. Tutelage is man's inability to make use of his understanding without direction from another. Self-incurred is this tutelage when its cause lies not in lack of reason but in lack of resolution and courage to use it without direction from another. *Sapere aude!* "Have courage to use your own reason!"—that is the motto of enlightenment.
>
> Laziness and cowardice are the reasons why so great a portion of mankind, after nature has long since discharged them from external direction (*naturaliter maiorennes*), nevertheless remains under lifelong tutelage, and why it is so easy for others to set themselves up as their guardians. It is so easy not to be of age. If I have a book which understands for me, a pastor who has a conscience for me, a physician who decides my diet, and so forth, I need not trouble myself. I need not think, if I can only pay—others will easily undertake the irksome work for me.[9]

---

9. Kant, *Practical Philosophy*, 11–12.

Dad would often say to me, "Son, don't just accept something because it is written in a book or by some so-called expert; think for yourself." I've always tried to follow that advice and have done so with respect to my Christian faith, subjecting it and its many interpretations and doctrinal variations to critical scrutiny.

The spirit of independent reasoning that Immanuel Kant encouraged and exemplified was the spirit of the ancient Greek philosophers. The birthplace of Western philosophy was the seaport town of Miletus, located across the Aegean Sea from Athens. What Thales and the other Milesian philosophers did was to set aside mythological explanations about the origins and nature of experienced reality and to look for more prosaic and, we might say, scientific understandings. It was thinking set free to range across any and all topics, including ethics, a priority for Socrates.

There is a spirit about philosophy that has also come to characterize contemporary science. It is this spirit that appears to be at odds with certain forms of the faith. What has surprised me over the years is how relatively rare is this spirit of independent and critical inquiry, and not just among people of faith. The critical questioning of beliefs is hard to find in almost any human grouping. People live within bubbles of belief and practice. Such is the human and very powerful need to belong, and to be safe in one's belonging, that bubble orthodoxies tend not to be questioned for fear of being excluded or, at least, viewed with suspicion.

And questioning can be dangerous. It is certainly challenging, especially in today's world where many of the world's philosophers and scientists have engaged in a centuries-old questioning of core Christian beliefs. It is no longer the case of a dominant Christianity questioning the legitimacy of philosophy's questions and conclusions; it is now the reverse. Moreover, for this reason and more, we live in highly anxious times where moving beyond the previously safe borders of one's belief system is scarier than it perhaps has ever been.

Reasons to Think Philosophy and Faith Are Incompatible

When I was just finishing my undergraduate studies at Moore College, I had the chance to begin a master's degree in theology. I chose to evaluate the contrasting approaches of an evangelical apologist, John Warwick Montgomery, and a philosopher, Van A. Harvey.

Van A. Harvey, until his death aged ninety-eight in July 2021, was the George Edwin Burnell Professor of Religious Studies (Emeritus) at Stanford

University. He was trained in philosophy and Christian theology. His Yale University PhD thesis was entitled "Myth, Faith, and History." John Warwick Montgomery, at the time I was writing my MTh thesis, was a lecturer in law at Luton College of Higher Education (now University of Bedfordshire) just outside of London, England. I tended, at that stage of my life, to side with Montgomery, whose basic thesis was that faith is grounded in historical fact, with the implication that faith and intellectual integrity (faith and reason) are compatible.[10] Harvey disagreed, arguing that they don't mix so well.

Harvey's book is entitled *The Historian and the Believer: The Morality of Historical Knowledge and Christian Belief.* The philosophical spirit of the ancient Greeks, refracted through the lens of Enlightenment thinking, gave birth to critical historical method, as it did to all the major sciences. Harvey argues that this spirit is incompatible with traditional Christian faith.

A major reason for this, for Harvey, has to do with the very nature of traditional Christian faith. Such faith, he observed, involves a committed acceptance of certain doctrines and beliefs, such as the Apostles' or Nicene Creeds. There is a passion about faith, a personal involvement, which Harvey argued is the opposite of the detached, scholarly commitment to finding the truth, which is characteristic of critical historical methodology. Entailed by it is the need to constantly suspend and modify judgment, often on the basis of scant available evidence. Harvey argued that there is a solidity about faith that can hardly be made dependent on the shifting and uncertain foundation of historical knowledge. He encapsulated the problem by asking:

> What should a person do when what he believes as a historian conflicts with his faith, or, as is more usual, when the probabilities of history do not seem to justify the certitude of faith? Can one and the same person hold the same judgement tentatively as a historian, but believe it passionately as a Christian?[11]

Traditional Christian faith and critical scholarship simply do not mix well, according to Harvey, and, in fact, ought not to mix. Harvey's major reason for saying this is that, in his opinion, traditional faith has the effect of "corrupting the balance of judgement which is the *sine qua non* of critical work."[12] Faith corrupts judgment because it involves a prior and

---

10. Montgomery argued that the case for Christianity is well established to the point of being proven by historically verified evidence. Though I still agree with him about the compatibility of faith and reason, I disagree about the strength of historical evidence, which is not so strong as he suggests.

11. Harvey, *Historian and Believer*, 18.

12. Harvey, *Historian and Believer*, 33.

personal commitment, which will inevitably inhibit open and independent investigation.

Could Harvey be right? There is some reason to think he might be. Although Christian theologians, down through the ages, have relied upon philosophy, certainly on its methods of careful reasoning, they have also almost always left the convictions and prescriptions of the biblical writers untouched and un-critiqued.

One good reason, or at least explanation, for this is that the Bible's stories and teachings are presented as revelatory and therefore authoritative. The Bible presents itself as containing the very words and actions of God. God speaks (Genesis); God meets, rescues, and displays his power (Exodus); God legislates (Exodus, Leviticus, Deuteronomy); God appoints, protects, disciplines, and reassures (the historical and prophetic books); God's Son is sent, activating an eternal plan to redeem humanity and the world (New Testament).

In many churches, the Bible is often referred to as "God's word." Bible readers conclude their readings with "This is the word of the Lord," and the congregation replies, "Thanks be to God." If the Bible is indeed God's word, it can hardly be questioned. Philosophy is thereby relegated to a clarifying or justificatory role. What the Bible is heard to say can be, and often has been, clarified using philosophical terms. The Bible has, additionally, been defended by apologetic efforts. But, we might ask, what happens when the biblical stories and prescriptions begin to be questioned, as they have been throughout history and especially since the Enlightenment? One reaction, with which I will finish this chapter, is the prioritizing of philosophy and/or science, and the outright denial of faith or theology.

A. C. Grayling's book *The God Argument: The Case Against Religion and for Humanism* does just that. Grayling is a professional philosopher and also something of a controversialist. His main academic interests are in the areas of epistemology, metaphysics, and philosophical logic. He has written numerous books. In *The God Argument*, Grayling posits that all religions are or should be a thing of the past. The only way to overcome the unavoidable tension between philosophy and religion is to ditch religion altogether.

While noting that religion has been a source of great inspiration and comfort, as well as much harm, Grayling argues that the case against religion goes deeper than its impacts.

> It is that religion's claims and beliefs do not stand up to examination. Briefly put, critical examination of religion's claims places

it in the same class as astrology and magic. Like these systems of thought, religion dates from [humankind's] less educated and knowledgeable early history, and, like them, it has been superseded by advances in our understanding of the world and ourselves.[13]

Grayling's book divides into two. In the first half, Grayling argues a case against religion; in the second half, the case for humanism. In arguing against religion, Grayling discusses what he understands is the nature of religious belief while also countering various arguments in favor of theistic belief. He concludes with these words:

> [Humanism] premises the value of things human, without the assistance of illusions about anything supposedly beyond this world and its realities. Humanism's desire to learn from the past, its exhortation to courage in the present, and its espousal of hope for the future, are about real things, real people, real human need and possibility, and the fate of the fragile world we share. It is about human life; it requires no belief in an afterlife. It is about this world; it requires no belief in another world. It requires no commands from divinities, no promise of reward or threats of punishment, no myths and rituals, either to make sense of things or to serve as a prompt to the ethical life. It requires only clear eyes, reason and kindness; and with them a determination to make the world the best place it can be for the flourishing of creativity, good possibilities and the affections of the human heart.[14]

Those are fighting words for sure, but they rather set up this book. Interestingly, Grayling is more closely aligned with Tertullian and Luther than he is with others of the theologians mentioned thus far. He agrees that philosophy and faith, Athens and Jerusalem, are incompatible. There can be no successful friendship between them. It is one or the other, and, in Grayling's opinion, philosophy and science prevail.

In this book, I will attempt to argue that Athens and Jerusalem don't need to be at war. They can coexist, even if not always comfortably. The traditional shape of Christianity may need to change. In fact, it will need to change. It is, I believe, the only honest way forward.

---

13. Grayling, *God Argument*, 2.
14. Grayling, *God Argument*, 238.

Questions for Reflection and Discussion

1. In deciding whether the questioning/questing spirit of philosophy and science is compatible with Christian faith, whom are you inclined to side with: Tertullian (faith and philosophy don't mix) or Justin Martyr (they do mix), and why?

2. In what ways have philosophy and/or science influenced your Christian or religious faith?

3. Is the passion and commitment of faith compatible with the ideally disinterested and critical spirit of philosophy?

Playing at the Edge
by Noel Davis

At the heart of God is a little child
who loves to dance and play.
It's true for each of us
however young we be.

Play *is* the edge
activity free of outcomes, quality controls,
agendas, resolving issues,
looking good and getting it right.

O to play, simply to play!

There's a heaviness about the way we're living
O-So-Serious getting his way
and Foolish looking rather flabby
restrained by Now-Let's-Be-Sensible
Playful so pale from too little sun
needing to leap and bound, while around, have fun.

How strange we are.

We love a playful spirit
love to be with those free at heart
who bring out the child in us
set us free from our restraints
have us laugh with life
be care free
indulge in nature's own therapy
invite mirth and merry mischief
into our set routine
delight in little things
that lighten up our day

A conflict has yet to be truly resolved by violence.
The sword's edge has never been the way.
A young man millennia back reminded us of this.
Came himself as a little child
invited us to play
to reclaim the child in us
so shrouded in the serious
desperate to be released
to play
there at the edge.

Chapter 2

Inquisitive Faith

I HAVE LONG CONSIDERED writing a book about honesty. The more I've lived, the more I have been alarmed by the prevalence of dishonesty. This has not just been among politicians, some of whom have come to believe, with good warrant, sadly, that they can get away with bald-faced, shameless, and sustained lying.[1] But we can all succumb to the temptation to be untruthful. We've all told lies to one another and to ourselves. We've all found ourselves in situations where it is more convenient, safer, or more advantageous to lie, and where it has been easier to retain doubtful beliefs when even a tiny bit of research would suggest that the truth lies elsewhere.

Honesty isn't easy. There will often be a cost involved in owning up to a lie or to the fact that we really don't know what we so confidently assert. Nevertheless, honesty is a value all religious traditions encourage, and which I also want to encourage in myself and others.

I have raised the question of whether Athens and Jerusalem, philosophy and faith, are or can be compatible. By way of attempting an answer, I propose that the value of honesty is a possible bridge between philosophy and faith, and this because honesty is as important to philosophy and to its scientific offspring as it is to faith and theology. In this and the following chapters, I'd like to consider what an honest faith might look like. What might my faith

---

1. Donald Trump, for example, now returned for a second term as US president, was fact checked by the *Washington Post* during his first term. It was found that by the end of his first term, he had accumulated 30,573 false or misleading claims, at an average of about 21 per day. Sadly, Trump's embrace of blatant dishonesty appears not to have impeded but to have helped him win this most recent election.

look like if something of the spirit of philosophy is given room to operate and flourish? Might there be a friendship between these two unlikely partners?

* * *

An honest faith implies the need to be inquisitive. To be inquisitive is to want to know the truth about something. It is a beautiful attribute, especially present in children who rightly feel they have so much to learn. Almost everything for them becomes a focus of fascination. It could also be that for us.

It was inquisitiveness that gave birth to philosophy. Samuel Stumpf, in his excellent history, *From Socrates to Sartre: A History of Philosophy*, explains its origins in these terms:

> Philosophy began with [humankind's] sense of wonder and curiosity expressed in the questions, "What are things really like?" and "How can we explain the process of change in things?" Many of the answers given . . . are not as important as the fact that they focused upon just those questions, and that they approached them with a fresh and new frame of mind that was in contrast to the great poets.[2]

Stumpf is perhaps a little hard on the great poets. One could argue that the earlier poets, such as Homer and Hesiod (both eighth century BCE), were similarly inspired by the above-mentioned questions. They too were inquisitive, the small difference being that their poetry was more obviously imaginative and overtly polytheistic.

One could argue, and I would, that the world's religions, ancient and more modern, similarly came to birth because of innate and God-given human inquisitiveness, an inquisitiveness that sought to make sense of life and death, and of this amazing though dangerous world we live in. Iain McGilchrist surmises:

> Religion, at its best, is a cultural expression of that enquiring impulse; of an awareness of and openness to a God or gods; of a context that transforms our understanding of the world, and which enables this sense to be shared and celebrated with others.[3]

---

2. Stumpf, *Socrates to Sartre*, 3.
3. McGilchrist, *Matter with Things*, 2:1219.

Judaism and Christianity fit this description well, as I will seek to show in succeeding chapters. For now, let's launch into what it means to be inquisitive.

Inquisitiveness is typically activated by puzzlement, by questions that demand answers, some of which are hard to find. Those who think they have all or enough of the answers are unlikely to be inquisitive. I think that is a pity. People are less likely to learn if they don't allow inquisitiveness to have its way. Let me share some of the things that have piqued my inquisitiveness over the years and up until now. All of these, I will pursue in later chapters.

Inquisitiveness and Human Origins

A long-standing stimulus for inquisitiveness has been information about the age and origins of humankind. I grew up happily content with the idea that God created human beings as well as all the other animals, plants, and organisms that populate the earth. It was a creation God could rightly describe as good, that is, until we humans offended and became the cause of all or most of the bad things that happen, like suffering and death. I keep hearing that description in sermons, and in the evangelical books and pamphlets I've encountered over the years.

This common Christian narrative fits the biblical description quite well. Genesis 1 has these intriguing verses:

> God blessed them, and God said to them, "Be fruitful and multiply and fill the earth and subdue it and have dominion over the fish of the sea and over the birds of the air and over every living thing that moves upon the earth." 29 God said, "See, I have given you every plant yielding seed that is upon the face of all the earth and every tree with seed in its fruit; you shall have them for food. 30 *And to every beast of the earth and to every bird of the air and to everything that creeps on the earth, everything that has the breath of life, I have given every green plant for food."* And it was so. 31 God saw everything that he had made, and indeed, it was very good. And there was evening and there was morning, the sixth day.

I've only recently noticed the highlighted verse 30. It was not just humans who were given green plants to eat. All the animals were as well, "everything that has the breath of life in it," with the implication that in God's original creation there were no carnivores. That amazed me, but this understanding is consistent with the second creation story of Gen 2–3, where humans could have lived forever, could have remained vegetarian, eating nonstop from the tree of life, had they not disobeyed God by eating from the tree of the knowledge of good and evil. Death was only then introduced into this formerly idyllic environment, presumably also animal death. In time, humans were allowed to kill and eat animals, but this was clearly less than ideal, certainly not the way God intended it.[4]

It is significant, I think, that the prophetic vision of the renewed earth involves vegetarian animals living peacefully with humans and each other.

> The wolf shall live with the lamb;
>   the leopard shall lie down with the kid;
> the calf and the lion will feed together,
>   and a little child shall lead them.
> 7 The cow and the bear shall graze;
>   their young shall lie down together;
>   and the lion shall eat straw like the ox.
> 8 The nursing child shall play over the hole of the asp,
>   and the weaned child shall put its hand on the adder's den.
> 9 They will not hurt or destroy
>   on all my holy mountain,
> for the earth will be full of the knowledge of the Lord
>   as the waters cover the sea. (Isa 11:6–9)

In Romans, Paul clearly draws upon Gen 1–3, and possibly also upon the vision of Isa 11, when he describes the consequences of Adam and Eve's sins, including upon nature itself.

> Therefore, just as sin came into the world through one man, and death came through sin, and so death spread to all because all have sinned. (Rom 5:12)

> I consider that the sufferings of this present time are not worth comparing with the glory about to be revealed to us. 19 For the creation waits with eager longing for the revealing of the children of God, 20 for the creation was subjected to futility, not of its own will, but by the will of the one who subjected it, in hope 21 that the creation itself will be set free from its enslavement to decay and will obtain the freedom of the glory of the children of God. 22 We know that the whole creation has been groaning together as it suffers together the pains of labor, 23 and not only the creation, but we ourselves, who have the first fruits

---

4. Interestingly, it is God who is depicted as the first to kill an animal, to provide clothing for Adam and Eve.

of the Spirit, groan inwardly while we wait for adoption, the redemption of our bodies. (Rom 8:18–23)

Paul's is a very anthropocentric picture of decay and death, which was believed to have been imposed upon the created order, and not that long ago, if the Bible's chronologies are followed.

What has caused me and multiple others to be inquisitive is that this explanation of human suffering and death does not mesh at all well with the complex and ever-emerging picture of human and animal origins, which we now reasonably believe is not only a very long history, in the hundreds of thousands, in fact millions, of years, but one which also involves suffering and death well before humans emerged. As Rutger Bregman, in his book *Humankind: A Hopeful History*, puts it:

> The basic ingredients for the evolution of life are straightforward. You need:
> Lots of suffering
> Lots of struggle
> Lots of time
> In short, the process of evolution comes down to this: animals have more offspring than they can feed. Those that are slightly better adapted to their environment . . have a slightly higher chance of surviving to procreate. Now imagine a friendly game of run till you're dead, in which billions upon billions of creatures bite the dust, some before they can pass the baton to their offspring. Keep this footrace going long enough—say four billions years—and the minuscule variations between parents and children can branch out into a vast and varied tree of life.[5]

Bregman goes on to note the challenge this story created for traditional Christian faith, including that of Charles Darwin:

> For Darwin the biologist, who'd once considered becoming a priest, the impossibility of reconciling the cruelty of nature with the biblical story ultimately destroyed his faith in God. Can you blame Darwin for putting off publishing his theory for years? Writing to a friend, he said it was "like confessing a murder."[6]

---

5. Bregman, *Humankind*, 52–53.
6. Bregman, *Humankind*, 53.

Pondering God's Rescue Plan

There are some additional puzzles to ponder. If one were to plot a biblical timeline, beginning in Genesis and going all the way through to Revelation, it would look something like this: After God creates an initially good and pain-free world, our first human ancestors, Adam and Eve, disobey God and lose the opportunity for immortality. They are expelled from paradise into our present world of suffering and death. God, nevertheless, initiates a graceful rescue plan for humankind, beginning with Abraham and climaxing with Jesus and a new creation. This unfolding plan was the centerpiece of the biblical theology I learned at theological college and have encountered ever since within evangelical circles.

The way in which this plan is frequently articulated is, however, problematic. Not only are there problems with the chronology, with suffering and death predating and not postdating humankind, but the following questions are also raised: Why did it take God so long to activate this plan, and to make humans aware of the plan? What about those who lived and died before the birth of the Israelite religion? On a most conservative dating, and on the assumption that Abraham and the other patriarchs are not mythical, the activation of God's plan is no more than about four thousand years old, whereas, by way of contrast, Australia's Aboriginal inhabitants have been on this continent for about sixty thousand years having earlier made the long trek from Africa. That's puzzling and well worth unpacking.

It has struck me more than once that those well schooled in the history of human life and civilization must find it entirely puzzling to attend a Christian church where the above described biblical timeline is expounded, especially if uncritically and literally.

On the Presence and Meaning of Myth

I've long been happy to consider Gen 1–3 and, in fact, Gen 1–11 as Judaic and now also Christian myth. These chapters include the stories of Adam and Eve, Cain and Abel, the worldwide flood, and the tower of Babel. As some textual evidence that these stories are mythical are the following intriguing few verses in Gen 6:

> When people began to multiply on the face of the ground, and daughters were born to them, 2 the sons of God saw that they were fair, and they took wives for themselves of all that they chose. 3 Then the Lord said, "My spirit shall not abide in mortals

forever, for they are flesh; their days shall be one hundred twenty years." 4 The Nephilim were on the earth in those days—and also afterward—when the sons of God went in to the daughters of humans, who bore children to them. These were the heroes that were of old, warriors of renown.

This definitely reads like a myth, like one of the Greek myths, for example. When Judy and I were in Athens, I bought some books on Greek mythology. I was only vaguely aware of the stories, but I was fascinated, especially by their insights into human nature, with the gods so humanlike. We didn't stay long in Athens. We travelled on to France, England, Ireland, and Scotland. While in Ireland and Scotland, I also made a point of buying more books and reading up on the mythologies of those lands. I was struck by how similar, and also dissimilar, were their myths to those from the early chapters of the Bible.

These non-biblical mythologies prompted me to think further about the role of mythology in the Bible. What I was also inquisitive about was other biblical stories, like the story of the exodus, which I've come to believe is not historical as described. That conclusion is certainly a growing consensus among biblical historians and archaeologists.

I was helped in my thinking by what appears to be an emerging understanding of myth in academic circles. For a long time, there has been a sharp distinction between myth and history. Theorists have thus had trouble defining the difference. Andrew Tobolowsky, in a helpful article published in 2016, noted that this problem of definition goes back to the Greeks, and it still bedevils us:

> In the present modern, post-modern, and post-post-modern worlds, the distinction between history and myth is generally arbitrated on the level of intentions: "history" bears the connotation of something intended to be true and "myth" something which may be descriptive of the truth but is not true in the sense of relating a true (actually occurring) event. Yet, while Greek historiographers show a clear concern for distinguishing truth and fiction (yes, even Herodotus), they often put the marker between them in places which utterly befuddle modern humans. There is very little evidence, for example, that it would have been possible to explain to an ancient Greek that the Dorians could not have been led south into the Peloponnese by the descendants of Herakles . . . because Herakles did not exist, ergo did not have sons, because beings with the strength to hold the

world on their shoulders, even if only for a minute, *even for worlds which, if we're honest, don't need holding up*, do not exist.[7]

The mixing of "history" and "myth," which the early books of the Bible appear to do, is not unusual, but it does necessitate the need to think further about myth and history. Historiography has become much more aware of the inevitable subjectivity involved in narratives of all sorts, with scholars increasingly suggesting that historicizing and mythicizing aren't that different. The genre border between them is shrinking. As a result, and in order to simplify matters, myth theorists now often deploy "myth" as a term for narratives about the past (distant and more recent) that present as fact but are not factual.

It struck me that if myth can be used as broadly as this, then many of the great stories of the Jewish Scriptures, including the story of the exodus, could be considered as myths. They don't describe actual events but, like all myths, contain truth we can continue to draw upon.[8]

What I remain inquisitive about is to what extent the New Testament contains myth, especially as defined above. As some indication of the presence of myth, the various writers of the New Testament, like early Greek historians, do not draw a distinction between stories we might consider mythical and stories that we'd be more inclined to describe as historical. Both Jesus and his followers, including those who wrote the New Testament, appear to have accepted the stories about Adam, Eve, Noah, the patriarchs, Moses, the exodus, and Jonah as factual. Perhaps they weren't even aware of the need (our need) to make a distinction.

There are other indications in the New Testament that myths, understood as nonfactual stories presenting as factual, are present and perhaps more widespread than we may have thought. I've long had doubts about the birth narratives, which are present in only two of the four gospels, Matthew and Luke. These stories are not referenced or alluded to elsewhere in the New Testament, and their details don't line up. I've wondered about the temptation narratives, which, incidentally, appear to assume a flat earth[9] and were not witnessed by any of the apostles. I've wondered about the transfiguration

---

7. Tobolowsky, "History, Myth," para. 3; emphasis in original.

8. It may be that actual events did occur, but they are described in mythological terms. A category that could be used in this case would be legend. They could also be described as mythologized history.

9. Matthew 4:8 describes the devil taking Jesus to a very high mountain to show him "all the kingdoms of the world and their glory," a feat in theory possible if the earth is flat.

narrative, within which Moses and Elijah join Jesus, again on a mountain. It is increasingly likely that Moses is a legendary figure about whom we know very little, if anything. Moses is included in the transfiguration story for fairly obvious reasons as the one believed to have been the transmitter of God's laws, with Elijah identified with the prophets. But what if we are now not even sure that Moses, and maybe even Elijah, existed? This is certainly something to be inquisitive about.

In recent years, I've become aware that the stories about Jesus are not unique in their ancient Near Eastern (ANE) context. For example, Richard C. Miller has scoured ANE literature and, like many before him, has found multiple instances of gospel-like ideas and events. Miller quotes Justin Martyr, who in his apology for the faith drew attention to these similarities:

> When we affirm that the Logos, God's first-born, begotten without sexual union, namely our teacher, Jesus Christ, was crucified, died, rose and ascended to heaven, we are conveying nothing new with respect to those whom you call the sons of Zeus.[10]

The logos idea is drawn from earlier Greek thinking. Justin provides other examples from his Greco-Roman heritage. While dismissing pagan gods as demons, he notes how familiar the gospel stories would have seemed to ancient readers.

Miller draws attention to what he describes as "translation fables." The term "fable," as Miller employs the term, "refers to culturally owned and cherished, even sacralised narratives, ranging from the playful and whimsical to the dramatic and dire." They are a form of myth, which Miller defines as "[sacred narratives or accounts that have served] to frame the present for a person, group, society, nation, or all of humanity." He continues, "Such a definition would thereby include eschatological myths, apocalyptic myths, cosmic myths, and aetiological myths." As Miller uses the terms in his book, the word "fable" adds to this description of myth the "qualification of self-consciousness, that is, the 'fable' exists as a myth to be understood as such."[11]

"Translation fables" are stories about the transfer of famous people to heavenly realms, who are commonly deified in the process. Miller describes these fables as "an elevated form of hero fabulation embroidering the exalted biography."[12] Common features of these fables include: heinous or ignoble

---

10. Justin, 1 *Apology* 21, quoted in Miller, *Resurrection and Reception*, 1.
11. Miller, *Resurrection and Reception*, 17.
12. Miller, *Resurrection and Reception*, 36.

injustice rectified by translation, metamorphosis, a missing body, turning into a star [or celestial object], post-translation speech, ascension, post-translation appearances, witnesses, odious or alternative accounts, and being taken up by the winds or clouds. Associated with these quite numerous fables[13] are tales of virginal conception and/or divine/human offspring.[14]

The gospels were released into a world awash with stories like these. Miller argues that the gospel authors created their own "translation fables," patterned on Greco-Roman fables. Moreover, in doing so, the authors were, he argues, aware of the essentially mythical nature of these accounts, as were the first readers of the gospels, who would not have understood the stories as factual.

In terms of my own understanding of the gospels, Miller's thesis is certainly interesting. It has without doubt made me inquisitive and willing to learn more. What I also find interesting is how modern readers of the Bible are increasingly having difficulty accepting the many miraculous stories that populate the gospels. Understandably, they appear incredible, not easily believed. This is one reason, among many, why people are failing to embrace, or are disengaging from, Christian faith.

Rapidly Declining Christianity

People are choosing to leave the faith in increasing numbers, including people who were once regular church attenders. Congregations are aging and shrinking almost everywhere across the Western world. What we are now witnessing is Christianity in rapid decline in Western nations such as Australia, the US, Canada, and England. Denominations that used to be thriving are failing to win converts, especially among younger generations. The Anglican Diocese of Sydney, which I was an active member of for many years, has often boasted about its ability to at least hold its own against the pull of an outgoing tide, but they too are now facing the stark reality that their church-going numbers are shrinking. Between 2013 and 2022, those

---

13. In ch. 2 of his book, Miller presents a gallery of seventy-seven translation fables, a sample of relevant examples but indicative of how widespread and well known these fables were.

14. Miller compares Matthew's account of the virgin birth of Jesus with that of Alexander the Great, as described in Plutarch's *Vita Alexandri*, a work contemporaneous with Matthew's. The two accounts are strikingly similar (*Resurrection and Reception*, 123–25). Elsewhere, Miller includes a list of more than sixty kings, queens, and other heroes who had gods as fathers, with mortal women as mothers (108–9).

numbers shrank by 18.5 percent.[15] Fewer than 1 percent of Sydney-siders are now attending an Anglican Church. That is a long way shy of Archbishop Peter Jensen's mission commitment, made in 2002 when he first became archbishop, to grow attendance at "Bible-believing churches" to 10 percent of the Sydney population within ten years.[16]

And it is not just church attendance that is in decline. The numbers and percentages of Australians identifying as Christian is also in steep and accelerating decline. Between the 2011 and 2021 censuses, the number of Australians who identify as Christian plummeted from 61.1 percent to 43.9 percent. That is a drop of 17.2 percent in just a decade. In 1971, Christians represented 86.2 percent of the Australian population. The contrast between then and now is stark. Just as stark has been the growth in those identifying as having no religion, from 6.7 percent in 1971 to 38.9 percent in 2021. If the trajectory continues, those with "no religion" will shortly surpass those identifying as Christian. It may take a little longer for no religionists to surpass those identifying with a religion. Those identifying with religions other than Christianity grew from 3.5 percent in 1996 to 10 percent in 2021.[17]

In my birth nation of Canada, almost thirteen million Canadians stated, in Canada's 2021 census, that they have no religious affiliation, up from about eight million in 2011, a similar sharp increase to what we are seeing in Australia. The percentage of people identifying as Christian dropped from 77.1 percent in 2001 to 53.3 percent in 2021.[18]

The situation in England and Wales is similar. In their combined census, also in 2021, 46.2 percent of the English and Welsh population said they are Christian, a decline of 13.1 percentage points since the 2011 census. The "no religion" category increased from 12 percent in 2011 to 37.2 percent.[19]

In the US, the decline has also been rapid. A 2020 study by Pew Research found that 64 percent of Americans identified as Christian, whereas in 1972, it was 92 percent. Thirty percent were now classified as "religiously unaffiliated." Approximately 6 percent of Americans identified with Judaism, Islam,

---

15. The attendance decline report submitted to the 2024 Synod of the Anglican Diocese of Sydney reported that across the diocese's 436 church centers, overall adult attendance declined by 6.7 percent between 2013 and 2023 and by 14.4 percent relative to population growth within the diocese (Sydney Anglicans, *Synod 2024*).

16. Diocese of Sydney, "2002 Ordinary Session," 4–6.

17. Information complied from Australian Bureau of Statistics, "2021 Census."

18. Information compiled from Statistics Canada, "Canadian Census."

19. Information compiled from Office for National Statistics, "Religion, England and Wales."

Hinduism, and Buddhism.[20] Belief in God is also declining. A 2022 Gallup poll found that 81 percent of Americans say they believe in God, the lowest percentage yet recorded. In 2023, when it gave respondents the option of saying they were not sure, it found that only 74 percent believe in God, 14 percent weren't sure, and 12 percent said they did not believe.[21]

More could be said about other Western nations, but this small sample is arresting enough. People are fast losing confidence in the church and in Christianity itself. Throughout the Western world, child abuse scandals have significantly contributed to this loss of confidence, eroding trust in religious leaders and their institutions. Here in Australia, a recently completed *Royal Commission into Institutional Responses to Child Sexual Abuse* was established in 2012.[22] Impetus for the commission was a journalistic investigation into abusive and predatory sexual abuse by priests in the Anglican Diocese of Newcastle, abuse that had been allowed to continue for at least thirty years.[23] Not surprisingly, this revelation and the resulting Royal Commission and its unearthing of widespread and ongoing abuse has resulted in significantly diminished trust, impacting women especially. A Macquarie University Report published on May 6, 2024, and entitled *Trust in Religion Among Women in Australia: A Qualitative Analysis* found that:

- About one third of Australian women have no trust in organized religion and religious leaders.
- Distrust is highest among younger women: almost half of all women aged eighteen to twenty-nine have no trust in religious leaders.
- Among religious women, around 10 percent have no trust in organized religion and religious leaders, while around half have "not very much trust" in either.
- LGBTIQ+ women have some of the lowest levels of trust in Australia. Almost two thirds have no trust in religious leaders.[24]

---

20. Pew Research, "Modeling the Future."
21. Jones, "Belief in God."
22. Its final report was submitted in Dec. 2017.
23. See further Manne, *Crimes of the Cross*.
24. Glesson and Ashton, *Trust in Religion*.

Deconstruction

What is going on? Something significant, that's for sure. As some evidence of its magnitude, there is a growing movement within Evangelicalism that is reflective of this rapid demise in Christian belief and identification. It is called deconstruction or faith deconstruction. It is not just Christians generally who are losing their faith; Evangelicals are as well, in large enough numbers to create alarm.

The term "deconstruction" has been borrowed from the French philosopher Jacques Derrida. Derrida's use of the word, in the field of textual criticism, was quite technical and not easy to understand for people (like myself) not schooled in continental philosophy. As it has been adopted by Christians, the word has come to refer to the process of reexamining one's faith, breaking it down, deconstructing it, and then maybe rebuilding it. Alisa Childers describes the process:

> Deconstruction is the process of systematically dissecting and often rejecting the beliefs you grew up with. Sometimes the Christian will deconstruct all the way to atheism. Some remain there, but others experience a reconstruction. But the type of faith they end up embracing almost never resembles the Christianity they formerly knew.[25]

Rachel Held Evans defined it similarly as "taking a massive inventory of [one's] faith, tearing every doctrine from the cupboard and turning each one over in [one's] hand."[26] It is a process that, at least potentially, involves questioning the whole foundation of one's faith and everything built upon it.

As I reflected on this new movement or phenomenon, a few things struck me. I realized that my previous two books could comfortably fit into this deconstruction genre, as could my whole adult life. I've been incessantly asking questions and also, thankfully, finding some answers. These are becoming the building blocks of my own attempted reconstruction, which the second half of this book will articulate.

It also struck me that this whole phenomenon is a clear case of philosophy interacting with theology and faith. It represents a quest for knowledge and/or wisdom, which sets aside external authorities, very much in the spirit of ancient and modern philosophy and/or science. Here are Athens and

---

25. Childers, *Another Gospel*, 24.
26. Held Evans, *Searching for Sunday*, 50.

Jerusalem going head to head, with their compatibility well and truly being tested.

Some Perplexingly Thin Cases

Returning to the theme of inquisitiveness, I have been intrigued by a whole host of things over the years, some of which are contributing to people leaving Christianity. Among those is the place of women in the church. What strikes me is how increasingly thin is the case against the full equality of women in the life of the church. In evangelical Anglican circles, within which I have lived and worked, it seems to me that their case against the full inclusion of women boils down to little more than reliance on the following passage from the Pastoral Epistles:[27]

> Let a woman learn in silence with full submission. 12 I do not permit a woman to teach or to have authority over a man; she is to keep silent. 13 For Adam was formed first, then Eve, 14 and Adam was not deceived, but the woman was deceived and became a transgressor. 15 Yet she will be saved through childbearing, provided they continue in faith and love and holiness, with self-control. (1 Tim 2:11–15)

Almost all of the evidence one could draw upon both from within the New Testament and from our own observations and experience would indicate that women should have unfettered opportunity to exercise their manifest gifts of leadership and teaching, and, should this happen or where it does happen, the life of Christian congregations will be enriched. Mercifully, most of Australia's Anglican dioceses now benefit from the ministries of female deacons, priests, and, in some cases, bishops and an archbishop. Why any church would hold out against this undeniable blessing remains a mystery.

It is especially mysterious given the weight that has had to be loaded onto 1 Timothy, which is unlikely to have been penned by Paul. Paul's authorship of the Pastorals is highly contested, with many and probably most New Testament scholars (conservative and liberal) convinced they are not the work of Paul, but instead of one or more of his disciples at a later date. The claimed apostolic authority of the above-quoted verses is thus called into question.

---

27. Also appealed to in building what becomes a quite complex case for excluding women from leadership and teaching roles within the church are some additional passages including 1 Cor 11:2–16; Eph 5:21–33; Gen 2–3.

It is a similar situation with issues of gender and sexuality, with debates still continuing about same-sex marriage and, more fiercely of late, the rights of transgender people. Those wanting to return to the way things used to be (or appeared to be) when men and boys were men and boys, with nothing in between or different, and women and girls were women and girls, with nothing in between or different, and when marriage could be only between a man and a woman (or two), have often appealed to the book of Leviticus, where categories do appear to be fixed and inflexible.

Adding weight to such an appeal is that Gen 1–3 describes an original binary male/female creation that is then beautifully unified in marriage. However, when inquisitiveness is allowed room to roam, an appeal to Leviticus is as fragile as is an appeal to the Pastoral Epistles, and this because the claimed origin of these laws is doubtful. Leviticus begins with these words:

> The Lord summoned Moses and spoke to him from the tent of meeting saying: speak to the people of Israel and say to them . . . (Lev 1:1)

The divine origin of these laws and their recording by Moses is unambiguously reiterated in the final chapters of Leviticus. The final verse states:

> These are the commandments that the Lord gave to Moses for the people of Israel on Mount Sinai. (Lev 27:34)

The problem is that almost no biblical scholar now believes that Moses was the transmitter of these laws at the time of the exodus. There continues to be debate about when these statutes, ordinances, and laws were written, but currently favored hypotheses suggest an extended period of composition,[28] with its current literary form originating in the exilic or postexilic period, that is, in the sixth century BCE or later.[29] This fact, if indeed it is a fact, is troubling, especially for those committed to a strong understanding of the authority of Scripture.

In the early stages of writing this book, I saw an advertisement for a conference that piqued my interest. A former Moore College student of mine, now a reverend doctor, John Dickson, was hosting a conference named after a podcast he runs called *Undeceptions*. The conference's theme was: "Making

---

28. It is widely accepted that a form of the book of Deuteronomy (which contains many of these statutes, ordinances, and laws) was discovered and perhaps even written at the time of King Josiah (circa 720 BCE), helping to fuel Josiah's reforms.

29. For an extended, up-to-date, and helpful treatment of this topic, see J. Wright, *Why the Bible Began*. Wright dates most of the Christian Old Testament to after the Babylonian exile.

Sense of Christianity." In broad terms the conference was seeking to meet the growing challenge of deconstruction.

It was a stimulating conference. John is a very able scholar, particularly in the area of ancient history. He had gathered an impressive array of speakers.[30] What really stood out to me was that more than half of the keynote speakers were female. That was refreshing, especially at an evangelical conference in Sydney. But what was even more surprising was that two of the three female keynote speakers, Dr. Rebecca McLaughlan and Rachel Gilson, were lesbian or, as they prefer to describe themselves, same-sex attracted. It struck me as a brave thing for John to do, especially when, on the opening night of the conference, current Archbishop of Sydney Kanishka Raffel was in attendance. The only speakers that night, apart from John, were these two same-sex attracted women.

What struck me even more forcefully as the conference unfolded was that, as far as I could see, the only reason offered against same-sex marriage, the only reason that Rachel Gilson and Dr. Rebecca McLaughlan (or anyone else) mentioned, is that they believed it violated the teaching and requirements of the Bible.

It must be acknowledged that the conference wasn't about same-sex marriage. Nevertheless, it was striking that there was no hint within the conference (in keynote addresses or in the breakout groups) of what Christian theologians have said and thought down through the ages about how abominably abhorrent same-sex sexual activity is, no hint that society's moral fabric would unravel or children be disadvantaged or youth corrupted. Nothing at all. In fact, Rachel Gilson, in her talk on that first night of the conference, acknowledged that she didn't understand why the Bible prohibits sex between people of the same gender. Despite her not knowing, she said she was willing to trust a God she had found to be trustworthy on other grounds.

This lack of external confirmatory evidence to support an ethical position is strikingly similar to what we've observed about the case against equality of opportunity for women. Both are perplexing for people looking on from outside the church. Younger people especially find Christian opposition to same-sex marriage baffling, to the point of being incomprehensible. For many, this opposition is reason enough to jettison or to not even consider Christian faith.

---

30. Dr. Rebecca McLaughlan, Dr. Sarah Irving-Stonebraker, Rachel Gilson, and Rev. Dr. Sam Chan.

A 2022 online survey conducted in the US identifies LGBTQ nonacceptance as the foremost initial or precipitating reason for leaving traditional Christian faith.[31] That certainly lines up with other surveys I have seen. What I also found interesting about this survey was the third most cited reason, which was lack of intellectual integrity or, in the terms of this book, honesty. Christians not displaying integrity might also partially account for the second most often cited reason, the behavior of Christians.

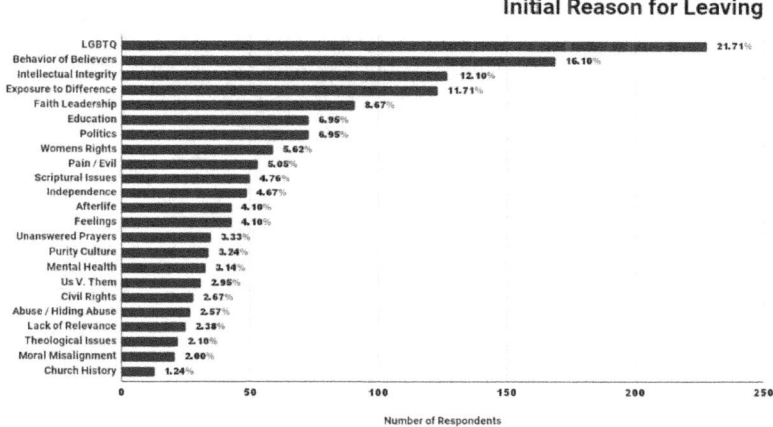

Initial Reason for Leaving

As I have looked through the above list, most of the expressed reasons resonate with me. They have aroused my inquisitiveness. Their cumulative impact has had me wondering again whether my Christian faith can meet the many challenges which have resulted in the current mass exodus from churches and from Christianity itself.

Questions for Reflection and Discussion

1. Why do you think Christian (including evangelical) faith is in such rapid decline in the West, and in what ways is that decline impacting you?

2. How would you explain the discrepancies between the increasingly accepted scientific account of human and animal origins and the biblical picture?

---

31. Flanery, "I Asked People," s.vv. "LGBTQ discrimination a big reason."

3. If you were to explain God's saving purposes for the world, how would you do that, and where would you start?

4. Has inquisitiveness been encouraged in your past or present communities of faith, and how has that impacted you?

5. What sorts of things (relevant to your faith) pique your inquisitiveness, and how have you sought to answer the resulting questions?

Sacred Time
by Noel Davis

We rise from the ruins of our catastrophies
recover from the pain of our woundings
the trauma of our tragedies
the shambles of our undoings
the bewilderment of our whys
the turmoil of our terrified minds
to birth each new beginning
beyond where we have been living
and with courage and trust
expand the inner and outer frontiers
of our including
that shatter our thus fars and no furthers
and have us glimpse our destiny.

Chapter 3

Humble Faith

Inquisitiveness puts us on the road to knowledge. It is a long road with many twists, turns, and possible dead ends. It is an endless road because whatever knowledge we acquire remains but a tiny fraction of what we could know. What was the case for our children is the same for us. Even at the end of our lives we don't know much.

That can be a little depressing for seekers after truth, which most of us are in one way or another. It is certainly humbling, and it should be. It is good to be reminded of our limits, our finiteness, and of our capacity for illusion and delusion. Even a superficial knowledge of human history will inform us of how many silly, crazy, and mistaken beliefs we humans have embraced down through the ages. Many and probably most of them were believable at the time, but they have since been abandoned, mostly with good reason.

I think of my own life and of beliefs I have held in the past, often with great conviction, but which I no longer believe, or, if I continue to believe them, I do so in a more nuanced way. Of the beliefs I presently have, some are sure to be mistaken.

Socrates and Humility

Socrates had a good understanding of the limits of his knowledge.[1] At some point in his philosophical career, a friend of his asked the Delphic oracle whether there was any living person wiser than Socrates. The oracle said

---

1. As far as we can tell. We are dependent on those who wrote about him, including Plato, who, to some degree, appears to have used Socrates as a mouthpiece for his own thoughts.

no. When this answer was conveyed to Socrates, he responded with initial disbelief.[2] This apparent revelation nevertheless helped to launch one of the greatest philosophical careers of all time. Socrates embarked on a journey to find someone wiser than himself.[3] What he found was that the sages he was able to seek out thought they knew more than they actually did. Socrates concluded that perhaps he was, after all, the wisest human. He at least knew he didn't know.

Socrates didn't believe he knew nothing, which is how he is often interpreted. When Judy and I were visiting Athens, I bought a T-shirt with the following quotation in Greek and English: "The only thing I know is that I don't know anything." Strictly speaking, that is self-contradictory. Socrates didn't think he knew nothing. Instead, he surmised that in not fully understanding important topics, such as how we should live, he remained ignorant. He couldn't describe himself as having knowledge.[4]

It was this ignorance, this lack of knowledge, that propelled Socrates into his quest for truth and wisdom. In setting out on this quest, Socrates was committed to the idea that achieving some knowledge was possible, in contrast to the relativism and skepticism of the Sophists. Socrates located the ability to know in the internal activity of the human soul, which he identified as the normal human powers of intelligence and character.[5]

Socrates's humble approach to knowledge acquisition has inspired philosophers and scientists ever since. In late 2023, there was a news item that caught my attention.[6] Physicists and cosmologists have long been theorizing about the origins of the universe, drawing on the ideas of Albert Einstein and others to delve back and back to within a fraction of a second of the big bang when space and time emerged and energy and matter began hurtling into the vastness of our still expanding universe. It is amazing that humans can do this sort of research, but what struck me about this news item was that current mathematical theories created to explain the nature and rate of the universe's expansion might need revising.

What has precipitated this rethink is that a gigantic supercomputer, reportedly with the power of seventeen thousand PCs, has been built at Durham University, England. It had spent the previous two years and fifty million process hours to run a simulation of the universe's initial explosion and

2. Plato, *Apology of Socrates*, 21a.
3. A quest described in Plato, beginning in *Apology of Socrates*, 21b.
4. Richard Kraut, "Socrates," in Audi, *Cambridge Dictionary of Philosophy*, 748.
5. See further Stumpf, *Socrates to Sartre*, 38–40.
6. It was an SBS news item on Oct. 25, 2023, with similar reports on other channels.

rapid expansion. Evidently, the simulation doesn't quite line up with what has been observed via the world's best telescopes. Current theories and reality are slightly but significantly at odds.

That's not completely surprising. Such discrepancies are frequent in scientific inquiry. It is that very thing that caught my attention in this news item. One of the cosmologists involved in this project, Durham University physics professor Carlos Frenk, said he was unconcerned that the theories and reality didn't line up (or didn't appear to). In fact, he seemed excited at what could turn out to be "cosmology at a crossroads." He said, "I welcome this. Because that is how we move forward. That is how we make progress in science."

Scientific enterprise, in the still vibrant spirit of ancient Greek philosophy, begins in ignorance and progresses through humble acknowledgment that we can always be wrong in our quest to know.[7] More often than not, the hypothesis we come up with today will need to be revised tomorrow.

Knowledge, Belief, and Humility

The very definition of knowledge is consistent with this essentially humble understanding and approach. The still widely accepted definition, often referred to as the standard definition, is that knowledge is "justified, true belief." Alvin Plantinga, the prominent American philosopher and epistemologist, whom I had the privilege of getting to know a little and whose theories became the focus of my doctoral studies, prefers the notion of warrant to justification. Both words identify the need to fulfil a crucial third step for belief to become knowledge. To know something is, first, to believe it. Knowledge's second requirement is truth. It has to be a true belief for it to be knowledge. To then fully rise to the level of knowledge, a belief also needs to be justified or warranted to an adequate degree.

What it is that gives true belief adequate warrant is a massive question. In terms of the sorts of knowledge we are dealing with in this book—the various objects of faith—warrant for these beliefs will mostly, if not always, boil down to whether or not there is adequate evidence for them.

---

7. Ideally, though not always in practice. Scientific enterprises have been as bedeviled as other intellectual disciplines, including theology, by plagiarism, falsification of results, poor methodology, and unreasonable and obstinate commitment to theories that should have been earlier abandoned.

It is worth noting that evidence can take various forms. Evidence can be propositional,[8] for example, in the form of eyewitness testimony, but it can also be nonpropositional, as is the case with direct experience, being appeared to by someone, for example. I know that I am encountering Judy, being appeared to by her, in those many instances every day when I see her, hear her, and am with her. I could put this into an argument, with various premises and a conclusion, but I really don't need to. The experiences themselves are sufficient. It could be that people have direct experiences of God that for them provide sufficient warrant for their belief that God exists. Plantinga argues that this is indeed how people come to a knowledge of God.

Whether this is so or not, the standard definition of knowledge (above) has itself encouraged philosophers, theologians, and apologists to think about what gives warrant to their various beliefs. This has been a most important quest because it is not just academic. It has everything to do with how we should live our lives. The literal meaning of philosophy is the "love of wisdom." The quest to live wisely is a noble one, but it is noteworthy that this, as with all such quests, is built on a foundation of not knowing, or of not knowing fully, in what should be a humble quest to know.

In this chapter on humility, it is therefore worth asking what we don't know or don't know fully. Here are just some of the things we are ignorant about, some of them drawn from the previous two chapters:

- We don't know who wrote the books of the Pentateuch—Genesis, Exodus, Leviticus, Numbers, and Deuteronomy—despite some of them being attributed to Moses. There are various hypotheses, including that Moses was the author or the major or original author, but the evidence suggests otherwise.

- We don't know anything about Moses, even whether he existed. The documents and stories attributed to him or about him are likely to have been written centuries later, with little to no external (to the Bible) evidence to confirm the existence of Moses or the exodus. Moreover, there appears to be increasingly persuasive counterevidence. We are left to conjecture about Moses and about whether a Moses-like figure might have been involved in a much smaller-scale escape from Egypt, but these conjectures don't even rise to the level of belief, let alone warranted true belief.

---

8. A proposition is a statement that can be either true or false. Propositions are used as premises in arguments, such as in a court case where various people claiming to be eyewitnesses make statements that the lawyer might use to build their case.

- We don't know who the authors of most of the books of the Bible were. The author we know most about is Paul, but New Testament scholars don't believe, or aren't confident, that he wrote any other than the following letters: Galatians, Romans, 1–2 Corinthians, Philippians, 1 Thessalonians, and Philemon. We don't know who any of the gospel writers were. It is also unknown who the authors of the non-Pauline letters were. There are many opinions and beliefs. Some people may think they know. I don't believe they do.

- We don't know, and can only make educated guesses about, what the writer or writers of Leviticus understood was so wrong about a man lying with another man as he would with a woman, and why women having sex with women doesn't get a mention.

- We don't know exactly when or how monotheism became dominant in Israel, replacing an earlier polytheism. There is a lively debate among scholars, with some suggesting the seventh century BCE and/or in the postexilic period, but we don't know and are left with theories, which, like all such theories, often need revising.

We don't know whether and to what extent the New Testament's portrayal of Jesus as divine reflects the actual thinking of Jesus during his lifetime. We will almost certainly have opinions and beliefs about this, including some understanding of what being divine could mean, but we can't say we know. Nor can we know whether post–New Testament theorizing about the Trinity accurately reflects what we find in the New Testament or in the Bible as a whole.[9] We also do not know whether this doctrine accurately reflects reality.

There is so much we don't know. When Christians stand up in church to say the Nicene Creed, it is significant that it begins with the words "We believe." The Apostles' Creed begins with "I believe." We would not be warranted to say "We (or I) know" these things. The Nicene Creed's statements of belief (reproduced here) are believed with varying degrees of warrant.

---

9. Metaphysical speculation about the relationship between Jesus (considered divine from the earliest days of the Christian movement) and God the Father was settled only after centuries of debate at the Council of Nicaea in 325 CE. That settlement, and the resultant doctrine of the Trinity, is still disputed to this day, with Orthodox churches having a subtly different take on it. The doctrine isn't to be found explicitly stated in the New Testament, though its defenders claim that the doctrine is true to what we find in the New Testament. At the very least, it does an acceptably good job of articulating a reality that is, nevertheless, an inscrutable mystery—three persons, one substance, not three gods, but one God.

> The Nicene Creed
> We believe in one God, the Father, the almighty, maker of heaven and earth, of all that is, seen and unseen. We believe in one Lord, Jesus Christ, the only Son of God, eternally begotten of the Father, God from God, Light from Light, true God from true God, begotten, not made, of one being with the Father. Through him all things were made. For us and for our salvation he came down from heaven; by the power of the Holy Spirit he became incarnate of the Virgin Mary, and became truly human. For our sake he was crucified under Pontius Pilate; he suffered death and was buried. On the third day he rose again in accordance with the scriptures; he ascended into heaven and is seated at the right hand of the father. He will come again in glory to judge the living and the dead, and his kingdom will have no end. We believe in the Holy Spirit, the Lord, the giver of life, who proceeds from the Father and the Son. With the Father and the Son he is worshipped and glorified. He has spoken through the Prophets. We believe in one holy catholic and apostolic Church. We acknowledge one baptism for the forgiveness of sins. We look for the resurrection of the dead, and the life of the world to come. Amen.[10]

The thing about the various Christian creeds is that they articulate beliefs that are considered crucial and central to Christian faith. They are not secondary beliefs like whether there was an actual Adam or a worldwide flood, or even whether there was an exodus, important though these beliefs might be. The beliefs articulated in the creeds are core beliefs.[11]

Should core beliefs be questioned? It is at this point that a possible friendship between Athens and Jerusalem might be seen to be in jeopardy. It may be okay for Athens to raise questions and create doubts about nonessentials, but creedal beliefs are core beliefs, without which someone could hardly be described as Christian, surely.

Not so surely, perhaps. Core beliefs are not necessarily more certain than noncore beliefs. Among the beliefs articulated in the Nicene Creed is belief in the resurrection of Jesus. That certainly is a core Christian belief. However, this belief has been seriously and sensibly questioned, not only by those who are not of the faith but by Christians as well. Was it a physical or

---

10. Standing Committee, *Australian Prayer Book*, 31.

11. It may be that some of them, such as the virgin birth, are not core beliefs, or are no longer core beliefs. However, being embedded within one of the historic creeds gives them a more authoritative status.

bodily resurrection as reported in the gospels? If so, what sort of body? Paul described it as a spiritual body (1 Cor 15:42–49). Some have speculated that the appearances were visionary, and not just in Paul's case. Others, including Christians, have suggested that evidence for the resurrection is not as strong as some may think or wish.

Alvin Plantinga, who, on nonpropositional grounds, believes that the resurrection happened, thinks that the propositional or evidential case for the resurrection is not strong, not even strong enough to warrant belief, let alone knowledge. Plantinga argues that even if one had a fine command of the vast literature on the historicity of the resurrection, one would "presumably think it pretty speculative and chancy, its probability being either low or inscrutable."[12]

That is a fairly pessimistic assessment. But it is by no means an outlier. Dale C. Allison, professor of New Testament at Princeton Theological College, has produced a large and impressive tome on this subject, entitled *The Resurrection of Jesus: Apologetics, Polemics, History*. It is the best book I have read on the subject. Allison, who does have a "fine command of the vast literature" on the subject, carefully considers the arguments of all major contemporary scholars (Christian and otherwise). He notes that these scholars lie along a spectrum from those who either "seek to establish, with some assurance, or beyond reasonable doubt, that God raised Jesus from the dead, to those who seek to establish, with some assurance, or beyond reasonable doubt, that God did no such thing." Allison concludes, after 365 pages of careful, respectful, and meticulous investigation, that neither of these projects succeeds. Allison is a Christian, who, in his words, believes "that the disciples saw Jesus, and that he [Jesus] saw them." Consequently, "next Easter will find [him, Dale Allison] in church" celebrating the resurrection.[13] Allison nevertheless agrees with Plantinga that the evidential or historical case, either for or against the resurrection of Jesus, is not strong enough to decide the issue one way or the other.[14]

---

12. Plantinga, *Warranted Christian Belief*, 276.
13. Allison, *Resurrection of Jesus*, 3.
14. Towards the end of his book, Allison writes that he would be "delighted" if he could share the optimism of scholars, such as N. T. Wright, who have argued that "logical scrupulosity yields their [resurrection] belief, [and] that to disagree means committing a ratiocinative blunder." Allison, unconvinced, concludes, "The evidence, which is not all on one side, does not demand their verdict. There is no coercive necessity here, and nothing absurd or self-contradictory in denying that Jesus rose from the dead" (*Resurrection of Jesus*, 356).

Another obviously key Christian belief is that God exists. Alvin Plantinga is only slightly more optimistic about arguments designed to prove this. In a long and distinguished career as a professional philosopher, Plantinga spent many years analyzing arguments both for and against the existence of God. He himself devised and revised versions of arguments in favor of God's existence and believed them to have merit.[15] He saw them as part of a cumulatively strong case for the existence of God. Nevertheless, Plantinga came to the conclusion that the very best one could say, on the basis of these arguments, is that God's existence is slightly more probable than not. In the light of this, the most reasonable thing to do, he argued, would be to suspend belief and be agnostic.

If Plantinga is right about the lack of evidential or propositional support for belief in God[16] and for belief in the resurrection, then this may well create a problem for those standing up week by week joining others in affirming their faith in the words of the Nicene and other creeds. It is likely to be especially problematic for those who believe that strong enough evidential support is *required* for one to justifiably believe these things. If warrant for one's beliefs is conditional on the strength of propositional evidence for those beliefs, then, arguably, Christians are in trouble.

If we acknowledge that we cannot be sure that God exists or that Jesus was resurrected, we can be even less sure about other of the creedal beliefs, including that God is three persons in one, or that Jesus was born of a virgin, or that we ourselves will be resurrected from the dead. It would certainly not be irrational to not believe these things or to believe them with a diminished degree of certitude.

But having said that, there are Christians who, with good warrant perhaps, believe they can still declare the words of the creeds with intellectual and moral integrity. It may be that they have carefully come to the conclusion that the propositional (or argument-based) evidence for these beliefs *is* strong enough and that Plantinga and Allison are wrong about this. Alternatively, they might not be relying on propositional or argumentative support for their beliefs, whether weak or strong, because of the belief that God's Spirit has witnessed directly to their spirit, and to the spirits of Christians

---

15. Plantinga speaks positively of there being "a whole host of good theistic arguments, all patiently waiting to be developed in penetrating and profound detail." In this context, he mentions over thirty examples of such arguments ("Christian Philosophy," 40–41).

16. Though I myself am persuaded by Plantinga on this point, there are others (as one might expect) who take a contrary view, including Richard Swinburne and William Lane Craig.

generally, that these creedal statements are true and trustworthy. That essentially is what Plantinga argues.

Drawing on ideas from the Protestant Reformer John Calvin and from statements by Paul in Rom 1,[17] Plantinga argues that humans believe in God because God has implanted within them a sense of the divine, the *sensus divinitatis*. They thus have adequate warrant for their belief in God. Plantinga also argues that belief in the Christian gospel, including belief in the resurrection, comes about by a similar nonpropositional method, in this case by the illuminating work of the Holy Spirit.

I am not convinced that Plantinga is right in either case, and argue as much in *Alvin Plantinga and Christian Apologetics*.[18] Nevertheless, Plantinga might be right, especially about his theory about how belief in God forms. With respect to belief in the Christian gospel, the question I'd ask is "Which particular gospel does the Holy Spirit warrant true belief in?" There are many different understandings of the gospel among Christians. A clergyperson friend of mine once told me about being quizzed by a fellow Evangelical about his understanding of the gospel. This person wanted to know whether my friend believed in the penal substitutionary theory of the atonement, which the questioner believed was nothing less than the gospel itself. Arguably, this is not the view of the New Testament, with a range of metaphors and understandings across its pages, but this does raise the question: Does the Holy Spirit directly verify a particular version of the gospel? I don't think this likely.

What I do think is that, as Christians, we need, as a mark of integrity, to honestly acknowledge that much of what we believe we don't know for sure. It is certainly not a good thing to be dishonest about one's beliefs.

False Certainty

I've noticed, and many others have as well, that too many Christian leaders, academics, and others have strayed in the other direction towards an overconfident expression of belief. I was in that camp myself early on. As a

---

17. These ones in particular: "For the wrath of God is revealed from heaven against all ungodliness and injustice of those who by their injustice suppress the truth. For what can be known about God is plain to them, because God has made it plain to them. Ever since the creation of the world God's eternal power and divine nature, invisible though they are, have been seen and understood through the things God has made" (Rom 1:18–20).

18. My ThD thesis, published in book form: Mascord, *Alvin Plantinga and Christian Apologetics*.

youngster and growing into adulthood, I believed that the only fully rational belief system was Christianity, and to not believe in God and to not believe in Jesus involved a deliberate suppression of the truth. That level of overconfident zeal is still present in Christian circles around the world, but it is a profoundly misleading and, in too many cases, dishonest zeal.

In uncertain times such as these, people are understandably on the lookout for something they can rely on, something strong enough to rest their faith upon. What this too often generates are churches that trade in certainty or near-enough certainty, as a proven method to win and keep converts. Claimed certainty works, for a while at least.

People looking on are puzzled by this, while also looking to explain it. A. C. Grayling, the atheist mentioned in chapter 1, observed:

> There is a human tragedy in this: the more they (religionists) suspect that they might be wrong, the more fiercely they adhere to it.[19]

Peter Enns, in *The Sin of Certainty*, also notes this tendency to over-inflate the strength of one's Christian beliefs. He agrees with Grayling that this is an essentially defensive phenomenon. Christians are on the back foot, and have been backed into smaller and smaller corners by the unrelenting accumulation of challenges to their faith.[20] As a result, an angry and overconfident fundamentalism has been spawned. As Enns describes it:

> Fundamentalists fought back. They said the modernists showed lack of faith in God by doubting that the Bible gives an accurate record of history. The Bible, *because* it is God's word, *must* get the past right. Otherwise the whole Christian faith collapses.[21]

What I have noticed is that this tendency towards overconfidence or claimed certainty spills out beyond Christianity's core beliefs to peripheral beliefs. God *most certainly*, it is claimed, is against same-sex marriage. God is against women having authority over men (in church at least), and all because of the supreme authority of the Bible. The plain-sense meaning of its texts must be defended at all costs. I'm amazed by the vehemence of support for these propositions, and by the anger and animosity expressed towards those who take a contrarian viewpoint.

19. Grayling, *God Argument*, 6.
20. Enns mentions Charles Darwin and critical biblical scholarship arising initially in Germany as some of the major challenges.
21. Enns, *Sin of Certainty*, 53; emphasis in original.

My own former Anglican Diocese of Sydney is willing, in fact is working towards splitting the worldwide Anglican Communion because of their certitude that what they believe is true. To believe otherwise is considered sinful. I am with Grayling in believing that, deep down, those adopting this defensive, aggressive Christianity know, or at least suspect, that they are wrong and are anxiously trying to suppress that knowledge or suspicion.

Jerusalem and Humility

Does the Bible promote epistemic humility?[22] Did Jesus promote humility in believing? Did Paul? Those are hard questions to answer. There is some reason to think not. As already noted, the Bible presents itself as divine revelation. God is frequently depicted as speaking, speaking the universe into being, speaking with Adam and Eve, with Abraham, the patriarchs, with Israel and Judah's kings and prophets, and through Jesus and Paul.

Marc Zvi Brettler,[23] in his book *How to Read the Bible*, gives one characteristic illustration of this.

> The most significant difference between modern law and biblical law is its imputed author. Exodus claims that the origin of its laws is divine. The Decalogue (the "Ten Commandments") is presented as unmediated revelation by God to all Israel; it is introduced by "God spoke all these words, saying . . ." The laws that follow the Decalogue . . . are presented as God's revelation to Moses that Moses is supposed to relay to Israel (20:19). The very structure of this part of Exodus places great emphasis on the direct-from-God revelatory nature of these laws.
>
> | | |
> |---|---|
> | Revelation | Chap 19 |
> | Decalogue | Chap 20:1–14 |
> | Revelation | Chap 20:15–18 |
> | Laws | Chap 20:19—23:33 |
> | Revelation | Chap 24[24] |

---

22. By epistemic humility I mean humility with respect to one's beliefs and ways of believing.

23. Mark Brettler is the Bernice and Morton Lerner Distinguished Professor in Judaic Studies at Duke University in North Carolina, and was formerly the Dora Golding Professor of Biblical Literature and chair of the Department of Near Eastern and Judaic Studies at the University of Brandeis in Massachusetts.

24. Brettler, *How to Read the Bible*, 61–62.

Brettler notes that this attribution of a nation's laws directly to God is unique in its ancient Near Eastern context.[25] And it is not just some but all of the Old Testament laws that are depicted as originating with God, either directly or via Moses.[26] Moreover, the reality of divine revelation is assumed to underlie Jewish wisdom and prophecy.

That assumption continues into the New Testament. Following are three examples. In the first, St. Paul identifies his own preaching as the word of God. In the second, the unknown author of 2 Peter identifies Paul's writings as scriptural, and therefore authoritative. The third example is the well-known 2 Timothy passage:

> We also constantly give thanks to God for this, that when you received the word of God that you heard from us you accepted it not as a human word but as what it really is, God's word, which is also at work in you believers. (1 Thess 2:13)

> There are some things in [Paul's writings] that are hard to understand, which the ignorant and unstable twist to their own destruction, as they do the other scriptures. (2 Pet 3:16)

> All scripture is inspired by God and is useful for teaching, for reproof, for correction, and for training in righteousness, so that the person of God may be proficient, equipped for every good work. (2 Tim 3:16–17)

One could certainly mount a prima facie case for saying the Bible itself lacks the requisite humility and questing spirit that would allow a sustainable and robust friendship between Athens and Jerusalem. They are perhaps irretrievably at odds.

To be honest, as I surely must be, given the title of this book, I am not convinced that Jesus and Socrates would have got along. Epistemic humility and the never-ending quest for truth so characteristic of philosophy and science might not have been one of Jesus's core values.[27] I don't see evidence of it in the gospel accounts. Jesus is presented there as speaking for God and, in John's Gospel, as God speaking. Jesus does challenge the beliefs and

---

25. Brettler, *How to Read the Bible*, 62.

26. Bernard M. Levinson notes: "[It] is not the Ten Commandments alone that the Hebrew Bible ascribes to divine revelation, [but] the entire legal corpus of the Pentateuch, in effect all biblical law" ("You Must Not Add," 12).

27. Some, drawing on post–New Testament Trinitarian thinking, may say, "Well, of course, Jesus wasn't a quester after the truth, nor is epistemic humility relevant to him as the omniscient Son of God, who is himself the Truth. And, of course, this is not to say that Jesus lacked humility."

practices of his contemporaries. He is Socratic in that sense. He is an acute and insightful critic of every human authority he encounters but not of the Scriptures, it would seem. Jesus was a skillful deconstructor, but his reconstruction was considered divine and thus unassailable.

Paul and Socrates have much in common, nevertheless. The Acts of the Apostles has Paul walking the same streets of Athens as Socrates once did. Though separated by centuries, they were similar in engaging passersby in robust debate and discussion. They both sought to move people towards truth as they understood it. I am sure they would have had a lively discussion had they coincided in time and place. But would they have become friends? I am not sure.

In the next chapter, I will do the next best thing to having them meet up in person and will imagine a dialogue between a present-day Socrates and a present-day Paul. Maybe that will illuminate what a friendship between Athens and Jerusalem could look like.

Questions for Reflection and Discussion

1. What comes to mind when you think about honesty and humility with respect to Christian faith?
2. What experiences have you had with overconfident expressions of belief, and how have these impacted you and others you know?
3. In what ways do you think the Bible is the word of God?

Saint Brendan's Prayer

Help me to journey beyond the familiar
and into the unknown.
Give me the faith to leave old ways
and break fresh ground with you.
Christ of the mysteries,
I trust you to be stronger than each storm within me.
I will trust in the darkness
and know that my times, even now, are in your hand.
Tune my spirit to the music of heaven,
And, somehow, make my obedience count for you.[28]

---

28. Merrell, *Celtic Blessings*, 30.

Chapter 4

Persistent Faith

AN HONEST FAITH REQUIRES persistence. There is a well-known human tendency to pull back from pursuing lines of inquiry. There are a host of reasons for this. It could be that currently held beliefs are comfortable or comforting, or that retention of one's beliefs is necessary or advisable for remaining in one's in-group. It may be that alternative beliefs are too scary even to contemplate. Particular beliefs may be considered crucial to one's belief system. Doubting them would thus threaten to completely upend the applecart of one's whole way of seeing things. It could be that one doesn't feel they have the time or the expertise to do the hard work of researching even a single strand of their belief system. They have enough on their plate already.

There are many possible reasons for not being persistent in asking questions. Some of these are doubtless acceptable. However, for those who are able, or who have time, or who have responsibility as caretakers of the belief system, it is important to be persistent in pursuing even the most frightening of inquiries. To not pursue them is to run the risk of continuing to believe what isn't true or, at the very least, to be left with the niggling suspicion that one might be misled or deluded, which thought then needs to be suppressed. This is both intellectually and psychologically unhealthy and, as noted previously, is what likely underlies present-day fundamentalisms.

If Socrates was still around, I'm sure he would discourage us from suppressing the truth through fear. He would encourage us to persist. As mentioned, Socrates believed that knowledge is possible. Persistence was therefore likely to be worth the effort. Socrates's method of persistent pursuit has become known as the Socratic method or *elenchus*. It involves a deliberate and disciplined process of dialogue, initially to clarify meaning, ultimately to secure knowledge. Socrates considered that this way of doing things was an exercise in intellectual midwifery. By it, the truth could be coaxed out.

Socrates, like Jesus, did not write anything down that we know of. We don't have any firsthand accounts of what Socrates believed and did, but a few others, including Plato, did know him well enough to inform us. Plato's earliest works, sometimes referred to as the "Socratic dialogues," have Socrates as the major protagonist or dialoguer.[1] Even if not verbatim what Socrates said, they definitely illustrate the method.

In the remainder of this chapter, I'll have a go at a contemporary example of such dialogue to help us in our pursuit of knowledge. A twenty-first-century "Socrates" has a long chat with a twenty-first-century "Paul," nicknamed PJ. For the sake of imagination, both are in their early thirties. A meetup had been arranged by mutual acquaintances.

Socrates: Hi, Paul. Nice to meet you.

PJ: Nice to meet you too, Socrates. Actually, you can call me PJ, my initials. No one calls me Paul, except for my mum and dad occasionally.

Socrates: No problem. Of course.

PJ: Excuse me for asking, but is your real name Socrates, or is that a nickname?

Socrates: It is my real name. My parents were both philosophy professors. They were admirers of Socrates long before I came along. I like the name.

PJ: I'll bet it has generated some fun conversations.

Socrates: It has. Your name has some pedigree as well.

PJ: You are right. My dad was an Anglican priest. Still is, actually. He is retired, that is, if they ever retire! Throughout his life he has always been a great admirer of the apostle Paul. I've come to share my dad's admiration for Paul.

Socrates: I see. We are a bit similar then in admiring our namesakes. I wanted to have a chat to you because I've spent most of my adult life studying philosophy, and, like many of my fellow "lovers of wisdom," I'm not so sure my studies are compatible with your Christian convictions. Someone suggested you'd be a good person to talk with about this. What do you think? Can you be a philosopher and a Christian?

1. Those identified as the Socratic dialogues are: Charmides, Crito, Euthydemus, Euthyphro, Gorgias, Hippias Major, Hippias Minor, Ion, Laches, Lysis, and Protagoras.

PJ: I believe so. I don't see them as incompatible.

Socrates: Well, the thing is, I've done some reading recently, as well as talking to Christian friends and acquaintances. Some have been helpful, but others seem to balk at my questions or simply pop them into the too-hard basket. Someone suggested you'd be different.

PJ: Thank you. I hope so. I have dabbled a little in philosophy.

Socrates: Excellent. So, to get started, how do you think the universe came into being?

PJ: I believe God created the universe.

Socrates: Okay. What are your grounds for this belief?

PJ: Well, I think that the cosmological[2] and teleological[3] arguments do provide some level of support, at least for the ideas that there was a first or underlying cause of the universe's existence and that there is at least some appearance of design.

Socrates: I think I'd agree with that—as you say, some support. I know that people have argued, scientists included, that the big bang theory is at least compatible with the idea of there being a Creator.

PJ: Yep. You'd probably also be aware, Socrates, of the work of Paul Davies, the cosmologist. He draws attention to the apparent fine-tuning of the laws of physics, which, if they had been ever so slightly different, would have rendered our universe uninhabitable.

Socrates: You are right, PJ. I have read some of Davies's books. I am certainly open to the idea that there is a God of some sort, a ground of all being, to use some of your theological language.

PJ: I realize that none of the arguments for the existence of God (or a god) prove that the God I worship, the God and Father of the Lord Jesus Christ, exists.

Socrates: You'd have to marshal a few more arguments, wouldn't you, to identify your God as creator?

PJ: True, but God (my God, as you say) would certainly be a reasonable candidate, don't you think? And I do think it's amazing that the laws of physics are such that a universe like ours can spawn creatures like us, with the amazing ability to think God's thoughts after him, so to speak! Paul Davies, at the end of one of his books, can't remember

---

2. Arguments to a first cause.
3. Arguments from apparent design.

which, concludes, "We are truly meant to be here."[4] He just couldn't bring himself to see the universe as a quirk of fate or accidental.

For me, the sheer wonder and beauty of nature leaves me feeling breathless and in awe and, to be frank, worshipful. At the very least, it has me thinking that belief in God is not irrational.

Socrates: I agree, though I also wonder what you make of the apparent cruelty and inherent wastefulness of nature. Suffering and death also seem to be built into its very fabric. This, as you know, has occasioned some pretty strong arguments *against* the existence of God.

PJ: You're right. I don't think that I or anyone else can fully refute those arguments. The best I can do is look to the Bible. There is a storyline there that at least offers some hope of us having a fuller explanation one day.

For me, it is the witness of the Bible, and of Jesus in particular, that is the grounds for my believing and continuing to believe in God, despite the challenge that evil and suffering poses.

Socrates: Oh, okay. Tell me more.

PJ: Well, I'll try to be brief, but there is a storyline that begins in the first book of our Bible and climaxes in the final book—a story that unfolds from Genesis to Revelation. It begins with a beautiful and fit-for-purpose creation that is initially devoid of suffering and death. Both suffering and death are then introduced because humans disobey God, and, as my namesake puts it, death and all the frustrations of our current existence are imposed. Paul describes creation as "groaning" until a promised future liberation. That's the Christian hope.

And, briefly, at the center of this story is the heart-transforming career of Jesus, who was also God, the divine Son of God, who willingly gave his life as a ransom to redeem humankind. This was to give each and every one of us the chance to be reconciled to God, have our sins forgiven, and share eternity with him.

Socrates: That is a pretty good summary. I think I've heard versions of it. I do have a question or two though.

PJ: I'll bet!

Socrates: I don't know how to put this, but haven't death and suffering been around from the very beginning? And who were these humans who sinned? You're not talking about Adam and Eve, are you?

---

4. Davies, *Mind of God*, 232.

PJ: I am. I grant you that suffering and death have been around from the very beginning, as you put it. And maybe I'm a bit silly, but I still do believe in a literal Adam and Eve, maybe not the first humans (or Homo sapiens) but the first humans whose free choices have adversely affected their descendants.

Socrates: Do you think so?

PJ: I admit it is pretty speculative. And it doesn't line up all that well with contemporary science.

Socrates: You do seem to have a bit of a problem there. I'll leave it with you. Can I go back to your original big story? You speak about Jesus as the "center" of this grand narrative. But don't you think God took a rather long time to send his Son into the world? It is hardly at the *center* of human history and of our prehistory. What do you think?

PJ: I have wondered about that. My dad has a possible answer to your question. I am not sure how good it is. He is what you call a Calvinist. He thinks, following Calvin and *maybe* the teaching of Paul, that ever since Adam's fateful choice (he also believes in a literal Adam) humans have been steeped in sin, mired in the blinding, deadening mud of their iniquity and rebellion against God and, as such, are thoroughly deserving of hell, which, except for redemption in Christ, they will experience forever in perpetual torment.

Socrates: That doesn't sound too good. Are they saying that it doesn't matter that God took so long to send Jesus? That God sent him at all is merciful. Is that the view of Calvinism?

PJ: I think so. It doesn't sound terribly good to me either. My dad is pretty hard-line, but, over the years, Christians whom I admire (as I do my dad) have tried to soften this aspect of the biblical story. They have done this, for example, by arguing that those who don't trust Jesus and his plan of salvation won't go to hell forever but will be annihilated, maybe after a little bit of punishment. Roman Catholics have purgatory, right? Others have suggested that God looks at the heart of every human being throughout history (and back into prehistory) and that some spark of implicit faith will have them in heaven rather than in hell or annihilated.

But, I have to admit, that's not Calvinism, according to which everyone is hopelessly sinful. It is only election and rebirth by the Spirit that will save some.

Socrates: I can see your problem.

PJ: Yep. Just while we are on this point, a friend of mine has recommended a book she thinks might be helpful. It's by a Roman Catholic theologian by the name of Richard Rohr, entitled *The Universal Christ*. From what my friend has told me, Rohr argues that Christ, and therefore God, has been ubiquitous within nature (including humankind) from the creation of the world on. God has therefore *always* been interacting with and through humans.

Actually, she emailed me some quotes. Let me grab them.

Yeah, here they are: Rohr writes, "[We] need to discard the notion of Christian salvation as a private evacuation plan that gets a select few humans into the next world."[5] "As St. Augustine would courageously put it in his *Retractions:* 'For what is now called the Christian religion existed even among the ancients and was not lacking from the beginning of the human race.' Think about that: Were Neanderthals and Cro-Magnons, Mayans and Babylonians, African and Asian civilizations, and the endless Native peoples on all continents and isolated islands for millennia just throwaways or dress rehearsals for 'us'? Is God really that ineffective, boring and stingy? Does the almighty need to wait for Ethnic, Orthodox, Roman Catholic, European Protestants, and American evangelicals to appear before the divine love affair could begin? I cannot imagine!"[6]

Socrates: That does sound a promising alternative. I might get ahold of Rohr's book. Getting back to what you said earlier, what struck me was how pessimistic a view of human nature your dad's Calvinism paints. I agree that humans can be pretty awful, and we all fall short of our own ideals, but people can also be quite wonderful. They can be generous, kind, compassionate, brave, and principled. My namesake was those things, it seems, though not perfect, of course.

My parents are both atheists, but they are the most wonderful of parents, the most wonderful of people. They are very kind and generous in their support for good causes like Black Lives Matter. They volunteer with a number of not-for-profits, some of them working with Indigenous Australians. My parents have a heart for our First Nations peoples.

And that more positive understanding of human nature is borne out across the globe with people of religious beliefs other than Christianity. The charitable work of Islamic people is well known, as is that of

---

5. Rohr, *Universal Christ*, 48.
6. Rohr, *Universal Christ*, 49–50.

Sikhs, Buddhists, and Hindus. Will they too be headed for hell despite all this, done in the service of God in many cases?

PJ: I'm not sure what to say. I've had similar thoughts. I'd like to think God takes into account people's at least relative righteousness. That seems to have been the case with Noah, Abraham, and Job. They found favor with God because of their righteousness. But, once again, this sort of thinking does contradict Calvinist ideas.

The thing about Calvinism is that it does a pretty good job of excusing God of any wrongdoing. Everyone who goes to hell deserves it. And, what's more, God's great mercy is highlighted in his gracious forgiveness of some. The cause of all evil ends up at the feet of humans or, before them, of the fallen angels overseen by Satan. It kind of works as a theodicy, but, frankly, it doesn't fit too comfortably with me or some of my friends.

Socrates: I can see why you (and your friends) aren't too comfortable with this. I wouldn't be. Is it okay if I change tack a little?

PJ: Sure.

Socrates: I'd like to assume that if there is a God, and particularly if there is a God as you understand God to be, one who is supremely good, gracious, and fair, then God wouldn't ask humans to believe things that are not true or where the evidence for those beliefs isn't strong. What do you think?

PJ: That would seem fair. What are you thinking?

Socrates: Well, I am thinking of my mum and dad. They are people of good will and are relatively righteous—to use your terminology. They have also thought long and hard about the existence of God, but have concluded that the evidence isn't strong enough for them to believe in God. They have also had a look at Christianity. My mum even had a Christian phase in her life as a teenager, but then went to university and did some reading and study. She concluded that the evidence for Christianity wasn't anywhere near strong enough for her to commit herself to it.

Just to give you one example, she compared the gospel stories to other ancient histories, biographies, and novels at around the same time as Jesus and found many similar themes: miraculous births, wonder-workers, miracles, eyewitnesses, empty tombs, people coming back to life and becoming divine.[7] She found similarities but also contradictions

---

7. For many such examples, and their similarity to the gospel stories, see Miller,

and hard-to-believe stories in the gospels. She felt she simply couldn't make what would have been a leap of faith.

My question to you, PJ, is: Would God condemn my mother for not believing, either in God or in the claimed truths of Christianity? I don't feel she has infringed any intellectual or moral duties in coming to her conclusions. My dad's journey is similar, though he didn't ever believe in God or Christianity.

PJ: That is a good question, Socrates, I have to admit. Many of my Christian friends, and my namesake, would say that to not believe in God, and to not accept Jesus, involves a suppression of the truth. I think that is how the gospel writers would see it as well. Jesus did more than enough to prove his divine bona fides.

There is a verse in Paul's Letter to the Romans that reads . . . I've got it here: "For what can be known about God is plain to them, because God has made it plain to them. Ever since the creation of the world God's eternal power and divine nature, invisible though they are, have been seen and understood through the things God has made" [Rom 1:19–20].

Socrates: Yeah, I think I can remember reading that sometime. There are a couple of things that stand out to me—not sure about yourself. It seems, it certainly seems, that in the scenario your namesake is describing the creation of the world coincides closely with the creation of human beings (as Gen 1 seems to suggest). But even you don't see it that way, right? The universe is billions of years old, the earth about 4.6 billion years old. Humans have been around for less time but still for a long time. As for human beings being able to intuit that a particular God (Paul's God) exists, that seems doubtful. As I understand things, ancestor worship probably came first, followed by various forms of polytheism, which appears to have been the religion of the Israelites prior to the emergence of monotheism.

Maybe you could press your friends with this question: Just looking at nature, with all of its wild and dangerous beauty, along with its apparent wastefulness and cruelty, what do they think can be reasonably inferred or intuited about the existence of God or gods? What do you think?

PJ: You are doing my head in, Socrates! I just feel I have to go with what the Bible says, even if I don't always understand it. It is much the same with the gospel. There is much about it that I don't get, like the

---

Resurrection and Reception.

stuff about hell and who goes there (or to heaven), but there are other things that are so precious, precious to me, precious to these friends of mine. Things like God's self-sacrificial love, forgiveness; the courage, compassion, and wisdom of Jesus; hope and trust that what is evil and bad in this world will be transformed into something that is beautiful and eternal; that there will be a new heaven and new earth one day where boundless joy, truth, and justice will have prevailed.

I know I am getting carried away, but these things just have the ring of truth about them. I've always believed—and Calvin and Paul also believed, I think—that one's conviction that these beliefs are true comes from the ministry of the Holy Spirit. That is how we know (and I mean know) that the gospel is true—and not just wishful thinking.

Socrates: Yeah, maybe. Do you think the Holy Spirit makes up for the lack of evidence for these beliefs? Is it like one of those experiences people claim they have when someone dies—maybe on the other side of the world—and their spirit is (apparently) alerted, and they somehow just know their loved one has died? They have no evidence except what their spirit tells them. Is it like that, perhaps?

PJ: Maybe. I don't know.

Socrates: So is my mum and dad's problem, and mine also, that we just haven't had the Holy Spirit tell our spirits that the Christian gospel is true?

PJ: Maybe, but maybe the Holy Spirit has tried, and you've resisted, you've rejected the message that could have saved you. I'm not saying that is the case. I'm just thinking aloud. My friends, my dad, would certainly say something like this.

Socrates: Okay. Maybe there is (or could be) something going on here which is beyond rationality—not irrational, but a-rational. I'd like to give that a bit more thought, but as a first thought, or first impression, this sounds a bit like a Holy Spirit of the gaps. The Holy Spirit comes along to bridge the gap between an unconvincing and a convincing case. Another question, PJ. Does the Holy Spirit make the unconvincing case suddenly *appear* convincing, or does it work independently such that you *just know* it is true regardless of whether there is evidence for it or not?

PJ: I tell you what, Socrates, you are exactly like I'd imagine your namesake was like! You are like a dog with a bone. I really don't know which of those two is right. I'd suspect the latter, because if the evidence, such as can be put into an argument, isn't actually strong enough to give warrant or justification for a belief or knowledge, then some supernatural sense of rightness or truth can't turn a poor case into a strong case. I judge it must be an alternative belief-forming process—a kind of direct line to the truth.

Just as a quick PS, some of my friends would say that the case for Christianity *is* strong and the only thing the Holy Spirit does is change a person's heart to be able to accept the truth of the gospel—which is sufficiently evidenced. A friend of mine has just finished N. T. Wright's long book on the resurrection.[8] Wright is a leading evangelical scholar, and he argues that, although one can't achieve mathematical-like certainty, the bodily resurrection of Jesus best explains the available historical data.[9] Others before him have argued similarly.

Socrates: I'm certainly no expert, PJ. I imagine that this has been debated, back and forth, for ages.

PJ: It has. I reckon I have read a dozen or so books about this over the time. I really don't know what to think, to be honest.

Socrates: I like those words, PJ. That's how I feel about a lot of things for a lot of the time. I think you are in good company in not knowing, in admitting you don't know.

PJ: Thank you. I mean it. Socrates, you asked me at the beginning of our long conversation whether I thought it possible to be a philosopher and a Christian at the same time. I said I thought they were compatible. What do you think?

Socrates: For me, the jury is still out, but I must say I am heartened by this discussion, which I found to be very honest and humble on your part. In acknowledging that you didn't know the answers to quite a few of the questions I raised, and in suggesting how they might be answered, you are being philosophical and a Christian at the same time.

PJ: Thank you, Socrates. That is kind of you.

Socrates: Not kind, just the sober truth. And before we head off, let me share some of my own ignorance and inquisitiveness. You earlier mentioned God's self-sacrificial love, along with other wonderful actions and attributes like courage, compassion, forgiveness, and joy. I don't presently believe in God. I don't know whether God exists or not, but

---

8. N. T. Wright, *Resurrection of the Son.*

9. Others who have argued similarly are Michael Green, Henry F. Schaefer, Stephen Davis, and Grant Osborne.

I do wonder whether there might be some ultimate source of beauty, goodness, and truth. What I do have some confidence in is that courage, compassion, and forgiveness are good things. Our world is a better place with them than without, and so maybe religion and philosophy can be friends, not just in the area of epistemology but in a common quest to help make this world a better place for us all.

I'm really glad to have had this talk with you today.

PJ: Me too. Thanks heaps. Let's do this again.

Socrates: For sure. How about we put something into our diaries. Maybe we could read a book in the meantime. Recommend something, and I'll make sure I read it. Until next time!

Questions for Reflection and Discussion

1. When have you had a discussion like the one above? Who were you most like, Socrates or PJ? What was the outcome of the discussion, and what did you learn?
2. Which of your inherited Christian beliefs have you found most difficulty with, and how have you sought to resolve or reevaluate them?
3. Do you think atheists are irrational? If so, or if not, why?
4. What do you think is the value and what risks might there be in persistent questioning such as the real Socrates encouraged?

In Memoriam A. H. H.: Prologue
by Alfred, Lord Tennyson

Strong Son of God, immortal Love,
    Whom we, that have not seen thy face,
    By faith, and faith alone, embrace,
Believing where we cannot prove;

Thine are these orbs of light and shade;
    Thou madest Life in man and brute;
    Thou madest Death; and lo, thy foot
Is on the skull which thou hast made.

Thou wilt not leave us in the dust:
    Thou madest man, he knows not why,
    He thinks he was not made to die;
And thou hast made him: thou art just.

Thou seemest human and divine,
    The highest, holiest manhood, thou.
    Our wills are ours, we know not how;
Our wills are ours, to make them thine.

Our little systems have their day;
    They have their day and cease to be:
    They are but broken lights of thee,
And thou, O Lord, art more than they.

We have but faith: we cannot know;
    For knowledge is of things we see
    And yet we trust it comes from thee,
A beam in darkness: let it grow.

Let knowledge grow from more to more,
    But more of reverence in us dwell;
    That mind and soul, according well,
May make one music as before,

But vaster. We are fools and slight;
    We mock thee when we do not fear:
    But help thy foolish ones to bear;
Help thy vain worlds to bear thy light.

Forgive what seem'd my sin in me;
    What seem'd my worth since I began;

For merit lives from man to man,
And not from man, O Lord, to thee.

Forgive my grief for one removed,
    Thy creature, whom I found so fair.
    I trust he lives in thee, and there
I find him worthier to be loved.

Forgive these wild and wandering cries,
    Confusions of a wasted youth;
    Forgive them where they fail in truth,
And in thy wisdom make me wise.

Chapter 5

Courageous Faith

SOCRATES'S PERSISTENCE (THE ANCIENT Socrates, that is) eventually got him into trouble. He was accused by some citizens of Athens of corrupting the youth and of attempting to replace the old gods, crimes that were deemed worthy of death by execution.¹ Socrates did not believe he was guilty of either charge and pled his case before a citizens' court of five hundred Athenians. As reported by Plato in *Apology*, Socrates describes himself as the city's gadfly:

> And now, Athenians, I am not going to argue for my own sake, as you may think, but for yours, that you may not sin against the God by condemning me, who am his gift to you. For if you kill me you will not easily find a successor to me, who, if I may use such a ludicrous figure of speech, am a sort of gadfly, given to the state by God; and the state is a great and noble steed who is tardy in his motions owing to his very size, and requires to be stirred into life. I am that gadfly which God has attached to the state, and all day long and in all places am always fastening upon you, arousing and persuading and reproaching you. You will not easily find another like me, and therefore I would advise you to spare me.²

In a final speech before his Athenian accusers, Socrates argued that his only crime was forcing Athenians to think:

> For if I tell you that to do as you say would be a disobedience to the God, and therefore that I cannot hold my tongue, you

1. Xenophon, *Memorabilia*, 1.1, 1.
2. Plato, "Apology of Socrates, 28–36," §§30–31.

> will not believe that I am serious; and if I say again that daily to discourse about virtue, and of those other things about which you hear me examining myself and others, is the greatest good of man, and that the unexamined life is not worth living, you are still less likely to believe me.[3]

Despite Socrates's efforts to dissuade his fellow Athenians, the majority voted that Socrates should be executed by drinking hemlock, which Socrates did voluntarily after rejecting a plan by his followers to engineer an escape from custody.

As I thought about the fate of Socrates—similar to the fate of Jesus and Paul—it struck me that something similar to the Athenian disquiet with Socrates is happening in our day with the growing numbers of people leaving Evangelicalism and, more broadly, the Christian faith. Along with efforts to understand this phenomenon are instances of angry accusation and of blaming those who are leaving. Citizens are again gathering at the foot of modern-day Areopaguses, Christians this time, in judgment on fellow and former Christians. And they are right in at least this respect that these doubters and leavers are most definitely influencing today's youth who are now jettisoning the faith, or versions of it, in large numbers.

A book was published in 2021 entitled *Before You Lose Your Faith: Deconstructing Doubt in the Church*. It was produced by the Gospel Coalition, an evangelical organization from the Reformed tradition, set up in the US to provide gospel-centered resources for churches. In its blurb at the end of the book, the coalition describes itself as seeking to be "timely, winsome and wise" in helping Christians to better understand the ever-relevant gospel. Those are admirable aims, but I found this multiauthored book disappointing. It was written to be given to people on the verge of giving up their faith. My impression was that it would hasten rather than hamper that process.

I say this because, despite efforts to be gentle, the overall tone of the book is accusative. One of the better chapters, by Karen Swallow Prior, concludes,

> The proper response to anti-intellectual Christianity isn't hyper-cerebral Christianity; it's cultivating an environment where sceptics are welcome, doubts are taken seriously, and we "have mercy on those who doubt" (Jude 1:22). The right questions asked in the right way can only lead to truth—and the Truth.

---

3. Plato, "Apology of Socrates, 37–42," §38.

Before you deconstruct your faith, know that there is no question too hard for Christianity.[4]

I like the scenario Prior paints, and agree that the right questions asked in the right way can lead to the truth, but, contra Prior, there are questions that remain unanswerable. There are also questions which are given unsatisfactory answers, as in this small book. What the book attempts to do is to defend what the authors describe as "traditional" or "historic" or "orthodox" Christian faith. They variously account for its widespread deconstruction. These are just some of those accountings:

- Only those who endure to the end will be saved (Matt 24:12–14). Some were abandoning the faith at its beginnings. We shouldn't be surprised, but we can be sad that it is still happening.[5]
- "A 'season of questioning' or a 'journey of doubt' can result in a stronger faith, but any reconstructed faith *will require* recovering Christian orthodoxy, not departing from it."[6]
- Those who embrace the faith of the European Enlightenment are replacing faith in God with faith in self, a faith unlikely to have been critiqued with the same vigor.[7]
- "Yes, God is a mystery. But he can also be known. He is known in Jesus. He is known in the pages of the Scripture. And when we seek him with all of our heart, we will find him."[8]
- "Historic Christianity is an ever stranger, ever more fringe, ever more unwelcome thing in today's world."[9] That is what makes it truly countercultural and radical—in contrast to the "'have it your own way' Burger King brand of faith"[10] that deconstruction will deliver.
- "[Our] desires don't own us. Jesus does,"[11] and regardless of whether same-sex attraction is permanent, same-sex marriage is out because of what the Bible affirms and forbids.

---

4 Karen Swallow Prior, in Mesa, *Before You Lose Your Faith*, 100.
5. Mesa, *Before You Lose Your Faith*, 2–3.
6. Trevin Wax, in Mesa, *Before You Lose Your Faith*, 8; emphasis added.
7. Trevin Wax, in Mesa, *Before You Lose Your Faith*, 12–13.
8. Ian Harber, in Mesa, *Before You Lose Your Faith*, 23.
9. Brett McCracken, in Mesa, *Before You Lose Your Faith*, 30.
10. Brett McCracken, in Mesa, *Before You Lose Your Faith*, 29.
11. Rachel Gilson, in Mesa, *Before You Lose Your Faith*, 47.

- "Your deepest longings can only be satisfied within a deep and rich Christian faith" that starts with God, champions unity, proclaims the gospel of historic Christianity, and follows God's word as the standard of truth.[12]

- "Paul 'credits' departing from the faith to deceitful spirits, teachings of demons, insincerity of liars, and seared consciences. Saving faith is a gift from God and people depart from the faith for spiritual reasons,"[13] and because they are not one of God's pre-chosen elect.

- "Whenever I read about someone deconstructing the faith, usually a predictable (and legitimate) package of issues tends to come up: the authority of the Bible considering history and science, miracles, evolution, and so forth. Then there are moral issues like Old Testament violence, or the Bible's perspective on sexuality or women. [As much as is possible] you should pay attention to Jesus himself—his concrete words and deeds in the Gospels—as you struggle."[14]

To be fair to this small book and to its various authors, this was an effort to make sense of what really is, for them surely, a puzzling and alarming trend. The authors have tried to understand it as best they can, drawing upon Scripture, which they consider authoritative. But to be frank and hopefully fair, I wouldn't give this book to someone seriously considering abandoning their faith or a version of it. They'd be even more likely to jump ship. In chapter after chapter, the blame for leaving is loaded onto the shoulders of leavers and doubters for being stumbled by peripheral issues or for selfishly and precipitously opting for inferior alternatives, while committing the greatest sin of all in not continuing to trust in Jesus—as they were perhaps predestined to do anyway.

What this book fails to do is to acknowledge that there really are big challenges to historic, orthodox, traditional Christianity. It fails to be genuinely empathetic towards fellow Christians, fellow human beings, many or most of whom are genuinely struggling to keep their faith alive or to have the sort of faith they can embrace with integrity.

I looked in vain for an honest and humble acknowledgment of the presence and strength of the large challenges that have been raised in this book thus far. One of those previously mentioned—the historicity of Moses, the exodus, and conquest—is worth examining again in a little more detail.

---

12. Thaddeus Williams, in Mesa, *Before You Lose Your Faith*, 84.
13. Jared Wilson, in Mesa, *Before You Lose Your Faith*, 124–25.
14. Derek Rishmawy, in Mesa, *Before You Lose Your Faith*, 132.

William G. Dever is well known as one of the doyens of biblical archaeology. He was born in 1933 and grew up in a fundamentalist home. His father was a clergyman. He himself became a cleric. He is a historian, a theologian, and an Old Testament scholar who has specialized in the history and archaeology of the ancient Near East. Dever describes his latest provocatively entitled book, *Has Archaeology Buried the Bible?*, as having been in the making for more than sixty years.[15] He is certainly an expert in its contents.

Dever notes that he began his archaeological career under the influence and supervision of one of America's leading biblical historians and archaeologists, G. Ernest Wright. Wright surmised that "[in] biblical faith, everything depends upon whether the central events actually occurred."[16] Dever asks:

> But what happens if the "central events"—patriarchal migrations, Moses and monotheism at Sinai, exodus and conquest, Israel's unique ethnogenesis—had not occurred?[17]

Dever argues that this is indeed the truth, and that biblical archeology's genesis as a discipline dedicated to proving the reliability of the Jewish and Christian Scriptures has ended in failure:

> Albright [one of the leading figures in this enterprise] is long gone (he died in 1971), and all of his achievements have been undermined. The archeological search for the historicity of the events in question has been all but abandoned. A revolution in viewing the Bible has indeed come . . . but hardly in the form Albright envisaged.[18]

With respect to the biblical stories of the exodus and conquest of Canaan, Dever notes that despite the fact that there is early evidence of a group described as Israelites, there is no evidence of an exodus from Egypt or a conquest of the land by former slaves.[19] Dever argues that the exodus

---

15. Dever, *Has Archaeology Buried the Bible*, vii.

16. G. E. Wright, *God Who Acts*, 126–27, quoted in Dever, *Has Archaeology Buried the Bible*, 4.

17. Dever, *Has Archaeology Buried the Bible*, 4.

18. Dever, *Has Archaeology Buried the Bible*, 3. Albright was fond of speaking of what he believed was a "revolution" in our understanding of the Bible being brought about by archaeological studies, which he believed would demonstrate the historicity of the pivotal stories of the Hebrew Bible.

19. The early evidence is from the Victory Stele of Pharaoh Merneptah, the son and successor of Ramesses II (the pharaoh of the exodus). The stele mentions that "Israel is laid waste, his seed is no more" (Dever, *Has Archaeology Buried the Bible*, 32). This wiping out was in Canaan.

tale faces insurmountable obstacles. The numbers supposedly involved (six hundred thousand adult fighting men, and thus as many as three million fleeing slaves) do not match up with reasonable possibilities—particularly with no trace of such an event anywhere. As Dever puts it:

> The problem is that anyone who has ever traversed the Sinai and camped there (as I have) knows that the vast and arid wastes of the desert could not possibly have supported even a small straggling band of a few hundred—certainly not for thirty three years. Even the few thousand modern Bedouin in the Sinai barely manage to survive. The Biblical story, read literally, is simply not credible.[20]

Dever notes that archaeologists have, for years now, searched diligently to identify and locate the Sinai desert sites mentioned in the Bible, including Mount Sinai, but without success. He concludes that Joshua's account of the conquest (which is internally contradictory and morally problematic) is fictional.[21]

These are uncomfortable conclusions for many Christians. Some will quickly reject them and will certainly question them, and that's not a bad thing. A good friend asked me, "But couldn't all these stories—these stories that you doubt, Keith—be factual?" I can understand the puzzlement and even alarm. But a courageous faith needs to look into the face of this challenge, needs to meet it head-on and ask, do the results of Dever's lifetime of research line up with what other experts in the field believe? Do their beliefs have good warrant?

There is no doubt that this is a challenge to historic Christian faith. There are just two major redemptive events in the Christian Bible. The first is the exodus. The second is the life, death, and resurrection of Jesus. The second is interpreted by the first. The persuasive power of the second is diminished if the first is nonfactual. There can be no doubt about the strength of this challenge, but the Gospel Coalition's book simply fails to mention it. In my opinion, none of the big challenges to traditional Christian faith is dealt with adequately. In neglecting these larger challenges, the book is deceptive. It is not an honest book nor courageous. We need to be both.

Some Christian friends of mine, one of whose sons is gay and whose story I shared in *Faith Without Fear*, gave me their copy of Steph Lentz's

---

20. Dever, *Has Archaeology Buried the Bible*, 31–32.

21. Dever, *Has Archaeology Buried the Bible*, 41. Archaeological evidence suggests that just one Palestinian city, Hazor, was destroyed, and not necessarily by Joshua, during the biblically described conquest period.

autobiographical *In/Out: A Scandalous Story of Falling Into Love and Out of the Church*. Once I started reading, I couldn't put it down.

Steph is courageous. She had to be, and honest. Steph was an inquisitive inquirer from her earliest days. In her words, she was "never satisfied with a short answer to any question."[22] Her early nurturing in the faith was within Sydney Anglicanism through Sunday school and into adulthood. She attended and became heavily involved in some of Sydney's prominent Anglican churches,[23] while simultaneously becoming aware, from about the age of nine, that she was attracted to people of the same sex. Even at that very young age she had an inkling that this might be a bit "off."[24]

In year six, during the Bible study segment of a youth group at St Swithun's, Pymble, Steph became a Christian. During a discussion of a passage from Philippians, she found herself deeply impacted.

> I was overwhelmed at the idea that God loves me. I wept as I pictured Jesus facing a terrible death so that I could be saved from eternal punishment. Why would Jesus do something that *good*? And for a person like *me*? That day it clicked for me. And it was dizzying. That was the day I became a Christian.[25]

In the days and years that followed, Steph increasingly struggled with the conservative Christian faith she had been converted into, which frowned on same-sex relationships. She secretly sought to make sense of the seemingly irresistible infatuations she kept feeling towards various women, some of whom she worked and ministered with. Steph couldn't turn that side of her life off, nor in fact can anyone, whether gay or straight. In an ultimately fruitless effort to deny herself, Steph became more and more deeply involved in Christian ministry, with her musical talents put to good use. She even attempted a straight marriage with a similarly keen young Christian man. It wasn't successful. It almost never is.

Steph became, momentarily, an advocate for the Sydney Diocese's position on same-sex marriage, at one point publicly entering into the fray of debates about this, only to be flayed (justifiably, she now thinks) by critics for being an unfeeling "gay basher." They had no idea about "what was taking place in [her] stormy heart."[26]

---

22. Lentz, *In/Out*, 5.
23. Including St Matthew's Manly, St Swithun's, Pymble, and St Andrew's Roseville.
24. Lentz, *In/Out*, 9.
25. Lentz, *In/Out*, 10; emphasis in original.
26. Lentz, *In/Out*, 49.

By increments and degrees, Steph began to ask increasingly searching questions about her faith. She had always been Socratic in this regard. This was despite this questioning being somewhat stifled by her belief that truth, and the Truth himself, is to be found in the Bible. This didn't stop the questions, however, and over time they became ever more acute. There is a chapter in her book entitled "Epistemology," which, not surprisingly, stood out for me. Steph was initially disappointed in her foray into epistemology to find that the evidence for theistic and Christian faith is not strong enough to compel belief. Some sort of leap of faith (as Pascal encouraged) is required, a leap that one might justifiably choose *not* to make. As Steph puts it, "[One might choose] not to leap on account of the chasm between the evidence and Christian beliefs."[27]

In the months and years before Steph courageously came out as gay to the board of Covenant Christian School, where she was teaching and consequently was fired from, Steph kept asking questions, ever more questions. She was persistent. It was fascinating to read her book because many of the people she mentioned I knew and had advocated with over the years. One of those was Joel Hollier, who was dismissed from his youth worker position at a Sydney Anglican church when he came out as gay.[28] Steff Fenton was another. Steff is a courageous and theologically skillful person whom Judy and I attended church with for a time at Holy Trinity, Dulwich Hill. Steff and Joel presented most helpfully (about gender and sexuality) to the NSW prison chaplaincy team that I had responsibility for prior to retirement.

Steph Lentz mentioned others both in the book and in later conversations whom I knew well, including John Dickson. They were something of a Who's Who of the Diocese of Sydney, a diocese she believes misled her.

Coming to a different understanding of gender and sexuality took up much of Steph Lentz's time and energy, but, as so often becomes the case, this opened the door to other hermeneutical and theological possibilities. As she describes it,

27. Lentz, *In/Out*, 68.

28. He was not alone in being so poorly treated. There have been any number of similarly devout Christians who have been fired, expelled, or sidelined when they have come out or been outed for being LGBTIQ+. Among those are Rev. Dr. Karen Pack, who was sacked (legally, under still-current anti-discrimination laws in NSW) from her lectureship at Morling (Baptist) College in 2020; Nathan Zamprogno, who in 2020, after twenty years of service, lost his job as a teacher at a Christian school in Sydney for being gay; and James Elliott-Watson, who was prevented from being a prefect and suspended from an independent school after he came out as gay. And this is not to mention many before them who have paid a similar cost, including formerly high-profile Pentecostal preacher and evangelist Anthony Venn-Brown, who lost his job when found to be gay.

> What I hadn't foreseen was that shifting my stance on homosexuality would destabilise other beliefs holding my worldview together.... The dodgy interpretations and shady motives that resulted in the church's anti-gay theology also led us astray in other areas. Failure to account for the context and literary form of the biblical texts, plus tussles over power in the church, had allowed arbitrary opinions to be promoted as divine truth. As I studied, the doctrines of sin and hell, the nature of gender and marriage, and even ideas about the Bible's origins began to teeter and sway. Previously, these ideas had been important pillars in the structure of my belief system. But now, in my giant game of Jenga, the whole tower was beginning to look alarmingly unsound.[29]

People talk about the slippery slope to unbelief. There is some truth to the analogy. Belief systems can fall to pieces under intense and fair questioning—as Socrates would encourage us to engage in. If the building isn't sound, it needs renovation. If the building is poorly constructed, its owners are likely to do all in their power to discourage questioning. It is because they too are aware of the building's fragility.

The truth is that the various challenges to historic or traditional Christian faith have been known about for centuries. For example, one of the founders of the European Enlightenment, the Jewish philosopher Baruch Spinoza (1632–77) raised questions about the historicity of the biblical miracles, including the story (from Josh 10) of the sun being stopped in the sky. He questioned the authorship of some of the books of the Bible, including the Pentateuch, which he attributed to Ezra and not Moses. He was sensitive to the genre of biblical passages and considered the Noah story as parable.[30]

Spinoza was willing to disagree with the Bible at various points, despite this contradicting the plain-sense meaning of biblical texts. In his day, that was quite shocking and revolutionary, but, four centuries later, many of his conclusions have been borne out by careful scholarship. This is well known by Christian academics and most Christian leaders. Unfortunately, the "owners" of the multiple Christian buildings we inhabit, Roman Catholic, Orthodox, Protestant, and Pentecostal, have all been slow to acknowledge and integrate this knowledge. They have failed to keep asking the sorts of questions that the spirit of Socrates would encourage them to ask. As John

---

29. Lentz, *In/Out*, 203–4.

30. Spinoza's groundbreaking contributions to early Enlightenment approaches to biblical interpretation are discussed by John Barton (*History of the Bible*, 409–17).

Barton notes in his excellent book, *A History of the Bible: The Book and Its Faiths*:

> Since the nineteenth century, biblical critics and theologians have danced around each other, trying to establish how a critical spirit can be reconciled with a desire to develop doctrine in a way that is true to the Bible. There has been a sort of concordat, under which those studying theology have to learn about biblical criticism, but the two areas have never coalesced, nor is it clear how they could.[31]

That is a great shame, and it has resulted in theological colleges failing to do this important work of acknowledgment and integration. As a result, students come and go from college with no real idea of how they might do that themselves. They learn about historical biblical criticism, and hopefully get the chance to interact with it a little, but they do so, in the case of more conservative colleges, largely on the defensive, because the "owners" of the college don't want them to ask too many questions. They'd prefer them to go out having critiqued and rejected critical approaches to the Scriptures. Sadly, graduates then go to congregations who themselves are not used to the sort of questioning and wrestling that is now long overdue.

In the early twentieth century, Adolf von Harnack (1851–1930), who himself was willing to wrestle, was reported to have said, "I bleach my students with historical criticism, but once ordained they gradually discolor again."[32] For many clergy, they are simply too frightened to venture out onto risky waters, with pressure from "owners" in both directions, from their denominational and training institutions and from the congregations they are sent out to serve. They've neither been prepared for nor supported in the increasingly urgent task of bringing all their sources of knowledge and belief into healthy alignment.

A good friend of mine who is an avid reader and who over time has read pretty much everything that has been written about biblical history, once cheekily prepared a document that he entitled "95 Theses of Contemporary Biblical Scholarship." In Luther-like style, he posted those theses, metaphorically, on the front door of Moore Theological College. He contacted a number of its former and current faculty, including some of its Old Testament lecturers, and shared his document with them. Included in it were theses about the exodus and conquest stories not being historical as described, and about the later-than-previously-accepted dating of the Old Testament

---

31. Barton, *History of the Bible*, 427.
32. Barton, *History of the Bible*, 411.

books and the anonymity of most of their authors, that is to say, many of the things I have included in the first half of this book.

The responses he received were fascinating. They were aware of the scholarship; most or much of it they accepted. What also struck my friend, and me also, was that graduates coming out of the college either weren't aware of this or had shelved what knowledge they had by the time they arrived in parish or in their various ministries around the world. My friend asked one of the recipients of the ninety-five theses, who had acknowledged that the exodus stories are not factual, how he preached when preaching on the exodus. His reply: "I preach as if it happened." I sincerely hope this clergyman does not leave the congregations he is preaching to in the dark about the nonfactual or mythical nature of the exodus narratives.

I have another friend who came into Christian faith from a religion other than Christianity. He was initially attracted by the gospel message of love, grace, and forgiveness and by the warm acceptance of the "Bible-believing" church he began to attend. But when he became aware of some of the big problems associated with this belief system, he felt he had been lied to. He'd been misled. He now refuses to have anything to do with (most) Christians and won't allow his children to attend Scripture lessons for fear that they too will be led astray.

Steph Lentz's experience was similar. Aware that many of the people she used to look up to are aware of the hermeneutical and epistemological issues that (for centuries now) have cast doubt upon their biblical worldview, Steph now challenges them to have the integrity to be truthful, and especially because the articulation of their views is so manifestly damaging to LGBTIQ+ people, including herself. She writes:

> The scholarship is there for the reading. That it behoves pastors and theologians to do the work is an understatement. That is their job. The onus is squarely on those who espouse a dehumanizing, dangerous theology to show their working. To continue to neglect this responsibility constitutes an egregious failure to fulfil their duty of care. What's inconvenient or uncomfortable for some is killing others.[33]

A brief PS to my comments about the Gospel Coalition book. I spoke positively about the chapter written by Karen Swallow Prior. It turns out, and I knew nothing of her before reading that book, that Karen has long been an

---

33. Lentz, *In/Out*, 188.

advocate for causes close to my heart. In her words, as reported in a Religion News article:

> I thought for a long time I could help the church (or at least my slice of it) change. I could take a community and denomination rife with racism, cronyism, misogyny and abuse and change it.
> How foolish I was.[34]

Prior had been a teacher (of literature) at the conservative Liberty University and then at Southeastern Baptist Seminary. Because of her efforts to encourage Evangelicals to keep thinking and rethinking their faith, and because of her evenhandedness and not coming down on one side or the other on various defining (for Evangelicals) issues, she was criticized, with one evangelical attack site saying this of her in 2021:

> *Given her support for homosexuality, her support for abortion doctors, her support for female clergy, her support for animal rights, and her support for Social Religion, anyone calling Prior a "Christian" is guilty of slander against Jesus.*[35]

Prior should be commended for her efforts and her courage. It has cost her. As I finish this section of the book, let me issue a challenge.

To parishioners, to those of you who sit in church each week, do begin to ask some of those searching, Socratic-like questions of your pastors and spiritual leaders. You can gently find out whether such questioning is compatible with the church, diocese, or denomination you are attending and whether Athens and Jerusalem are or can be at peace with each other. Ask and keep asking until you get an honest answer. And even then, keep asking.

To clergy, to all pastors and preachers, if you are unsure, go back to your theological teachers and trainers and ask them what they think about these challenges to traditional Christian faith. And if you already know the answers to those questions, even with a degree of uncertainty that is impossible to avoid, have the courage to tell the truth from the pulpit and in your Bible studies and home groups. Do not lie to those you are shepherding. Do not lie to yourself. Have the courage to be honest. It may cost you your job or advancement in your career, but you'll have kept your integrity.

To theological lecturers and students, don't stop asking questions of each other. Theological colleges should be the safest of environments to do that. Principals, boards, and staff members, make sure it is safe. Only then will

---

34. Prior, "Don't Go Into a Relationship," paras. 11–12.
35. Poletti, "#1 Female Evangelical Scholar," para. 11; emphasis in original.

the honest, humble quest for truth be safeguarded. Only in the integrity of such courageous action can Christianity survive and thrive.

Questions for Reflection and Discussion

1. When have you needed to be courageous in asking and seeking answers to hard questions about your faith? What was the result?
2. What cost would you have to pay to be fully honest with yourself and others about your doubts and emerging convictions about your faith? What would you lose if you kept silent?
3. How might you encourage honesty and courage within your friendship group and/or faith community?

REFORMING JERUSALEM

Tertullian's challenging question "What has Athens to do with Jerusalem?" certainly requires an answer. In some ways, these two ways of seeing and interacting with the world have never been farther apart or more conflicted. What hope is there of concord or peace? I believe there is hope and will seek to demonstrate why in this second half of the book.

Hope will, however, be contingent on change, change that many will find threatening. The headings of these next chapters are reflective of what a re-forming faith will need to be, that is, imaginative, loving, liberating, and hopeful. A re-formation or even reformation of sorts is needed. The faith of a reforming Jerusalem will be different than what we have inherited and become familiar with. It will need to be different to be an honest faith.

For the Interim Time
by John O'Donohue

When near the end of the day, life has drained
Out of light, and it is too soon
For the mind of night to have darkened things,

No place looks like itself, loss of outline
Makes everything look strangely in-between,
Unsure of what has been, or what might come.

To this wan light, even trees seem groundless.
In a while it will be night, but nothing
Here seems TO believe the relief of dark.

You are in this time of interim
Where everything seems withheld.

The path you took to get here has washed out;
The way forward is still concealed from you.

"The old is not old enough to have died away;
The new is still too young to be born."

You cannot lay claim to anything;
In this place of dusk,
Your eyes are blurred;
And there is no mirror.

Everyone else has lost sight of your heart
And you can see nowhere to put your trust;
You know you have to make your own way through.

As far as you can, hold your confidence.
Do not allow your confusion to squander
The call which is loosening
Your roots in false ground,
That you might come free
From all you have outgrown.

What is being transfigured here is your mind,
And it is difficult and slow to become new.
The more faithfully you can endure here,
The more refined your heart will become
For your arrival in the new dawn.

Chapter 6

Imaginative Faith

IMAGINATION IS A KEY to understanding Christian faith. It is also a key to securing an honest and sustainable faith. Imagination is another of inquisitiveness's siblings. Inquisitiveness is perhaps the elder sister who initiated the process which led to both religion and philosophy. Imagination wasn't far behind. She was required to help make sense of a reality which is profoundly puzzling. It is why stories are needed. It is why Plato composed his "likely stories," including the well-known allegory of the cave out of which humans need to emerge.[1]

Imaginative Storytelling

The Bible is chock full of stories. The earliest of them simply needed to be imaginative and in story form because those who composed them had no way of knowing their prehistory, let alone the prehistory of the earth and universe. By almost any understanding of myth, these stories are mythical.

I once thought that the employment of myths more or less stopped at the end of Gen 11, and that myths thereafter only played a small part in the biblical storyline. However, under influence from a broader understanding of mythology,[2] many more of the Bible's stories are coming to be understood as mythical in the sense of being nonfactual or not literally true but still likely to be truth full.[3] I'm now of the opinion that the Bible's storyline

---

1. Plato, *Republic*, bk. 7.
2. As articulated in ch. 2, 16–19.
3. I personally found Richard C. Miller's definition of myth helpful. Myths, as he defines them, are "sacred narratives or accounts that have served to frame the present

as a whole is one long largely mythical epic, not altogether dissimilar to the *Odyssey*,[4] *The Lord of the Rings*, or the Narnia chronicles. The biblical writers are every bit as imaginative as Homer, J. R. R. Tolkien, and C. S. Lewis. The difference, and it is significant, is that the biblical story does slide into our more prosaic world, perhaps as early as the book of Judges and certainly by the time of the Israelite and Judean kings. Mythology and history increasingly merge, but never do they entirely separate.[5] We find them still together in the New Testament.

For some, this way of looking at things is threatening, but when you think about it some more (persistence), it could hardly have been otherwise. Imagine if the ancient writers had kept themselves to events and people they could independently verify, with all the necessary documentary and other evidence. One would end up with a very boring and much shorter document. Think for a moment about all the wonderful, beautifully crafted biblical stories, including the detailed, psychologically perceptive, and thematically fascinating patriarchal narratives. The long story of Joseph, at the end of the book of Genesis, is an epic in itself. A history shrunk down to just the ascertainable facts would not only be boring, it would need to be constantly revised with historical hypotheses replacing each other ad infinitum.

The biblical writers have done much better than that. They've told a big story, an epic story, with one of its chief characters, Moses, depicted as writing it, recording it, eye-witnessing it, and skillfully theologizing about it. It is not unusual for ANE writers to attribute works to more famous people. This practice spills into the New Testament with Matthew, John, Peter, Paul,

---

for a person, group, society, nation, or all of humanity." They can thus incorporate eschatological, apocalyptic, cosmic, and aetiological myths (*Resurrection and Reception*, 17). This contrasts with popular understanding of myths as stories that are not true. As we increasingly recognize, myths are very often profoundly true. They can elucidate the truth more powerfully and insightfully than more prosaic efforts to communicate truth.

4. A relatively new (for many) and promising development within New Testament studies is research into the influence of Greco-Roman culture, including its histories, poetry, and mythology, on the New Testament authors, including the clearly well-educated authors of the four gospels. An interesting thesis, which still requires further study and review, is that the author of Mark's Gospel was influenced by, drew upon, and possibly even patterned various gospel stories on themes and episodes from Homer's *Odyssey*. See, for example, MacDonald *Homeric Epics*; and MacDonald, *Gospels and Homer*.

5. Frank Moore Cross, in his helpful book *Canaanite Myth and Hebrew Epic*, notes that "epic in interpreting historical events combines mythic and historical features in various ways and proportions" (vii). Understood in this way, epic is an apt description of the overarching narrative of the Bible.

and James having works attributed to them that they themselves probably did not write.

But back to the big story, it is not just a big story. As with the *Odyssey*, *The Lord of the Rings*, and Narnia, the biblical story is a story with serious intent. It is a story that tells an even bigger story. For its Jewish and earlier Israelite writers, it was their way of telling their national story and of using this story to illustrate their understanding of life. It became their nation's dreaming, akin to the mythologies of our First Nations' peoples, akin also to the more recent ANZAC myth that we Australians draw upon in imagining our nation's origins.[6]

The theological imagination of the authors did not only look backwards. It also looked forward in trustful hope to a better future, as the nation's mythology was pressed into the service of apocalyptic expectation.[7] The biblical epic is much more than a history therefore, however understood. It is cosmology, anthropology, theology, eschatology, and apocalyptic. In the hands of its Jewish and Christian authors, it became the world's story, a big story indeed.

It is not that there aren't problems with it, as the first half of this book has begun to lay out. Whether fraudulently or not, many of the Bible's authors have misled us by attributing their writings to others. Many of us grew up thinking the Bible was perfect, without error, and that it wouldn't mislead us, that indeed God would not mislead us. But the Bible is not perfect, or if it is perfect, it is perfect in unexpected ways.

We often hear about "Bible-believing" Christians and "Bible-believing" churches, but that must surely mean believing in the Bible as it is, not as we might like it to be. And the biblical writers *just were* hugely imaginative. Imagination is endlessly present and active throughout the pages of the Bible, and it resulted in two characteristics of the Bible that Bible-believing Christians should be aware of. First, the biblical authors frequently revise

---

6. What is interesting about the ANZAC myth, which is also often described as a legend, is that it is about real events (Australian and New Zealand soldiers involved in an unsuccessful military campaign at Gallipoli in 1915) but told in such a way as to define something of Australia's national ethos.

7. As Andrew Judd, in his helpful recent book, points out by way of a question: "But how do you describe the indescribable or communicate a reality beyond anything in world history? With an array of otherworldly images that speak to the imagination, of course!" He goes on, "Apocalyptic texts . . . [bring] together a rich feast of symbolic material. They are full of visions, dreams, hidden meaning, animal symbols, meteorology, angels and demons. Some of the imagery seems to be drawn from Ugaritic motifs or Hellenistic propaganda, but adapted to the Bible's monotheistic worldview" (*Modern Genre Theory*, 161–62).

opinions earlier expressed, and second, they more than occasionally differ from each other. The biblical authors hold a diversity of opinions. Understanding this has huge implications, some of which we will explore.

The Ever-Revising Nature of Scripture

We don't know how many human authors the Bible had. There may have been hundreds involved in writing, redacting, tweaking, and finalizing the Bible's sixty-six books. We also don't know exactly when they were written, with all sorts of theories about underlying sources that were drawn upon over time until the final form of these books was eventually reached. This complex composition history has left some interesting literary footprints, allowing scholars to speculate about the early development of ideas, some of which were discarded, others of which came to full expression later in the piece. We are talking about composition over hundreds of years.

Polytheistic Remnants

Biblical studies are a bit like archaeology or geology. Scholars are looking for telltale signs, now fossilized in the text or, as Tom Holland describes them, "preserved like insects in amber."[8] Some of these texts speak of an earlier polytheism, which later monotheistic scribes chose to not fully edit out. The presence of these earlier remnants has allowed biblical scholars such as William Dever to construct an increasingly credible picture of the development of Israelite history. Dever contends that the biblical version of Israel's history is an ideal history, "a portrait not of what Israel actually was, but of what it *should* have been had it conformed to orthodox Yahwism. [It is] a theocratic history, history viewed primarily as the acts of Yahweh, Israel's creator and sole deity."[9] Moreover, it was "almost never the reality, [it was] an ideal that they projected back upon a largely imaginary past."[10]

Dever notes that Israel's earliest popular folk religion honored the older Canaanite deities, including El and his consort Asherah, who were the parents of the lesser gods, including Yahweh.[11] Also honored were a rival pair, the

---

8. Holland, *Dominion*, 62.
9. Dever, *Has Archaeology Buried the Bible*, 125.
10. Dever, *Has Archaeology Buried the Bible*, 126.
11. Tom Holland notes that Yahweh was initially a storm god worshipped in the form of a bull by the inhabitants of Edom to the south of Canaan, as alluded to in 1 Kgs 12:28 (*Dominion*, 62).

storm god Baal and his wife/warrior companion Anat. There were also a host of lesser gods and goddesses. Summing up, Dever writes:

> Most biblical scholars now conclude that polytheism—or what some call "poly-Yahwism," *many versions of* Yahwism—was the norm throughout the history of ancient Israel. Not until the destruction of Jerusalem and the temple and the exile, when Israel had finally learned a painful lesson, did monotheism finally emerge triumphant. That monotheism in Scripture, and in practice, is what prevailed in later Judaism, and, of course, in its offshoot, Christianity.[12]

We may never know how exactly it came about that Judaism embraced monotheism and why it turned its back so forcefully on polytheism. Perhaps it had to do with carving out a place for itself in an aggressively corrupt, dangerous, and polytheistic world.[13] From where I am sitting, it was an entirely positive development. It was progress, ultimately a gift to the world. It delivered us the beauty of Gen 1–3 with its full-of-faith story about an essentially good God and an essentially good creation. It imagined humans into the image of this supremely good and gracious deity, creating by far the most dignified view of humankind ever imagined. The impact of that view continues to reverberate all the way to our present day.[14]

This brilliantly beautiful way of seeing things, new to the world, wasn't without problems or potential for challenge. In fact, some of those problems were of its own making. Polytheism doesn't have the same problems. If the world is populated with many gods, good, bad, and in between, then evil in the world and among humans is more easily explained. But if there is just one God, and this God is totally good, and also supremely powerful as the sole creator of the universe, whence then comes evil, and, once it has arrived, why hasn't it been removed? It is those big questions that inform and challenge the biblical epic from go to woe.

---

12. Dever, *Has Archaeology Buried the Bible*, 127; emphasis in original.

13. J. Wright notes that well into Israelite and Judean history, Yahweh was believed to have a female consort, Asherah, who had earlier been El's consort. It appears that under the reforming reign of Judean King Josiah, Asherah worship was outlawed, while the Canaanite pantheon was reduced to one. Wright suggests that this was "part of an effort to focus on a single transcendent entity that could unite the nation" (*Why the Bible Began*, 84).

14. Tom Holland does a fine job in *Dominion* of articulating the impact of Judeo-Christianity within Western cultures.

Deuteronomistic Revisions

We see this perhaps most strikingly in what has become known as the Deuteronomistic history, which has become a common way of describing the book of Deuteronomy and the books that follow, often referred to as the Former Prophets: Joshua, Judges, 1 and 2 Samuel, and 1 and 2 Kings. The architect of this description was German scholar Martin Noth (1902–68). Noth observed similarities in style and theology across these various books. He also noted that the book of Deuteronomy had more in common with the books that followed than with the first four books of the Bible. His ideas have been widely accepted, though not without differences and modifications, as we'd expect. Nevertheless, what the Deuteronomistic history does have in common is the strong message that obedience to Yahweh will result in blessing and that disobedience will result in calamities such as the exile, which is predicted in Deuteronomy. It is now widely accepted that Deuteronomy and the Deuteronomistic history were written, or more likely, completed after the Judean exile. If so, they were written, in part at least, to explain this catastrophic event for the Jewish nation.

The Deuteronomistic history can therefore be understood as a form of theodicy,[15] defending God, and belief in a good God, by attributing suffering to human sinfulness and failure. It is this thesis that is challenged and modified throughout the pages of the Bible. There is a quite stark example of this in the wording of the Ten Commandments in Deuteronomy and in the earlier-written Exodus. The Exodus version provides the following incentive for obeying the command to not bow down or serve other gods:

> For I the Lord your God am an impassioned God, visiting the guilt of the parents upon the children, upon the third and upon the fourth generation of those who reject me, but showing kindness to the thousandth generation of those who love me and keep my commandments. (Exod 20:5–6)

The author or authors of Deuteronomy react against the implied notion of intergenerational punishment, and they aren't alone in this. According to the prophet Ezekiel, "Know that all lives are mine; the life of the parent as well as the life of the child is mine: it is only the person who sins who shall die" (Ezek 18:4).[16] Deuteronomy makes the same point even more decisively:

---

15. A theodicy is an effort to defend the goodness of God in view of the existence of suffering and evil.

16. Ezekiel not only challenges the idea that children are punished for the sins of their parents, he also takes issue with the idea that blessing accrues to the children of

> Know, therefore, that the Lord your God is God, the faithful God who maintains covenant loyalty with those who love him and keep his commandments to a thousand generations, 10 and who repays in their own person those who reject him. He does not delay but repays in their own person those who reject him. (Deut 7:9–10)

The contrast couldn't be plainer, and the rationale appears to be that punishing people for their parents' sins is unjust and unworthy of a wholly good God. Theodicy at work again.

The need for theodicy is perhaps even more acute in this context than elsewhere. The above verses from Exodus are embedded within the Ten Commandments, purportedly delivered on Mount Sinai by none other than God. As already noted, these laws and, in fact, all Old Testament laws are described as coming directly or indirectly from God. This creates an obvious difficulty for future biblical authors, including the prophets. How can any of these laws be critiqued or modified without undermining their divine authority? Bernard Levinson notes the problem and suggests that later authors needed to be somewhat subtle in modifying earlier problematic texts such as Exod 20:5–6.[17] In the case of Ezekiel, it was by the indirect approach of critiquing a well-known parable:

> The word of the Lord came to me: what do you mean by repeating this proverb concerning the land of Israel, "The parents have eaten sour grapes, and the children's teeth are set on edge?" As I live, says the Lord God, this proverb shall no more be used by you in Israel. Know that all lives are mine; the life of the parent as well as the life of the child is mine: it is only the person who sins who shall die. (Ezek 18:1–4)[18]

Levinson observes that "Ezekiel therefore uses the proverb as a strategic foil for the far more theologically problematic act of effectively annulling a divine law. The prophet in effect 'de-voices' the doctrine's original attribution to God, and then 'revoices' it as folk wisdom."[19]

It is worth noting that contemporary Jews and Christians have similar challenges. The biblical authors were indeed creatively imaginative in depicting God as the direct lawgiver and in locating these laws within the mythical

---

obedient parents. See, for example, Ezek 14:12–20.

17. Levinson, "You Must Not Add," 43–44.
18. Ezekiel 18 spells this out more fully.
19. Levinson, "You Must Not Add," 33.

stories of the exodus and conquest. But from the vantage point of almost three millennia, some of those laws ought to be challenged, particularly those with patriarchal assumptions. The relative devaluation of the life of a slave,[20] or the assumption that women, children, and slaves are the property of men, we no longer find acceptable.

Returning to the note of theodicy, the defense of God's goodness is not restricted to issues of justice. In fact, the Deuteronomistic emphasis upon justice, on God rewarding goodness and punishing badness, can obscure an equally important aspect of God's goodness, which is mercy. Anthony Bartlett, in his insightful book *Signs of Change: The Bible's Evolution of Divine Nonviolence*, expounds the story of Jonah, which Bartlett describes as "pure story or fable."[21] In it, God's mercy and compassion for all peoples, including some of the most violent of them, the Assyrians, is highlighted. An implicit contrast is thereby set up with the actual Jonah, who in 2 Kgs 14 provides prophetic encouragement for King Jeroboam II's military campaign to restore Israel's borders.

The thing about borders is that they keep people out and benefit those who are in. Jonah, of the book of Jonah, is sent out on what was intended as a mercy mission, to extend mercy beyond Israel's borders. The possibly postexilic author of the book is also likely to have had the seventh-century prophet Nahum in view. Nahum had absolutely no time for Nineveh, except to rail against it, which he does so vividly at the outset of his book:

> An oracle concerning Nineveh. The book of the vision of Nahum of Elkosh.
> A jealous and avenging God is the Lord;
>   the Lord is avenging and wrathful;
> the Lord takes vengeance on his adversaries
>   and prolongs it against his enemies. (Nah 1:1–2)

It would be no exaggeration to say that Nahum hated Nineveh, a revulsion shared by his fellow Israelites. Nahum lived and prophesied at the time of Nineveh's demise at the hands of the Babylonians and Medes, and no tears would have been shed for it.

---

20. Just to give one small example, Lev 19:20 legislates that "if a man has sexual relations with a woman who is a slave, designated for another man but not ransomed or given her freedom, an enquiry shall be held. They shall not be put to death, since she has not been freed." In the very next chapter, "if a man commits adultery with the wife of his neighbor, both the adulterer and the adulteress shall be put to death" (Lev 20:10).

21. Bartlett, *Signs of Change*, 123.

The writer of the book of Jonah had a very different and deliberately contrasting view. The fictional Jonah had to be dragged kicking and screaming, in fact, had to be vomited back in the direction he was fleeing from, in order to express God's unfathomable love for the unlovable. The book concludes with a rebuked Jonah and God's tender love explained:

> Should I not be concerned about Nineveh, that great city, in which there are more than a hundred and twenty thousand persons who do not know their right hand from their left and also many animals? (Jonah 4:11)

Biblical authors could take issue with their fellow authors. They did so in ongoing efforts to bring their understanding of God into line with their experience and ongoing reflections. The Deuteronomistic perspective was too neat and unconvincing for the authors of Ecclesiastes and Job. They went out of their way to critique simplistic understandings of the causes of evil and suffering. They were critics, friendly critics, of their own Jewish traditions.[22] At the very least, they called for nuance while also not providing us with final answers.

The debate between Job and his comforters/accusers is representative of Bible-long conversations, with Jesus also contributing. The idea that suffering and calamity are the result of sin and failure, and blessing the reward for righteousness, simply does not match reality. When a person born blind was brought to him, Jesus was asked whether it was this person's sin or his parents that had caused his blindness. Jesus replied,

> Neither this man nor his parents sinned; he was born blind so that God's works might be revealed in him. (John 9:3)

The point to make is that Scripture is not static nor monochrome. Its voices are often contrasting. Moreover, across time, understandings develop. In terms of biblical hope, there is movement within and beyond the Old Testament from a this-worldly to an otherworldly hope. The fact that the righteous do not always prosper, and that the unjust frequently do, and that everyone eventually dies anyway, prompted the introduction of notions of heaven and hell as places where God's justice and mercy could coalesce and find full expression.

---

22. Another instance of intra-biblical critique is the book of Ruth, which Robert Alter argues represents an argument against the exclusionary policy on foreign wives propagated by Ezra and Nehemiah (*Strong as Death*, 59).

Christological Expansions

Another example of the ever-revising nature of the Bible, and of the need for imagination, is the New Testament's deification of Jesus. Scholars mostly agree that belief in the resurrection of Jesus was Christianity's originating impetus, without which Christian faith would not have come to be. Within days of his crucifixion, a number of Jesus's closest disciples, male and female, reported experiences of being appeared to by the risen Jesus. The apostle Paul later also reported a life and career-defining encounter with a risen Jesus.

The immediate and longer-term challenge created by these reported encounters was the need to make sense of them. It is no exaggeration to say that each and every book of the New Testament was actively engaged in this process of making best sense of what initially was an unexpected event. The earliest Christians had a number of resources they could draw upon, both from within and outside of Judaism. Most obviously to hand were messianic expectations. There was a widespread belief among first-century Jews that a descendant of David would liberate the nation from oppression, which it was again experiencing under Roman rule.

Two other resources close at hand were the suffering servant figure of Second Isaiah and the Son of Man figure of Dan 7:13–14. Prior to the claimed resurrection of Jesus, messianic expectations had not included the suffering servant or the Son of Man. However, the Suffering Servant Songs were quickly appealed to for their obvious explanatory power. Paul built his understanding of the gospel around them. Son of Man was a preferred self-designation of Jesus in the Synoptic Gospels, suggesting that this was a title Jesus applied to himself.

None of these descriptions involved or implied the attribution of divinity. The suffering servant was depicted as an individual human sufferer and identified as the nation of Israel. The Son of Man was the son of a human father, that is, a human being, gifted with everlasting dominion, glory, and kingship. The messiah was a human king to be. The common description of Jesus as Son of God, used often in the New Testament, also did not imply divinity. King David was a son of God. The Israelite kings were sons of God. Israel was a son of God. Luke describes Adam as a son of God (Luke 3:38). In an ardently monotheistic religion, such as Judaism had become, the idea that a human being could be divine, except in a secondary sense, is unlikely to have been countenanced, especially early on.[23]

---

23. Though it is interesting that Jewish authors were not averse to calling humans God. See, for example, Ehrman, *How Jesus Became God*, which, in ch. 2, has many

It is an entirely different story for contemporaneous Greco-Roman culture, within which emperors and other heroes were commonly divinized. As mentioned in chapter 2, there existed numerous "translation fables" in which deserving, normally famous, and often legendary human beings were divinized and taken heavenward. The story of Romulus, the founder of the city of Rome, is a typical example. Romulus mysteriously disappeared from a parade of his troops to become the god Quirinus. There were claimed eyewitnesses to his translation, which was a common feature of these fables. Another common feature was the absence of a body and/or an empty tomb. Another was nobility in the face of an unjust death. In the context of the times, the empty tomb or the centurion's declaration in Mark 15:39, "Surely this man was God's son [or a son of God]," is not surprising given widespread knowledge of translation fables.

Judaism had its own translation fables, which the authors of the gospels may well have drawn upon. Philo, for example, in one of his books about Moses, describes Moses as having been taken up into heaven to become a divine being, not equal with God but given divine-like honors, not dissimilar to the Son of Man figure.[24]

With all of these resources at hand, it nevertheless took Christians a long time to arrive at a doctrine of the Trinity and to have it authorized, with differences, by the Western and Eastern Churches. James D. G. Dunn, in *Christology in the Making: A New Testament Inquiry into the Origins of the Incarnation*, notes that even with all of the above-mentioned resources at their disposal, there was still significant ground to be covered before arriving at the Trinitarian agreements of the Council of Nicaea in 325 CE. Even the idea of an incarnation took time to emerge. It did not previously exist within Judaism. None of the major titles applied to Jesus in the New Testament, including Son of Man, Son of God, and Messiah, was considered to be preexistent.[25] Titles applied to beings who were preexistent, including Spirit, Wisdom, and Word, never reached the status of divine beings in Jewish thought:

---

examples of Jewish authors calling humans God. There are also instances within Scripture of this, such as Ps 45:6 where God addresses the king in these terms, "Your throne, O God, is forever and ever." There is also an instance in John 10:34–36 where Jesus is reported as quoting (in fact misquoting) Ps 82:6 where some gods of the heavenly assembly are divested of their divinity for unjust rule. Jesus takes the verse as applying to its human readers.

24. Michael Bird notes that Philo in describing Moses as God qualifies this to say, "Moses is God in relation to Israel" (Philo, *On the Life of Moses*). Bird summarizes this as "He has god-like power over Israel" (Ehrman et al., *When Did Jesus Become God*, 70).

25. Dunn, *Christology in the Making*, 252.

> They all remain in the literature of our period (Philo included) ways of speaking of God's powerful interaction with his world and his people, God's experienced immanence through nature and revelation, in Torah, prophet and saving act, which yet did not infringe his transcendence. Their pre-existence is the pre-existence of God, of God's purpose to create and redeem.[26]

It is therefore entirely understandable that it took some considerable time for Christians to imagine and then to embrace an incarnational and Trinitarian understanding of Jesus. They could well have decided differently. They could have simply accepted Jesus as the divinely authorized Messiah, who was also the suffering servant and Son of Man, and, as such, also a Son of God like David or Adam or any favored human being. They could have gone a step further, with good precedence, and declared Jesus as a second-level deity, like Moses. They could have taken an adoptionist position, with Jesus adopted into divine sonship at his baptism, transfiguration, or resurrection. There are certainly Scriptures that hint at such a possibility. Because there were these many options, they were debated back and forth for centuries, up until and even after the Council of Nicaea. It was the position of Arius, a churchman from Alexandria in Egypt, that lost out in the debates occurring at Nicaea. Arius argued that Jesus was a second-level deity having been created by God as his Son, who then created the universe. Arius would have had no trouble marshaling supportive biblical texts.

What does seem clear is that early Christian thinkers were required to cogitate long and hard, with their imaginative powers fully utilized. In a useful small book, entitled *When Did Jesus Become God?*, Bart Ehrman and Michael F. Bird approach the question of Jesus's divinity from quite different perspectives.[27] Erhman is a former Evangelical who now describes himself as agnostic or atheist. Bird was an atheist before becoming an evangelical Christian. He had previously considered Christianity an oppressive human construct. What I found interesting about the book is that Ehrman and Bird were agreed that within and beyond the New Testament there was significant theological development.

We can see that development in the gospels. Mark's Gospel, the earliest of the four, has the true identity of Jesus more or less hidden (the messianic secret). About the most one can say from a close reading of Mark is that Jesus was the Son of God *because* he was also the Son of Man and suffering servant. The disciples didn't really have a clue. Some years later, when the

---

26. Dunn, *Christology in the Making*, 252–53.
27. Ehrman et al., *When Did Jesus Become God*, 70.

Gospel of John was written, a much fuller picture was painted of a preexistent Word of God, and of a Jesus who claimed equality with God. Dunn notes that John's Gospel is the only New Testament document that is unambiguously incarnational. In summing up his book-long discussion of these matters, Dunn writes:

> [As] the first century of the Christian era drew to a close we find a concept of Christ's real pre-existence beginning to emerge, but only with the Fourth Gospel can we speak of a full blown conception of Christ's personal pre-existence and a clear doctrine of incarnation.[28]

John's Gospel is certainly an outlier. It is strikingly different than Mark. Jesus is depicted as fully forthright about his divine identity in many long speeches, leaving not only his disciples but hostile listeners in no doubt about his elevated claims. Ehrman points out the anomaly of Jesus being so clear about his godlikeness and even God-ness in John when there are no such explicit disclosures in Mark's Gospel, nor in Luke or Matthew. Bird acknowledged the anomaly and expressed his view towards the end of the book:

> I think the Gospel of John is a mixture of memory, midrash, and mysticism. . . . I think there is a historical tradition in John, but it is being pushed through a thick interpretive layer. So what we get in the Gospel of John, even on the lips of Jesus, is not just the words of Jesus, not just the voice of Jesus, but sometimes the impressions Jesus made on his earliest followers are incorporated in the narrative. So I think there is a historical tradition in John. Some say that John is historically worthless. I wouldn't go that far. But John is different than the Synoptics.[29]

What is so interesting about these comments, and what we have seen thus far, is the indispensable role of imagination, the clear need to be imaginative, not just for the biblical authors but for theologians and philosophers living beyond the New Testament, including ourselves. A process begun within the pages of the Bible continues beyond them.

Eschatological Adjustments

Imagination and the need to revise one's views are also present and necessary for the New Testament's eschatological expectations. From the earliest

---

28. Dunn, *Christology in the Making*, 258.
29. Ehrman et al., *When Did Jesus Become God*, 76; emphasis added.

days of the Christian movement, and arguably inspired by words from Jesus himself, was the expectation that Jesus would return and that the end would arrive shortly after the firstfruits resurrection of Jesus. One of our earliest New Testament documents, Paul's First Letter to the Thessalonians, puts it this way:

> But we do not want you to be uninformed, brothers and sisters, about those who have died, so that you may not grieve as others do who have no hope. 14 For since we believe that Jesus died and rose again, even so, through Jesus, God will bring with him those who have died. 15 For this we declare to you by the word of the Lord, that we who are alive, who are left until the coming of the Lord, will by no means precede those who have died. (1 Thess 4:13–15)

Paul appears to be drawing upon a memory of Jesus's words that would later be included in the Gospel of Mark:

> "Those who are ashamed of me and of my word in this adulterous and sinful generation, of them the Son of Man will also be ashamed when he comes in the glory of his Father with the holy angels." And he said to them, "Truly I tell you, there are some standing here who will not taste death until they see that the kingdom of God has come with power." (Mark 8:38—9:1)

This "word of the Lord" assuring his disciples that some of them would still be alive when he came in glory was interpreted by Paul to mean that Christ's return was imminent. In words he would later use in his Letter to the Romans, the "night is far gone, the day is near" (Rom 13:3).

That "day" did not arrive during Paul's lifetime, and the expectation of Christ's imminent return was increasingly qualified within the developing New Testament. It is always a useful exercise to roughly date the New Testament books. It is then revealing to plot expectations of Christ's return along that timeline. In Paul's undisputed letters, the expectation is of an imminent return. In later letters attributed to him, this expectation wanes. By the time the Second Letter of Peter was written,[30] its writer felt the need to account for the apparent delay in Jesus returning by noting:

> But do not ignore this one fact, beloved, that with the Lord one day is like a thousand years, and a thousand years are like one day. The Lord is not slow about his promise, as some think of

---

30. Sometime in the early second century CE, many scholars believe.

slowness, but is patient with you, not wanting any to perish but all to come to repentance. (2 Pet 3:8–9)

When the gospels were written, between about 70 CE and 110 CE, expectations were already adjusting. Dr. James Tabor, in an online lecture I attended, drew attention to subtle but important differences in the gospel writers' reporting of Jesus's teachings about the end. Mark is different than Paul in indicating that certain things needed to happen first before the glorious return of the Son of Man. Included in Mark's portrayal were events happening at or near the time he was writing such as the desecration of the temple and the fearful events of Rome's sacking of Jerusalem in 71 CE.

Mark's account is consistent with an imminent return. Less so for Luke's and Matthew's accounts. In Luke 21 and Matt 24, Christ's return is pushed still further into the future. The later-written Gospel of John includes no expectation of an imminent return of Jesus, but rather has him leaving the earth to prepare a place for his disciples to join him:

> Do not let your hearts be troubled. Believe in God; believe also in me. In my Father's house there are many dwelling places. If it were not so, would I have told you that I go to prepare a place for you? And if I go and prepare a place for you, I will come again and will take you to myself, so that where I am, there you may be also. (John 14:1–3)

The Diversity of Scriptural Opinion

That the Bible was constantly being revised throughout its history suggests what we have already noted, and that is that the biblical writers often differed from each other. Sometimes, those differences were small and simply involved tweaking or nuancing earlier understandings. At other times, circumstances precipitated more radical reimaginings.

Doctrinal Disagreements

One of the more profound differences of opinion relates to the doctrine or doctrines of the atonement, which in broad terms is about how the relationship between God and humans can be restored. There are some surprising differences. In late 2023, I attended an online course on textual criticism hosted by Bart Ehrman. Ehrman was particularly looking at the New Testament and its 5,700 or so manuscripts, none of them originals, all of them copies, most of them copies of copies. The manuscripts were all originally copied by hand, and mostly not by expert copyists. As a result, there are about half a million textual variants across those 5,700 copies.

Most of the variations are simple mistakes of spelling, grammar, and syntax, but some are significant. Sometimes copyists assumed the role of scribe and added or subtracted things, perhaps assuming that earlier mistakes had been made or to clarify matters that the text in front of them appeared to have muddied. In the following case, it appears that some details have been added to Luke's account of Christ's passion, possibly to correct a perceived lack.

Our English Bibles mostly have these verses in brackets to indicate the likelihood that the verses were not original. But, as we will see, their addition is impactful, very much so. The verses come as Jesus withdraws to the Mount of Olives shortly before his death:

> When he reached the place, he said to them, "Pray that you may not come into the time of trial." 41 Then he withdrew from them about a stone's throw, knelt down, and prayed, 42 "Father, if you are willing, remove this cup from me, yet not my will but yours be done." [43 Then an angel from heaven appeared to him and gave him strength. 44 In his anguish he prayed more earnestly, and his sweat became like great drops of blood falling down on the ground.] 45 When he got up from prayer, he came to the disciples and found them sleeping because of grief, 46 and he said to them, "Why are you sleeping? Get up and pray that you may not come into the time of trial." (Luke 22:40–46)

Verses 43 and 44 have been added. I can remember referring to these verses in an Easter sermon or two. I did so to highlight the intense psychological anguish Jesus would have been experiencing prior to his crucifixion. I would have pointed out that Jesus was no coward, and wasn't simply afraid of the physical torture of crucifixion. He wasn't the first or the last to die in that way. But this use of the verses, understandable perhaps, runs completely contrary to what we find in Luke, which perhaps explains why they were added.

As said previously, the author of Luke's Gospel relied on the earlier Gospel of Mark as one of his major sources. It is where he uses Mark in the Passion narratives that is most revealing. In the scene at Gethsemane (Mark 14), Mark goes out of his way to show Jesus as extremely distressed and agitated (v. 33). Jesus describes his soul as being deeply grieved, even to the point of death (v. 34). He throws himself face down to the ground and cries out to Abba Father that if possible the hour might pass from him and that the cup (of imminent suffering) might be removed (vv. 35–36). Luke, in his version of this story, removes all mention of Jesus's distress. He introduces the scene by having Jesus show concern for his disciples that they might not come into a time of trial (Luke 22:40). Luke has Jesus kneeling rather than throwing himself down on the ground and, in contrast to Mark, has him praying just once, not three times. Luke removes the reference to Jesus asking that the hour might pass and the cup be removed. He retains Jesus's stated willingness to do his Father's will.

By these omissions, Luke can be seen to emphasize the calmness and complete control of Jesus. Rather than being devastated by grief or fear, Jesus expresses concern for his disciples, both at the beginning and end of this passage. He later interacts compassionately with bystanders and witnesses of his crucifixion, including two insurrectionists. One of these he promises will join him in paradise that same day. Luke contains three of Jesus's seven "words" from the cross, including "Father, forgive them for they know not what they do" (Luke 23:34) and "Father, into your hands I commend my spirit" (Luke 23:46).

Mark has just one "word" from the cross: "'Eloi, Eloi, lama sabachthani?' which means, 'My God, my God, why have you forsaken me?'" (Mark 15:34). Jesus is depicted by Mark as being forsaken by everyone. There are no disciples, male or female, at the foot of the cross. There are only mocking soldiers, finger-wagging passersby, and sarcastic scribes and Pharisees.

What increases the starkness of these contrasting accounts is that Luke had Mark's Gospel in front of him but chose to mute the terrible aloneness and anguish of Jesus's betrayal and death, so much so that scholars have described Luke's account as a "passionless passion." While that certainly helps to explain why a later scribe would include a story about Jesus perspiring blood and needing an angel to be sent, one is certainly left wondering whether something else is going on here. It seems there might be.

There are other notable omissions in Luke's use of Mark. Luke fails to include the interaction between Jesus and his disciples that climaxes with:

> For the Son of Man came not to be served, but to serve and to give his life as a ransom for many. (Mark 10:45)

Matthew's Gospel includes this episode and these words, but Luke doesn't. Throughout his Gospel and the Acts of the Apostles, Luke appears to avoid references to Jesus's death as sacrificial, as a death for or in place of others, so much so that advocates for the post–New Testament doctrine of penal substitution struggle to find evidence for that theory in Luke's writings.

Many are convinced that Luke did not consider the death of Jesus to be an atoning event.[31]

In years past, I did notice, and it surprised me that the notion of Jesus dying to pay the penalty for our sins appears to be entirely absent from Luke's description of gospel preaching, either by Jesus or by his disciples. In the evangelistic sermons of Peter and Paul in Acts, the overwhelming emphasis is upon the resurrection of Jesus and his consequent lordship and authority to forgive. The need for there to be a sacrifice for this to happen is not mentioned, either in gospel preaching or associated explanation. What makes this all the more remarkable is the very positive portrayal of Paul in Acts. Paul in his letters certainly expressed the belief that Jesus's death was, in some sense, sacrificial. It seems that Luke didn't, or at least wanted to avoid that metaphor. This was perhaps because he considered sacrificial language to be pagan or because he did not see redemption in those terms.

The Gospel of John is different again. There is a reference to the Lamb of God taking away the sins of the world (John 1:29), but as for how this might happen, that is another question. Rev. Dr. Margaret Wesley, in an unpublished conference paper entitled "Her Hour Has Come," suggests that the imagery of birth and nursing, found throughout John's Gospel,[32] is key to understanding the Johannine view of redemption.[33] In the story of Nicodemus, in John 3, Jesus declares that there can be no entry into the kingdom of God without a second birth, a spiritual rebirth into God's family. Those so reborn are "not born of blood or the will of the flesh or the will of man, but of God" (John 1:13). It is this spiritual birthing of individuals into the family of God that is the key to individual and world transformation. It is how the Lamb of God will fulfil his destiny.

In summary, what we find in the Bible, what "Bible-believing" Christians need to be cognizant of, is that the Bible contains diverse perspectives. These came to be expressed over time, always in response to circumstances, some of which were extremely challenging, all of which required faith-inspired reflection. Hence the importance of imagination, the ability to imagine what

---

31. In my limited reading around this topic, I've noticed that even conservative commentators acknowledge the problem. Why, for example, if Christ's death was understood by Luke to be an atoning act of self-sacrifice for others, does he leave out one of the clearest expressions of that view in Mark 10:45? Why doesn't it appear explicitly in Luke-Acts? One evangelical writer I read surmised that Luke was, at least, not averse to the conclusion that Jesus's death was a sacrificial death for the good of others. That was the most he could say. See further Kimbell, *Atonement in Lukan Theology*.

32. John 1:18; 6:51; 7:37–39; 13:23–25; 19:25–35; 20:17.

33. Wesley, "Her Hour Has Come." Delivered at Fellowship of Biblical Scholars conference, Sydney, Sept. 2023.

must or might be the case, especially in a world where suffering and evil continue to prevail. Biblical ethics, soteriology,[34] epistemology,[35] and eschatology[36] were all forged on the anvil of necessary theological imagination.

Implications for Hermeneutics

Hermeneutics is the science or art of interpretation. Many Christians look to 2 Tim 3:16–17 to find their understanding of how the Bible should be read and interpreted:

> All scripture is inspired by God and is useful for teaching, for reproof, for correction, and for training in righteousness, 17 so that the person of God may be proficient, equipped for every good work.

While these verses are unlikely to have been written by the apostle Paul, it is nevertheless worth reflecting on what inspiration might mean. As explained more fully in *Faith Without Fear*, I am of the view that a notion of the Bible's inerrancy cannot be successfully defended.[37] However, I am not averse to the idea that the whole process of biblical and postbiblical reflection is, in some sense, inspired by God, that the impulse to faith and the desire to know, which is simply part of who we are as humans, is what inspired biblical writers on their quest of faith and knowledge. In my own life, I have a sense of the gently guiding presence of God and that I am on this long journey of faith as well.

As a result of my reflections over time, I found myself agreeing with German theologian Jürgen Moltmann. Moltmann differentiates between two types of hermeneutic. The first, a "hermeneutics from above," locates the authority of the Bible in God's direct communication with humans through the Scriptures, understood to be God's written word. The authority of the Bible lies in the God who speaks. This was the view of another great German theologian, Karl Barth. A "hermeneutic from below," by contrast, highlights the humanity of the Scriptures, viewing them as time and culture-bound testimonies of faith. This is Moltmann's view, and it is how I now understand the Scriptures.

---

34. Studies about the theme of salvation.
35. The study of knowledge.
36. The study of "last things," including death, judgment, heaven, and hell.
37. In ch. 2 of Mascord, *Faith Without Fear*, entitled "The Error of Inerrancy," I argue that, at best, theories of inerrancy die the death of a thousand qualifications.

The big question for me and for those who think likewise is: How can we take anything that the Bible says seriously? How can we use it to guide our lives? Is it "useful for teaching, for reproof, for correction, and for training in righteousness"? I am convinced it is useful for those purposes. My reason for saying this is because of some help offered by another influential scholar, French philosopher Paul Ricoeur (1913–2005).[38] Ricoeur divided the hermeneutical (or interpretative) process into three steps.[39] Ricoeur's hermeneutical arc, as it is sometimes called, begins with a first or naïve understanding, a "first naïveté," which generally occurs when one first encounters a text like the Bible. The first stage of Ricoeur's arc is nonreflective or pre-contemplative. It is like one's first impression of someone one has just met.

But first naïveté gives way, and has given way historically, to a second stage of Ricoeur's hermeneutical arc, which is critical engagement. We begin to subject the text to critical analysis. We take a step back from the text. Ricoeur refers to this as distanciation. We analyze the text as if it were a specimen to be put under the microscope of critical analysis. We make use of all the critical tools now at our disposal in the wake of the scientific and historiographical revolutions arising out of the European Enlightenment.[40]

The first half of this book could definitely be viewed as an instance of step two, critical engagement, as might all instances of attempted deconstruction. This process, which is now happening at pace around the world, needs to happen. The contention of this book is that it simply must take place. It is a requirement, perhaps like never before, of an honest and re-forming faith. To give it a more august history, this is a process of faith seeking understanding, a quest that St. Augustine encouraged us to journey on. We certainly cannot stay with a naïve or Sunday-school faith. There can be no return to a first naïveté. But we also don't need to remain within step two.

There is a third step, to a "second naïveté," which Ricoeur calls appropriation. Appropriation involves returning to the text to be challenged and transformed by it. To enter a second naïveté, one must move beyond the

---

38. What follows in this and the next paragraph (from "Ricoeur's hermeneutical arc" to "European Enlightenment") is partially drawn, almost verbatim, from Mascord, *Faith Without Fear*.

39. For an early articulation of this process, see Ricoeur, *Symbolism of Evil*.

40. In the case of our study of the Bible, we can helpfully draw on the burgeoning results of textual criticism, literary criticism, genre criticism, redaction criticism, historical criticism, rhetorical criticism, and narrative criticism, the now-large and growing family of disciplines associated with the historical-critical method. These now include queer literary criticism and gender studies, feminist literary criticism, liberation theology, and Indigenous literary criticism.

otherwise endlessly critical and suspicious hermeneutic of the Enlightenment to reengage earlier texts, including the ancient text of the Bible.[41] Being responsibly critical has its place, but one need not forever remain at a distance from the text. One can become attentive to what the Bible and God might say to us.

In my previous book, *Faith Without Fear*, I explained that appropriation involves personalizing what one encounters in the text of the Bible. The constant challenge of interpretation is the need to overcome the distance between the past to which the text belongs and the interpreter. But this can be done, according to Ricoeur, by allowing the text to facilitate self-understanding, by taking what is initially foreign and appropriating it to become familiar and one's own.[42]

Aiding this process of appropriation and self-understanding is the realization that the meaning of texts is never fixed or invariable. In the subtle and ever-evolving interplay between interpreter and text, texts have a life of their own somewhat independent of the intentions and understandings of the original authors. Texts are able to speak with renewed and renewing insight into each new situation and to each new reader. Just as the Bible is itself dynamic, the relationship between the Bible and us—its readers—is dynamic, endlessly dynamic.

Ricoeur's model of hermeneutics has been immensely helpful as I have sought to understand the Bible and its imaginative and intensely hopeful storyline. It has also been helpful to discover that the Bible's own hermeneutic is not dissimilar to Ricoeur's. As I am about to argue, the biblical writers were first-class appropriators.

The Biblical Hermeneutic

Those who wrote the Bible were constantly involved in appropriating texts, both scriptural and non-scriptural. They drew not only from earlier biblical texts but also from oral and extra-biblical written traditions. These they sometimes copied. At other times, they were critiqued, rejected, and/or nuanced. Unlike us, they did not seem interested in what the original human authors meant. They certainly did not employ grammatical-historical

---

41. Ricoeur took issue with some previous hermeneutical approaches, such as those represented by Freud, Marx, and Nietzsche, for being both suspicious and reductionistic in their approach to mythical or symbolic consciousness. See, for example, Ricoeur: *Freud and Philosophy*, 32–36; and "Critique of Religion."

42. Ricoeur, "Existence and Hermeneutics."

or historical-critical methods.[43] Not surprisingly, Jesus and the authors of the New Testament employed interpretive techniques current at the time they wrote, that time being the Second Temple period of Jewish history, the period between the completion of Jerusalem's Second Temple in 516 BCE and its destruction by the Romans in 70 CE. These interpretive techniques included allegory, typology, and *pesher midrash*,[44] which was an exegetical practice used at Qumran. By this method, Old Testament texts were read and interpreted in the light of current events, which were seen to be their eschatological fulfilment.

Like the Qumran community, Christians developed their own *pesher* exegesis, scouring their authoritative texts for prophetic references to Jesus. Their experiences and understandings of Jesus also supplied them with hermeneutical principles that guided their interpretation of Scripture. Paul, for example, in seeking to make room for gentiles, proposed a distinction between the "letter which kills" and the "life-giving spirit," a distinction that allowed him to sideline the Jewish law for a new and more glorious covenant of the spirit (2 Cor 3). The prioritizing of faith over law keeping similarly allowed Paul to make room for gentiles. His use of the Scriptures in support of his case is not always convincing.[45] But it is imaginative, and needed to be. Paul, as with all the disciples, was faced with a new situation, which required a rethink. In this, he was no different than previous biblical authors.

Paul's approach was also not dissimilar to Ricoeur's recommended approach. Both approaches involve creative reappropriation. We can follow suit. The Bible itself would encourage us to do so, to be both critical and imaginative. Like the biblical authors, we too can use our God-given gifts to reexamine our traditions and then to step through to a second naïveté of hopeful possibility.

---

43. The first of these two broadly defined methods is favored by Evangelicals, the second by more liberal scholars. They both involve examining biblical texts in their historical and literary context.

44. *Pesher*, meaning solution or deciphering, *midrash*, meaning exegesis or interpretation. For more information, see R. Hays and Green, "Use of Old Testament," as well as E. Earle Ellis's excellent monograph, *Old Testament in Early Christianity*. A publication that wrestles with the implications of *pesher midrash* for an evangelical hermeneutic is Enns, *Inspiration and Incarnation*.

45. For example, Paul's interpretation of Gen 15:6 in Rom 4 appears neglectful of texts such as Gen 26:4–5, where God promises numerous offspring "because Abraham obeyed my voice and kept my charge, my commandments, my statutes, and my laws." Some would argue that Paul misrepresents both this verse and Judaism itself in arguing as he does.

Marc Brettler, in the afterword to his book *How to Read the Bible*, provides an example of how someone might do this:

> Many who have just completed this book would guess that I, as its author, lack religious convictions altogether. After all, it is easy to read the previous pages as an acute case of "Bible bashing." I have emphasized the composite nature of the Bible, treating it as a human, rather than a divine, work. I have contextualized it in the ancient Near East, rather than treating it as a timeless book. I have made the following claims: the beginning of Genesis is a "myth"; the Exodus did not happen, and Joshua did not fight the battle of Jericho and make the walls come tumbling down. Further, I have stated that much of the material in the Bible's historical texts is not historical; that not everything found in the work known as Amos (or Isaiah, or Jeremiah, or Ezekiel) was written by Amos (or Isaiah, or Jeremiah, or Ezekiel), and that David composed none of the psalms. I have asserted that not only is the Song of Songs a secular work, but that the Bible is also, for it was influenced by (secular) ideology as much as by religion.
>
> I am, in fact, an observant Jew. I take the Bible quite seriously in my personal life. It stands at the core of who I am as a person, and as a Jew.[46]

Brettler explains that he views the Bible as a "source book" with respect to his scholarship, but as a "textbook" for his life, authoritative for him in choosing how to live. In explaining how he does this, he comes very close to Ricoeur's notion of appropriation. Brettler chooses options that the Bible offers. He notes that the biblical writers themselves were selective and critical in what they accepted from previous texts. He concludes,

> So, too, as I engage the Bible: After carefully considering its texts, I use selection to adopt some texts as more meaningful than others.
>
> Sometimes, when confronting a particular issue, I find that *all* the biblical texts are problematic for one reason or another. In such cases, I must acknowledge that the Bible is an ancient text; it hails from a society fundamentally different from ours. Perhaps it has not always aged well. Therefore I must actively "translate" the text into terms that fit our society. This is extremely difficult to do with integrity, yet in some areas, especially concerning matters of sex and gender (what "real men"

---

46. Brettler, *How to Read the Bible*, 279.

and "real women" do), it is the only workable approach. I then distinguish what the text originally *meant* (in its original historical context) from what it now *means* (taking into consideration certain key difference between ancient Israelite antiquity and modern times). I assign the new meaning by modernising the text quite carefully.[47]

What Brettler is doing, I am attempting as well. But this is not just for individuals. It is too large a task for any one person on their own. It requires the expertise and relevant knowledge of many. It is a job for theological colleges, universities, denominations, churches, and other faith communities. We will need storytellers and critical analysts of all sorts. And in all this, imagination is required.

A re-forming faith simply must be imaginative. Only then will a friendship between Athens and Jerusalem be possible. Only then might this friendship flourish and a sustainable faith be re-formed. Only then might inadequate and even damaging understandings of the past be left behind.

Questions for Reflection and Discussion

1. What do you think of the idea of the Scriptures containing one long imaginative and largely mythical story? What would you say to support or counter this idea?

2. What do you think are the implications of acknowledging evolving and diverse understandings throughout the Scriptures?

3. Can you think of instances in your reading of the Bible where you have followed something like Ricoeur's process of first naïveté, followed by critical engagement, followed by a second naïveté? Was it helpful, and, if so, in what ways? If not, why do you think that was?

4. Of the two broad hermeneutics, a hermeneutics from above and a hermeneutics from below, which do you think is most helpful and most likely to get you in touch with the text of the Bible, and why?

---

47. Brettler, *How to Read the Bible*, 281–82; emphasis in original.

Satisfying Our Deepest Longing
by Noel Davis

No amount of money, possession
knowledge or prestige
can satisfy our deepest longings.
Our hearts know this.

The satisfaction we seek comes from love
the experience of being loved
and being loving
living care and kindness
knowing we belong.

It is our love that breaks through barriers,
boundaries, divisions and differences
and creates a life generating and potent community
in which trust dispels our fears and anxieties
and we feel free to be ourselves
open and vulnerable with each other.

Of what use is it to discourse learnedly on the Trinity, if you lack humility and therefore displease the Trinity? Lofty words do not make a man just or holy; but a good life makes him dear to God. I would far rather feel contrition than be able to define it. If you know the whole Bible by heart, and all the teachings of the philosophers, how would this help you without the grace and love of God?[48]

---

48. Kempis, *Imitation of Christ*, 27.

Chapter 7

Loving Faith

WE HAVE GOOD REASONS to be doubtful about many things, but few of us are likely to doubt the importance of love. Both Jesus and Paul identify love—love for God and love for neighbor—as the essence of what is required of us as humans. These are the two great commandments. In comparing faith, hope and love, Paul declares that love is the greatest of these (1 Cor 13:13). St. Augustine expanded the reach of love into biblical interpretation. He argued that no interpretation is valid, no matter how exegetically clever, if it results in the violation of the commandment to love.[1] Love is a key to sound interpretation, as it is to life.

Also not to be doubted is that neighbor love needs to be informed. It needs to be informed by knowledge, knowledge about what is good for our neighbor. How will their best interests be served by our actions and words? The answer to that is often complex. There are all sorts of assumptions and beliefs that will need to guide us in deciding how best to love our neighbor. Our theology and anthropology will inform the decisions we make.

This was vividly illustrated for me when I listened to the podcast *The Witch Trials of J. K. Rowling*, which investigates Rowling's fall from grace with many of her fans because of things she'd tweeted and said (and keeps saying) about transgender people.[2] Somewhat surprisingly, the podcast's pre-

---

1. Note, for example, Augustine, *Confessions* 12.25: "When so many meanings, all of them acceptable as true, can be extracted from the words that Moses wrote, do you not see how foolish it is to make a bold assertion that one in particular is the one he had in mind? Do you not see how foolish it is to enter into mischievous arguments which are an offence against that very charity for the sake of which he wrote every one of the words we are trying to explain?"

2. Phelps-Roper, *Witch Trials*.

senter, Megan Phelps-Roper, is the granddaughter of the founding pastor of Westboro Baptist Church, internationally infamous for its very public anti-gay rhetoric. Westboro's website highlights "[the] duty to love our neighbor as ourselves," but it immediately qualifies that requirement by noting that "[this] involves 'rebuking' our neighbor."[3] They have certainly done that. In some commentary on the podcast, Megan Phelps-Roper tells her story:

> I was born into the Westboro Baptist Church, a tiny congregation founded by my grandfather. [It] was a world unto itself. From the age of five, I protested with my parents, siblings, and extended family on sidewalks across America—including outside the funerals of AIDS victims and American soldiers. We held signs with messages like "God Hates Fags," and earnestly believed we were doing the Lord's work—that our protests were an expression of love, warning the world from sins that would do them harm.[4]

It is hard to deny the sincerity and perseverance of this now-almost-defunct community. Whether what they were saying and doing was informed by knowledge, grace, or good understanding is another matter. Phelps-Roper now believes it was not. I agree.

We might, in what follows, try once again to bring Athens and Jerusalem together.

Love and Womanhood

I am amazed that women continue to be prevented from assuming leadership in Christian churches, and not just in some, but most. It is only within Protestantism that just some churches now allow women unrestricted leadership and authority. Over 60 percent of the world's Christians identify as Roman Catholic or Orthodox. In not one of their churches can a woman become a deacon or priest. In 2020, Pope Francis created a second Vatican commission to consider ordaining women as deacons. In October 2023, the pope was reported as saying that "holy orders is reserved for men."[5] His opinion was that any change to this would "undermine the essence of the Church," according to which women mirror the bride of Christ. They therefore cannot be deacons, priests, bishops, or popes, or so this pope believes.[6]

---

3. See https://www.godhatesfags.com/.
4. Phelps-Roper, "Witch Trials," para. 19.
5. Brockhaus, "Pope Francis," para. 2.
6. Brockhaus, "Pope Francis," para. 8. Brockhaus draws her information from an

Orthodox churches are no closer to changing their long-held practice of ordaining only men to the priesthood. Most evangelical churches are similarly disinclined to change.

How might love be the key to unlocking this impasse? What conclusions might we come to if we allow ourselves to fully engage in the second and third steps of Ricœur's hermeneutical arc, which are critical engagement and reappropriation? The temperament and method of Socrates would certainly aid us in that process. What if we allowed ourselves to be guided by contemporary knowledge and experience, as the biblical authors clearly were? One might even employ a grammatical-historical approach, which, at its best, takes full account of text and context.

I touched on this issue in chapter 2 but for the sake of convenience have gathered some of that information and more, and displayed this in a diagram. These are some of the things that would need to be taken into account in coming to an informed conclusion.

When things are laid out like this, it becomes obvious, to me at least, what a sensible or wise choice might be. You begin to wonder how this could be resisted. Young people leaving the church or sensibly vowing never to step foot inside a church are understandably mystified. They are also likely to see that behind this stubborn resistance is something more sinister.

Teaching on female subordination contributes to domestic violence and to lesser forms of hurtful discrimination.	Jesus only chose men to be his apostles. The apostles, apart from Junia, were male.	The Pastoral Epistles (including 1 Timothy) are unlikely to have been written by Paul—and are thus intentionally or unintentionally misleading.
Women have more than proven their ability to assume leadership and authority at all levels of responsibility in church and world.	**Women and a Love-Directed Hermeneutic**	The prohibitions in 1 Tim 2:11–15 may have been temporary and circumstantial. They don't line up well with Paul's undisputed letters nor with his and the early church's practice where women did teach and exercise authority.
In recent years, and possibly for much longer, women have felt called by God to pastoral and leadership roles.	Up until the 1970s, most Christian theologians considered women inferior to men, not able to lead, and more gullible than men. Few now interpret the relevant verses to that conclusion.	Women have had a subservient role within most Christian churches for almost all of church history.

---

interview for a book published that year, the English title of which is *The Shepherd: Struggles, Reasons, and Thoughts on His Papacy*.

In reading the Pastoral Epistles, it is hard to avoid a similar disquiet. It certainly looks as though whoever wrote those letters was reacting against the refreshing (to us) elevation of the status of women by Jesus and Paul. Plausibly, it was considered by this or these unknown authors that things had gone too far and brakes therefore needed to be applied. There may well have been an apologetic impulse given the status of women in Greco-Roman society. Steff Fenton, in their at-this-stage unpublished manuscript "Gender Expansive Faith," describes the dominant and consistent gender ideology that prevailed at the time:

> Discourses about Graeco-Roman masculinity described a series of binary opposites for man and woman, masculinity and femininity: "free/enslaved, native/foreign, superior/inferior, hard/soft, active/passive, dominant/submissive, inviolable/violable, impenetrable/penetrable, sexually insertive/sexually receptive, hairy/smooth, and self-disciplined/ruled by the emotions." So, the Roman Empire upheld that masculinity was the norm, the ideal and the superior, and that women were inferior, leading to the idea that they need to be cared for and ruled. At the core of its society was a binary definition of gender.
>
> From this philosophy, the Empirical administration institutionalised male dominance over women and children in the family, as well as society more broadly. Specifically, the structure of the Roman Empire had a male emperor at the top. Underneath him, society was organised by a strict social code which assigned status, praise, and blame, and prescribed social roles, according to gender. As such, the Roman Empire was a kingdom that governed hierarchically, and this social hierarchy delineated personal value, morality, status, autonomy, and rights according to one's gender. The "primary paradigm for understanding the dichotomy between the ideal and less ideal [was] a gendered one" In other words, patriarchy was the fog that stirred within all areas of social life.[7]

Women were considered inferior, their bodies' softness associated with love of luxury. Their perceived slowness of minds was thought to affect their ability to think clearly, which was also adversely affected by their emotions and degenerate morals.[8] When one reads again those controversial verses

---

7. Fenton, "Gender Expansive Faith," unnumbered page.

8. Fenton, "Gender Expansive Faith," unnumbered page, drawing on Kuefler, *Manly Eunuch*, 21.

from 1 Timothy, one is certainly struck by how similar sounding they are to Greco-Roman orthodoxy.

> I do not permit a woman to teach or to have authority over a man; she is to keep silent. 13 For Adam was formed first, then Eve, 14 and Adam was not deceived, but the woman was deceived and became a transgressor. 15 Yet she will be saved through childbearing, provided they continue in faith and love and holiness, with self-control. (1 Tim 2:12–15)

Should an advocate for female subordination reply that this alignment with surrounding culture is not accurate, the plain-sense meaning of these verses wasn't missed by any of Christianity's greatest theologians. Their exegetical conclusions line up well with Greco-Roman orthodoxy as the following quotations make clear.

> Tertullian: "And do you not know that each of you [each woman] is Eve? . . . You are the devil's gateway: you are the first deserter of the divine law."[9]
>
> Chrysostom: "[A man is to have] pre-eminence in every way. [Women are] captivated by appetite. [They are] weak and fickle . . . collectively."[10]
>
> Augustine: "Whether it is in a wife or a mother, it is still Eve the temptress that we must beware of in any woman . . . I fail to see what use woman can be to man, if one excludes the function of bearing children."[11]
>
> Aquinas: "Woman is defective and misbegotten, for the active power in the male seed tends to the production of a perfect likeness in the masculine sex, while the production of a woman comes from defect in the active force."[12]
>
> Luther: "Adam is approved [by God] as superior to Eve."[13] "As the sun is much more glorious than the moon (though the moon is glorious), so the woman was [created] inferior to the man."[14]

---

9. Tertullian, "On the Apparel of Women," in Roberts and Donaldson, *Ante-Nicene Fathers*, 14:90.

10. Chrysostom, "Homily 9 on 1 Timothy 2:12" (trans. James Tweed), in Pusey et al., *Library of the Fathers*, 12:63–64.

11. Augustine, *City of God*, 454.

12. Aquinas, *Summa Theologiae*, pt. 1a, q. 92, a.1 reply to objection 1.

13. Luther, *Commentaries*, 278–79.

14. Luther, *Luther's Commentary on Genesis*, 1:34.

Calvin: "[Women] are born to obey, for all wise men have always rejected the government of women as an unnatural monstrosity."[15]

What should a person, guided by love, conclude from all this? They would surely be misled by the orthodoxy of the past. They could most sensibly disregard the opinions of many of their favorite, though misled theologians. Guided by a better-informed love, they would have more than enough reason to disregard more recent, increasingly shrill, and needlessly stubborn proponents of a long-discredited patriarchy. Guided by love, they might also look more carefully at the relevant biblical texts as evangelical egalitarians have done so helpfully in recent years.[16]

As evidence of the positive impact of having one's hermeneutic guided by love, one can simply witness how liberating, affirming, encouraging, and deserved are successful efforts to achieve equality for women in the church. Love seeks the flourishing of the other, in this case of more than half of all Christian congregations. Our society has left us behind in this matter. It is time to catch up.

Love and Gay, Lesbian, and Bisexual Persons

Love can also be the key to deciding to include, honor, and celebrate the lives of gay, lesbian, and bisexual humans, as it is also for people who are transgender/gender diverse/gender expansive, who will be considered in the section to follow. The same sorts of hermeneutical considerations apply. Looking at all the facts together, it is again, I think, a relatively easy endeavor. A few things to note by way of relevant background.

Gratifying Progress Has Already Been Made

Christian teaching and behavior have massively contributed to the damage done to our lesbian, gay, and bisexual sisters and brothers, reaching all the way back to the very beginnings of the Christian movement. Christian theologians and thought leaders have consistently taught that any and all variations from biblically established sexual and/or gender norms are inherently defective and/or sinful, and that those who depart from them, and especially those who in our terms are homosexual, are worthy of contempt

15. Calvin, *Second Epistle of Paul*, 217.
16. See, for example, the scholarly work of Margaret Mowczko (https://margmowczko.com), Craig Keener, and Kevin Giles (some of whose works are included in the bibliography). Another valuable resource is Pierce et al., *Discovering Biblical Equality*.

and the most severe censure. To quote (again) from some of Christianity's greatest thought leaders:

> Tertullian: "All other frenzies of lusts which exceed the laws of nature and are impious toward both bodies and the sexes, we banish from all shelter of the Church, for they are not sins so much as monstrosities."[17]
>
> Chrysostom: "When God abandons a man, everything is turned upside down! Therefore, not only are their passions satanic, but their lives are diabolic. So I say to you that these are even worse than murderers, and that it would be better to die than to live in such dishonor. A murderer only separates the soul from the body, whereas these destroy the soul inside the body. There is nothing, absolutely nothing, more mad or damaging than this perversity."[18]
>
> Augustine: "Sins against nature, therefore, like the sin of Sodom, are abominable and deserve punishment whenever and wherever they are committed. If all nations committed them, all alike would be held guilty of the same charge in God's law, for our Maker did not prescribe that we should use each other in this way. For even that fellowship which should be between God and us is violated, when that same nature of which He is author is polluted by the perversity of lust."[19]
>
> Aquinas: "For if the sins of the flesh are commonly censurable because they lead man to that which is bestial in him, much more so is the sin against nature, by which man debases himself lower than even his animal nature."[20]
>
> Luther: "The vice of the Sodomites is an unparalleled enormity. It departs from the natural passion and desire, planted into nature by God, according to which the male has a passionate desire for the female. Sodomy craves what is entirely contrary to nature. Whence comes this perversion? Without a doubt it comes from the devil. After a man has once turned aside from the fear of God, the devil puts such great pressure upon his nature that he extinguishes the fire of natural desire and stirs up another, which is contrary to nature."[21]

17. Tertullian, *De pudicitia*, quoted in McNeill, *Church and the Homosexual*, 89.

18. Chrysostom, *Epistulam ad Romanos*, quoted in McNeill, *Church and the Homosexual*, 89–90.

19. Augustine, *Confessions*, 65.

20. Aquinas, *Super Epistolas S. Pauli Lectura*, 26–27.

21. Luther, *What Luther Says*, 1:134.

By any measure, these are dreadful, horrific statements. We rightly recoil from them because they so completely misrepresent what we now know about homosexuality. These statements make me shudder when I think of my many gay, lesbian, and bisexual friends and fellow Christians whose lives and lifestyles are so normal, whose spiritualities are so genuine, whose depth of maturity is so deepened by the awful abuse and misunderstandings they've had to endure.

In light of the harrowing but consistent and church-history-long messaging cited above, it is noteworthy that this sort of rhetoric is increasingly rare in Christian circles, except within the dying enclaves of Westboro Baptist-like churches. To their credit, Rachel Gilson and Rebecca McLaughlan, the two lesbian keynote speakers at the earlier mentioned *Undeceptions* conference,[22] said nothing like what Christianity's great but misinformed theologians of the past wrote and thought. They did not argue that families and society would unravel as a result of same-sex marriage or that the increasing visibility of lesbian, gay, and bisexual people was evidence of corruption, godlessness, and declining moral standards. They acknowledged that their own orientation was hardwired and not fixable. Rachel Gilson, both in her speeches and in her chapter in the Gospel Coalition's book, *Before You Lose Your Faith*, could say no more than that our desires don't own us, Jesus does, and, regardless of whether same-sex attraction is permanent, the Bible forbids sex between people of the same gender. Even though we might not understand, we simply must trust that God knows best. That was the most she said.

Learning From and Lovingly Applying What We Now Know

The case against same-sex marriage appears to be getting thinner and thinner. We have become increasingly aware that same-sex sexual orientation is as old as humankind. It is not a matter of personal choice. There is, furthermore, mounting evidence that there are not just two neatly opposite sexes.[23] The mythical and clearly idealized description of early coupling in Gen 2, and Jesus's appeal to it, do not rule out alternative marriage customs. The

---

22. Described in ch. 2.

23. Sex normally refers to the biological and physiological characteristics that have been used to define humans as either male or female. People with an innate variation in sex characteristics show us that there are more than two experiences of biology or physiology, i.e., sex. We also know that people have many variations of gender identity. Gender identity tends to be understood in terms of how people perceive themselves as either male, female, or something else like nonbinary or genderqueer.

Bible is more flexible in its understanding of marriage than are its twenty-first-century devotees.

Understanding this should assist us as followers of the compassionate Christ to enter more fully into the lives and painful experience of our lesbian, gay, and bisexual fellow Christians. It should encourage us to honestly seek to understand why self-loathing, self-harm, and suicide are particularly common among those who have grown up in conservative religious and/or Christian homes or churches.

It should also encourage Christians to rethink their hermeneutic. If it is the case that when we look outside the Bible and fairly examine contemporary evidence we cannot find any good reason to resist same-sex marriage, while also finding many good reasons to embrace it, including the requirement of a better-informed love, then surely it is time to consider a hermeneutic (like the Bible's) that is responsive to contemporary knowledge and experience. It is well past time for an improved hermeneutic such as Ricoeur would recommend.

This ever-mounting evidence should also encourage us to reconsider what the author or authors of Leviticus might have meant by their prohibition of sex between men. If what they had in mind was that God has created fixed and invariable boundaries between species, which simply must not be breached or treated as exceptions, then surely it is time to take full account of scientific evidence to the contrary, and especially when the authority of the book of Leviticus is undermined by the likely false attribution of Mosaic reception and recording of the Levitical laws.

Drawing much of the above together while adding a little more is the following diagram.

Gay, lesbian, and bisexual Christians have been members of churches throughout church history, but have had to hide their sexual identities to avoid inevitable rejection, expulsion, and, even now, imprisonment and execution.	Diversities in sexual orientation have existed for as long as we can tell and are natural variants among humans and other animals; not the result of evil or God-denying choices. They cannot be "fixed" by therapy or having them prayed away.	For nearly all of church history, all major Christian theologians, and Christians in general, have considered same-sex sexual activity as the most heinous of sins, contravening nature and deserving of the severest of punishments.
Gay, lesbian and bisexual Christians continue to suicide as a result of rejection by their families and churches—and as a result of internalizing teaching that depicts them as broken and/or corrupt and displeasing to God, and with no prospect of sexual and interpersonal intimacy.	**Gay, Lesbian, and Bisexual Humans and a Love-Directed Hermeneutic**	Homosexuality has been viewed, and still is by some Christians, as personally, interpersonally, socially, and spiritually degrading, and as evidence of corruption, godlessness, and declining moral standards.
Our growing acquaintance and friendship with LGB neighbors, churchgoers, and work colleagues has confirmed how otherwise normal, non-corrupt, and in fact special they are. They enrich our personal, corporate, and church lives.	Since marriage equality has been legislated for across the world, society hasn't fallen apart; the mental health of lesbian, gay, and bisexual people has improved; families with same-sex parents are doing remarkably ….."	Christians are increasingly finding it difficult to understand why churches, both historically and today, appear so adamantly anti-gay, anti-same-sex marriage, and even willing to split churches over what is now a very much contested issue. Newer generations find it almost impossible to excuse or comprehend this. Many Christians struggle to find a good reason to keep holding their stance, except for the conviction that this is what the Bible teaches.
The Bible itself accommodates a variety of marital customs, e.g., polygamy, levirate marriage, ownership of wives.	The passages in Leviticus that condemn as an abomination sex between men are unlikely to have been conveyed directly by God to Moses and therefore lack moral authority.	

Love and Gender-Diverse Persons

What does it mean to love gender-diverse people? Minimally, once again, it means being as fully informed as one can be. The word commonly used to describe gender diverse is transgender. It is an apt word. The prefix "trans" suggests a reality that goes between or across. Another phrase that is becoming increasingly common is gender expansive. It is a phrase Steff Fenton prefers, using it in "Gender Expansive Faith." The descriptors trans, gender diverse, or gender expansive describe people whose gender differs from what was presumed or assigned to them at birth. They are umbrella terms used to cover a range of genders such as nonbinary or genderqueer. Steff, who identifies as gender expansive, came to realize this about themself over time. They do, however, remember a revealing moment in early primary school when they were having a bedtime prayer with their father. As they describe it:

> One of my earliest memories was a time in early primary school when my dad tucked me into bed at night. Our evening tradition during my childhood was to share a prayer at the end of the day, often giving thanks for the things we enjoyed and also acknowledging the hardships that were present across the world. We prayed about being kind, thoughtful, and generous to others, as a way of recognising and sharing the love we received from God. This one night, I recall bringing to my father a question I had been pondering, "Dad, is it possible to be a boy when I go to heaven?" Originally, I had interpreted this desire through the lens of my sexuality – wanting to date the girls instead of the boys at primary school. With hindsight I realise this was equally about my gender identity. My mother had been formed by the feminist movements of the 70's and 80's so her three darling 'girls' (me and my two sisters) could do, wear and be anything we felt comfortable in. For me, that meant I lived my childhood in Maui and Sons overalls playing every kind of sport with the boys I went to school with. That night with my dad, little Steff sprouted some words which I recall now with great fondness. I believe that was my first childlike voicing of an intrinsic desire to be gendered as something other than a girl. I love that it so beautifully stemmed from within one of the rituals of my Christian spirituality: prayer. At five years old, little Steff mumbled a prophecy, a sacred possibility, of gender expansive faith.[24]

Transgender descriptors are recent and therefore not found in the Bible. The closest biblical descriptor is eunuch, and it is quite close. In ancient Rome, contemporary to the time of Jesus and before, eunuchs were widespread and well known. Their description closely matches contemporary understandings. Steff sums up their own extensive discussion of how eunuchs were described and understood in the Roman world of the first century CE:

> As we have seen, ancient literature grappled with the sprawling nature of the eunuch's gender identity and expression. They were considered men who had lost their masculinity, half-men, women, unmen, non-human, all of the above and none of the above. They were considered neither male nor female, or changing between male and female, and in this way, eunuchs embodied a more flexible range of gender identity than ancient

---

24. Fenton, "Gender Expansive Faith," unnumbered page.

patriarchy allowed or expected. The eunuch's gender expansive identity went beyond the two-gender system into a third, fourth, fifth and even more gender categories. They could not be easily categorized or controlled within patriarchy's binary gender ideology.[25]

Because eunuchs did not neatly fit within the male/female binary, they thereby threatened the patriarchal model, which in turn condemned them. As emasculated oddities, they were held in contempt, considered inferior and even dangerous. They were described as carnal, irrational, unnatural, voluptuous, fickle, manipulative, and deceitful. They were considered soft, lecherous, adulterous, unkind, immodest, weak, impotent, deceitful, cowardly, and incapable of virtue.[26]

In Jewish thinking, they were considered defective, as a result of which they were excluded from worship. Deuteronomy 23:1 instructs: "No one whose testicles are crushed or whose penis is cut off shall be admitted to the assembly of the Lord." With respect to the priesthood, Lev 21:17, 20 mandates: "No one of your offspring throughout their generations who has a blemish . . . or crushed testicles . . . may approach to offer the food of his God." Philo, in his commentary on Lev 18:22 and 20:13, describes eunuchs as effeminate and unable to enter the congregation because they are:

> men who belie their sex and are affected with effemination, who debase the currency of nature and violate it by assuming the passions and the outward form of licentious women. For it expels those whose generative organs are fractured or mutilated . . . and restamp the masculine cast into a feminine form.[27]

It is horrifying to read such brutal prejudice, but more horrifying still is that similar sentiments continue to be expressed today, especially within, and with the encouragement of religious communities. Ever since same-sex marriage was legislated for in Australia, the US, Canada, and elsewhere, there has been a strong and sometimes vicious counterreaction to this and other challenges to patriarchal orthodoxy. Our lesbian, gay, and bisexual fellow citizens and congregants remain in the cross fire, but increasingly it is the even smaller minority of trans citizens who are bearing the brunt of hateful and misinformed attacks. In the US, for example, 2023 marked

---

25. Fenton, "Gender Expansive Faith," unnumbered page.
26. Fenton, "Gender Expansive Faith," unnumbered page.
27. Philo, *Special Laws* 1.325, quoted in Fenton, "Gender Expansive Faith," unnumbered page.

the fourth consecutive record-breaking year for anti-trans legislation.[28] Involved in these legislative efforts are some of the following: an outright denial of gender-affirming care, including hormone treatment and surgery; not allowing people to identify with their gender of choosing; mandating de-transitioning for minors; criminalizing parental support; banning participation in sports; disallowing education about gender and sexual identification within schools; denying that transgender and nonbinary people exist; insisting that there are just two genders, two sexes.

The situation in the US has gotten only worse since the election of Donald Trump, who, in his reelection campaign, targeted transgender citizens while spreading misinformation and repeating lies such as the following delivered at a Bronx barbershop: "They take your kid. There are some places, your boy leaves for school, comes back a girl . . . without parental consent." Standing somewhere in the background to this dishonest, damaging, and cynical campaign were the recommendations of Project 2025, a movement committed to increasing the power of the president while implementing sweeping culture adjustments, all in a conservative Christian direction. Under the heading of "Restore the family as the centerpiece of American life and protect our children" are the following imperatives:

> The next conservative President must make the institutions of American civil society hard targets for woke culture warriors. This starts with deleting the terms sexual orientation and gender identity ("SOGI"), diversity, equity, and inclusion ("DEI"), gender, gender equality, gender equity, gender awareness, gender-sensitive . . . and any other term used to deprive Americans of their First Amendment rights out of every federal rule, agency regulation, contract, grant, regulation, and piece of legislation that exists.[29]

Time will tell whether these imperatives are ever actioned, but the situation is certainly grim for trans Americans. And what is happening in America is certain to reverberate elsewhere. Things are already bad in parts of Africa[30]

---

28. See https://translegislation.com/bills/2023. See also "2024 Anti-Trans Bills Tracker," current home page of https://translegislation.com. As of this writing, it was noted that 664 bills were being tracked, with 45 of them already passed in 2024.

29. Dans and Groves, *Mandate for Conservative Leadership*, 5.

30. For example, in late May 2023, Uganda's President Yoweri Museveni signed one of the world's toughest anti-LGBTIQ laws, including the death penalty for "aggravated homosexuality." This was in a context where Uganda and more than thirty African countries have already made same-sex relations illegal. The new law goes further by stipulating capital punishment for "serial offenders" and a twenty-year sentence for

and Eastern Europe, but even here in Australia we are likely to feel the impact. Friends and relatives often pass articles on to me, and one of these arrived in my in-box in September 2023, written by Al Stewart. It was a review of *Irreversible Damage: The Transgender Craze Seducing Our Daughters*, by Abigail Shrier (2000). Stewart I knew from his time on the staff of St Matthias, Centennial Park, which was prior to a short stint as Anglican bishop of Wollongong. At the time of writing this article, he was national director of the Fellowship of Independent Evangelical Churches in Australia.

The review article was one of a series on "gender confusion" sponsored by American Evangelical Randy Alcorn. Alcorn introduced the article under the heading "The Social Contagion Targeting Girls, and What Parents Can Do to Protect Their Children." He raised the stakes involved by claiming the deadly intentions of none other than Satan:

> As I've often said about abortion—and I believe is also true of transgenderism—we are not dealing here with "one more social issue," but a unique and focused evil in which Satan has deeply vested interests. This is another example of how the evil one has a special hatred of children, and in this case, targets them with gender confusion. He wants to kill them, and he lies to facilitate and cover his attempts to destroy them.[31]

Alcorn's level of alarm is matched by Al Stewart, who in his review appears uncritically accepting of rapid-onset gender dysphoria (ROGD), the so-called contagion or craze sweeping the US. According to this theory, "girls begin to identify as 'trans' in friendship groups or clusters, even though there was no sign of gender dysphoria earlier in their lives."[32] Stewart simply quotes Shrier to the effect that this phenomena is factual and evidentially well supported by recent rapid increases in adolescent women identifying as trans. He also claims, following Shrier, that there are widespread examples of unscrupulous psychologists, counselors, and online advocates advising young girls that if they think they are trans, they are; that they should "try out" breast binders; that testosterone is amazing, that it will solve all their problems; that if their parents loved them, they would support their trans identity; that deceiving parents and doctors is okay.[33] If this was true and widespread, it would indeed be alarming, but Stewart:

"promoting" homosexuality.

31. Randy Alcorn, "Note from Randy," para. 2, in Stewart, "Social Contagion Targeting Girls."
32. Stewart, "Social Contagion Targeting Girls," para. 6.
33. Stewart, "Social Contagion Targeting Girls."

- Fails to mention that Shrier's book relies heavily upon a yet-to-be confirmed hypothesis suggested in a 2018 paper by Lisa Littman that was published in a peer-reviewed open-access journal (*PLOS One*). Littman hypothesized a potential new subcategory of gender dysphoria with young women in particular falsely claiming to be trans as a result of peer influence, especially online.

- Fails to acknowledge the significant scholarly backlash against Littman's paper. Shortly after its publication, *PLOS One* issued a comment that questioned Littman's methodology. Six months later, *PLOS One* reissued the study with a large correction emphasizing that Littman's paper was a "descriptive, exploratory" paper that had not been clinically validated.[34]

- Fails to tell his readers that Littman's research was based on parent surveys recruited from explicitly anti-trans or trans-skeptical websites and forums. Children were not interviewed.

- Fails to mention the more than sixty leading psychology organizations who have taken issue with this untested theory, including the American Psychological Association, who have called for the elimination of the term;[35] or the 2021 *Journal of Pediatrics* study that found no evidence for ROGD's existence;[36] or the *MIT Technology Review* article published in August 2022, which details how Littman's poorly constructed paper went viral, feeding into toxic and right-wing Christian and not-so- (or not-at-all-) Christian politics, or the large-scale study published in the journal of the American Academy of Pediatrics in September 2022, which concluded against the "social contagion" theory, while also finding that the proportion of adolescents who were assigned female at birth and have come out as transgender has not increased.[37]

- Could have also mentioned research such as a 2022 study that found that family acceptance and appropriate medical intervention can have lasting benefits, with researchers reporting that trans and nonbinary youths who went on puberty blockers or hormones had 60-percent lower odds of depression and 73-percent lower odds of suicidality, compared with those who did not.[38]

34. The Brown University retraction: Brown University, "Updated."
35. Kesslen, "How the Idea," para. 4.
36. Bauer et al., "Do Clinical Data."
37. Kesslen, "How the Idea," para. 4.
38. Tordoff et al., "Mental Health Outcomes."

- Completely ignores the voices and lives of the overwhelming number of transgender people and their medical and other companions, a deadly neglect considering how urgent and often life threatening are the issues facing those who are truly trans.[39]
- Lacks the necessary nuancing that more responsible studies do well. The issue of best quality care is complicated, but this, in itself, ought to caution us against premature and possible destructive conclusions.

Alcorn and Stewart have thus failed in their duty of care to their trans fellow citizens and fellow Christians. They have failed the second great commandment of loving neighbors as they love themselves. They have transgressed the ninth commandment against bearing false witness. They have failed to be honest, and, sadly, theirs is just one of any number of misinformed articles and programs causing hurt and damage, contributing to the suicide deaths, assaults upon, and even the murder of people, thus bringing the Christian gospel, which they say they value, into disrepute.[40]

Sadly again, Stewart gives the game away towards the end of his one-sided review, by writing, "Shrier doesn't offer a consistent understanding of gender as rooted in our creation as male and female in the image of God."[41] That surely, is the underlying agenda, this ever more vehement, ideological push, which, while ignoring counterevidence and with a manifestly faulty hermeneutic, continues to insist that there are just two genders and that everything else is broken and not as God intended.

After receiving the online article by Al Stewart, I sent it on to the highly capable trans activist and Christian theologian and pastor Rev. Dr. Josephine Inkpin. Jo was understandably distressed by the review. She observed:

---

39. Stewart could have mentioned, but didn't, Australian research that more honestly addresses these real issues, including Bretherton et al., "Health and Well-Being." Among the findings were the following: Despite 47 percent having tertiary qualifications, the unemployment rate was 19 percent, with 33 percent reporting discrimination in employment due to being trans. Discrimination in accessing health care was reported by 26 percent, and verbal abuse and physical assault were reported by 63 percent and 22 percent, respectively. Lifetime diagnosis of depression was reported by 73 percent and anxiety by 67 percent. Sixty-three percent reported previous self-harm, and 43 percent reported attempted suicide. This later reality explored in Cheung and Zwickl, "Why Have Nearly Half."

40. For better information and to counter misinformation such as the above I'd recommend this very useful handbook: Trans Justice Project, *Anti-Discrimination Handbook*.

41. Stewart, "Social Contagion Targeting Girls," final para.

To be honest, this article reads like a form of conspiracy theory, prompted by lack of understanding, and some deliberate confusion. Shockingly there is no mention of the real issues facing transgender people and the research that backs up their/our real needs.

In essence, I think [the article] is a clear example of a moral panic, highly hypocritical coming from a quarter which has so strongly resisted women's self-expression and advance, and which clearly seeks to use the, certainly sad, distress of an extraordinary tiny number of young females to hurt so many other young people of all kinds of gender identity and expression.[42]

Something Is Wrong with One's Hermeneutic If People Are Hurt

As noted earlier, St. Augustine argued that love is a key to biblical interpretation. Although he himself was misinformed and led astray by his own Christian and pagan culture, Augustine was certainly right about the priority of love. Moreover, we now have evidence and understandings that he and his fellow theologians did not have, and we can therefore better apply his suggested hermeneutic. We can say with some confidence that if any interpretation, however well exegetically grounded, results in people being hurt or even killed, that interpretation or way of interpreting must be rethought. If it leads to dishonesty and the hardening of hearts, it is to be rejected. If it does not lead to the flourishing of God's creation in the lives of his much-loved creatures, it must be exposed as "not of God." The following diagram draws together relevant considerations.

---

42. Josephine Inkpin, email to author, July 19, 2024.

Gender-Diverse Humans and a Love-Directed Hermeneutic

Gender-affirming care might include (i) social affirmation, such as changing names, pronouns, hair, or clothing, (ii) legal affirmation, such as changing one's legal name or gender, and (iii) medical affirmation, with hormones, puberty blockers, or surgery. Some trans people come out as children, others later, some don't ever feel a need to.

Detransition (after surgery) is rare. Surveys indicate that very small percentages, as low as 2 percent, of trans people who undergo gender-affirming surgery regret doing so, with detransition rare and often temporary. Moreover, common factors for those who do detransition are external factors like family pressure and social stigma against transgender people.

Medical gender affirmation has been widely politicized. Unscrupulous ideologues exist on all sides of this complex issue. Nevertheless, gender affirmation has the best results when done in an environment where people are given time and freedom to explore, while having support from family, loved ones, and qualified medical professionals.

There is no single or agreed explanation for why some people are transgender. Nevertheless, research suggests that biological factors, hormone levels, prenatal brain development, and early and later experiences in life variously contribute to gender identification.

Poorly researched, evidence-lacking, peer-rejected "transgender contagion/rapid-onset gender dysphoria" theory continues to be circulated in efforts to further marginalize and discriminate against trans people, creating further harm and misunderstanding.

There are significant improvements in mental health during and after transition, especially in supportive environments.

Some people (up to 30 percent of Gen Z) experience their gender in a way that does not align with the sex they were assigned at birth, for example, being assigned female at birth but having an experience of gender that is male.

There is no direct biblical attention given to gender diversity. However, the Levitical prohibition of cross-dressing suggests discomfort with people living and acting in ways that are inconsistent with their perceived sex and/or gender.

In Australia and across the world there are strong and often ugly campaigns being waged against transgender rights, to the point of denying gender diversity; banning talk; banning from sports, bathrooms, etc.

Large-scale surveys have found that among LGBTIQ+ people, those who are transgender experience the highest levels of suicidal thoughts and behaviors, as much as two times as much as those in the LGBTIQ+ community who are cisgender.

Love-Directed Advocacy

For most people, it is likely to take time to fully integrate and investigate the information noted above—about women; about those who are lesbian, bisexual, gay; about those who are trans, gender diverse, and intersex. And most people have not even heard of hermeneutics, which I have argued is of key importance in these matters. Phillip Jensen was notorious for asking, "Hermon who?" As became obvious, Phillip's feigned ignorance wasn't entirely feigned. Graduates of Moore College, including Phillip, mostly have a poor grasp of hermeneutics. It is not surprising therefore that many churchgoers, of multiple denominations, have received very little education about hermeneutics and have simply accepted that the way their pastor has treated the Bible is the way they should.

And so, not only is the subject matter complicated, so are the various interpretive methodologies that can sensibly be employed to address these matters. What this means is that one needs to be diligent and patient in working through the issues oneself, while being gentle and encouraging of others as they launch out along this investigative path.

My own story is illustrative of the need for this. At various stages of my life's journey I was opposed to the ordination of women to the priesthood. For about half of my life, I would have been horrified to think that I'd one day be advocating for LGBTIQ+ equality. Those acronyms weren't even around for much of my early life. And so, I urge patience, gentleness, and love in your dealings with those you disagree with. For almost all of us, it takes time to change. Love and respect can be a catalyst to change.

Still, once you do get to a place where you have made up your mind, gentle advocacy is to be encouraged. We must not be like the priest or the Levite who walked on the other side of the road, past the stripped, beaten, and half-dead Jew who had been callously thrown into the gutter. Love won't let us. God won't excuse us.

My story again: As, over time, I came to see the injustices and harm involved in long-standing attitudes towards women and LGBTIQ+ people, I knew I needed to speak, even though I also knew it might cost me. Within four years of writing *A Restless Faith*, I worked on a second book, *Faith Without Fear*, which was launched on March 4, 2016, by Hon. Michael Kirby. I had briefly indicated my support for LGBTIQ+ equality in *A Restless Faith* but elaborated more fully on that support in *Faith Without Fear*. I also wrote a series of articles in support of marriage equality,[43] and expressed this support in interviews at the time.[44]

I was most definitely becoming an advocate. Perhaps a little surprisingly, I was invited to meet up with then Archbishop Glenn Davies. Archbishop Glenn was preparing a prayer service for victims of the Orlando massacre. Forty-nine people had been killed and fifty-three injured when, in the early hours of June 12, 2016, a lone gunman entered the Pulse Nightclub in Orlando, Florida, and began shooting. Archbishop Glenn was planning to offer an apology to the LGBTIQ+ community, which he did.

43. For example, Mascord, "Bible Is True Prejudice."
44. For example, on ABC's Religion and Ethics Report—aired June 12, 2016—interviewed by Noel Debien (Mascord, "Interview").

It was an okay meeting, but shortly thereafter, a friend I had just gotten to know, Natalie Cooper, expressed an entirely different take on this planned apology. She wrote to me:

> Angry, angry, angry that the memorial service for the victims of Orlando will be held this evening in the heart of the Anglican Diocese. This Diocese, via GAFCON, has exported contempt for LGBTIQ+ people worldwide, the outcome of which is the tragedy we witnessed in Orlando.

Natalie anticipated that Glenn would not acknowledge the dehumanizing of LGBTIQ+ people, nor the role of his diocese in this tragedy. "What a slap in the face," she wrote. She was right.

In his public apology, the archbishop stated, "[As] Australians, we abhor violence in all its forms—domestic violence, street violence, xenophobic violence, religiously motivated violence, and especially violence against members of the LGBTI community." One could certainly say amen to that. But then he went on to say "*if* any members of our churches have participated in such acts of violence against women, against young people, against ethnic minorities, against religious minorities or against those from the LGBTIQ+ community I offer my heartfelt apology."[45]

If, just if. No acknowledgment of centuries of abuse and derision resulting from horrific teaching by Christianity's great theologians. No acknowledgment of his church's silence when LGBTIQ+ people were targeted and murdered in and around Sydney, with the NSW police force and the "priests" and "Levites" of Anglican (and other churches) saying nothing or little, of Anglican Christians in Sydney taking their own lives in despair at teaching that had them believe they were defective, broken, and evil. There was so much that Archbishop Glenn could have said but didn't.

Steff Fenton could have provided the archbishop with any number of reasons to apologize, including the following:

> In the twelve years after I told my church "I'm queer", I watched as my entire LGBTIQA+ community were muddied and abused by my Church leaders. In sermons, books, newspaper headlines, doctrine lists on church websites, employment contracts in schools and not-for-profits, and political and legal campaigns, we were being labelled as the evils of human gender and sexuality. I watched them use strength and dominance to humiliate and exclude us. For years they told our families that the way to love

---

45. Powell, "PM, Premier," para. 11; emphasis added.

us was to withhold parental care and compassion, increasing our rates of homelessness. They fired us from our jobs, created environments where our children were bullied and punished in their schools, they sent us to unqualified counsellors who taught us to internalise their shameful messages and to suppress our internal sense of selves through pseudo-psychological approaches. Church leaders counselled us into entering heterosexual marriages, then blamed us when those families unravelled. They wielded spiritual practices and sacred texts against us, threatening to isolate us from our communities and networks of support if we did not conform. Today, Christian leaders continue to enforce these teachings into all their official documents and coach their followers not to waver when LGBTIQA+ people express their distress and plead for change. Churches have directed and continue to direct out-of-proportion resources into these efforts against us, so we would understand ourselves as the problem, rather than them.[46]

Equal Voices

It was for reasons such as this that a new movement came to birth. On June 19, 2016, Natalie Cooper visited Holy Trinity Anglican Church, Dulwich Hill, in Sydney. Natalie is the sister-in-law of Sydney Anglican Bishop Michael Stead, who, like Archbishop Glenn, has led the charge against same-sex marriage and the full inclusion of LGBTIQ+ Christians within the lives of their (and others') churches. Natalie and I had been chatting, but we conversed again after church with a soon-to-be married couple, Irene Stein and Regina Barry. We wondered whether we might be able to create a movement of LBGTIQ+ Christians and their allies to advocate for equality within Christian churches. We also thought that, as we had opportunity, we would support marriage equality, which would shortly be voted on in Australia.

A meeting was arranged for July 7, 2016, at Irene and Regina's home, then just across the road from the church. Some very fine and long-term gay advocates were invited. We were joined for that first meeting by Malcolm McPherson, Benjamin Oh, Francis Voon, and Rev. Margaret Mayman. At a subsequent meeting on August 10, the name *Equal Voices* was suggested by Fr. Peter Maher, another long-term and highly respected advocate, who was lost to the movement, and to all those many who loved him, on November 8, 2022. We mourn his passing and honor his life. The Anglican, Roman

---

46. Fenton, "Gender Expansive Faith," unnumbered page.

Catholic, Uniting, and Metropolitan Community Churches were represented at these early meetings.[47] The movement came quickly to include LGBTIQ+ Christians and their allies from most major Christian denominations in Australia, with both denominational and geographical hubs set up over time. It was exciting to be part of it and to take a leading role within it for a number of years.

Some Cost to Pay

At about this time, and really I shouldn't have been surprised, I noticed that my name and details had been removed from the Anglican Diocese of Sydney's just-published yearbook. Diocesan protocol insists that if a name is to be deleted, the person concerned (if still alive) is notified. I wasn't. Thinking that perhaps it was an oversight, I sought an explanation. I was told by Bishop Michael, whom I had taught when he was a student at Moore College, that there was uncertainty about whether I could affirm my ordination vows. Strange that this wasn't asked of me prior to my name being removed from the yearbook. I assured him I could. Prior to writing back to him, I again carefully considered the vows I had taken (in 1984 and 1986). I then explained to Michael that I could indeed promise them again, although with new understandings. I found it quite interesting to think about the following vow:

> Will you be ready to drive away all false and strange doctrines that are contrary to God's word, and to this end both publicly and privately to warn and encourage all within your care?

It struck me that this was indeed something I remained committed to. In fact, it was what my advocacy was all about, and so this is what I wrote in my letter back to Bishop Michael:

> This is an aspect of ministry to which I do feel I am called, which is why I wrote *A Restless Faith* and *Faith Without Fear*. As you know, I drew attention not only to the limitations, but also to the damaging and misleading consequences of inerrancy, especially

---

47. Equal Voices, as an ecumenical movement of LGBTIQ+ Christians and their allies, was well and truly standing on the strong soldiers of prior and still continuing movements such as Acceptance, Changing Attitudes (Anglican), the Uniting Network, the Rainbow Catholics Interagency, Freedom 2b, Metropolitan Christian Churches (MCC), the GLBTIQA+ Interfaith & Intercultural Network (GIIN), and Ambassadors and Bridge Builders International (ABBI). Natalie and I were relative novices, but keen for the vision of a national and multidenominational movement that could be a voice for inclusion alongside efforts from Buddhist, Jewish, and Muslim advocates and organizations.

when yoked to a plain-sense literalist approach. To the extent that this way of thinking (or doctrine) makes it more likely that Christians will believe things which are simply not true, it needs to be exposed as false.

What I have written on the more contentious topic of homosexuality is, perhaps surprisingly, in the same category of wanting to "drive away all false and strange doctrines." [Here] is a strong example of where the church has seriously and damagingly got things wrong.

My letter did not quite meet the purposes I intended. Bishop Michael asked that I wait until Archbishop Glenn could find time to read *Faith Without Fear*. In the meantime, I kept busy organizing for the launch of Equal Voices in early 2017. There was also much to do ahead of the same-sex marriage plebiscite.

On August 30, 2016, I received a letter from Archbishop Glenn informing me that a license to preside and preach in Sydney would not be renewed. Glenn noted that my egalitarian views (with respect to the ministry of women) were not a barrier to the granting of a license, but he said he was disturbed by my view of the Bible as "an ancient text," with some stories not likely to be factual, despite Jesus and Paul apparently believing they were. Coming to this conclusion, "presumably on the fallible ground of human reason," was considered unacceptable. But more disturbing still for Glenn was the following statement from *Faith Without Fear*: "The Biblical writers weren't disabused of their erroneous cosmological, anthropological and *theological* [Glenn's emphasis] ideas."[48] Glenn elaborated:

> That you consider the Biblical writers to be capable of theological error is breathtaking, and I believe undercuts not only the teaching of the Bible, but Articles 6, 20 and 34 of the Thirty-nine Articles. Along with Paul, all Anglicans should be able to assert, "I believe everything laid down in the Law and written in the Prophets (Acts 24:14)."

I must say I was intrigued by the archbishop's response. That the biblical writers disagreed with each other, and thereby were taking issue with the theology of other authors is hardly contentious, as this present book points out. Moreover, biblical anthropology and cosmology feed into theology, and these most definitely vary throughout the Bible. It was quite staggering that Glenn was not sufficiently aware of this as a former theological lecturer.

Almost as a PS, Archbishop Glenn noted my advocacy for same-sex marriage, which he claimed was simply not possible given that "same-sex

---

48. Mascord, *Faith Without Fear*, 207.

relationships are prohibited in Scripture." That may well be the case, but how we can best understand that prohibition has everything to do with one's hermeneutic, and Glenn simply does not address that issue, a serious weakness.

Archbishop Glenn did offer the opportunity to have a limited license to continue ministering the sacraments and preaching at Holy Trinity, Dulwich Hill, on the condition that I "desist from teaching in that parish any doctrine which is contrary to that which has been received by the Anglican Church of Australia." I wasn't willing to accept that condition.

I was okay with all of this. It allowed me unfettered opportunity to advocate for causes dear to me. It was encouraging, in this context, to learn of a letter of protest written to Archbishop Glenn and signed by sixty-eight Anglican priests and church leaders from across Australia. They noted that Anglicans across this country and around the globe hold a variety of positions in good conscience about marriage equality. To de-license a fellow clergyperson for holding one of those diverse views had "deeply shaken" the church, the letter stated, while also noting that free and open discussion about this contested issue was unhelpfully inhibited by this action.

The days and months that followed were busy. There were more interviews,[49] articles to write,[50] a National Apology to LGBTIQ+ Australians to organize,[51] along with the launch of Equal Voices.[52] Without doubt we contributed an alternative Christian voice to the nationwide debate about same-sex marriage. We were overjoyed by the result. To the postal survey question "Should the law be changed to allow same-sex couples to marry?," 61.6 percent of Australians ticked yes. Of those who voted (in record numbers), 38.4 percent ticked no. It was yes in all Australian states and territories, a decisive outcome, with high percentages of Christians voting yes.

Advocacy means seeking to persuade others about things one believes are right. I have continued to advocate, in one way or another, since those days.

 49. On Sept. 28, 2016, I was interviewed along with Rev. Rod Bower on ABC's *Drum* by Julia Baird (Mascord, "Video").

 50. Including Mascord, "Ever Shrinking Case."

 51. On Feb. 24, 2017, a very moving Service of Reconciliation and Apology was held at St James, King Street, in Sydney's CBD. We were grateful for the leadership and support of Rev. Andrew Sempell, who, with the unanimous support of his Parish Council, hosted the event. Archbishop Glenn and his fellow bishops in Sydney were invited but declined to attend. Nevertheless, some clergy from the diocese did attend, and at least one Australian Anglican bishop came in via Facebook.

 52. Equal Voices itself was officially launched by Hon. Michael Kirby on Apr. 3, 2017, with Rev. Dr. Margaret Mayman presiding. It, too, was an extraordinarily moving event, the launch of a movement still continuing.

I had to take a step back between 2018 and 2022 when I moved from being a parole (or community corrections) officer to becoming the NSW prison chaplaincy coordinator. Being responsible for a multi-faith, multi-perspectival prison chaplaincy team meant that I needed to be more circumspect in articulating my particular beliefs, not shared by all those I managed.

I am now retired and enjoying it immensely. I have been hugely encouraged by the ongoing support of the Anglican Diocese of Newcastle,[53] which has licensed me to minister, preside, and preach in the Parish of Taree. In retirement, I will continue advocating in love for those causes dear to my heart.

The Priority of Love

As I reflect on the need for loving advocacy, it is more than likely that almost everyone involved in arguing for or against the above-mentioned causes would say that their advocacy is informed by love. Maybe so, although I must acknowledge that *I've* not always been loving, certainly in attitude. Love, nevertheless, remains an ideal I continue to strive towards. A key difference between those who support and those who oppose LGBTIQ+ and female equality is how one understands the Scriptures. If, as I have argued, the Scriptures are best understood as dynamic, self-correcting, and open ended, then what love requires will (or may well) be quite different than what many of us (myself included) may have once thought when guided by a more static or traditional understanding of the Bible.

Questions for Reflection and Discussion

1. How do you think love for God and love for neighbor should work its way through disagreements about gender and sexuality?
2. In what ways has your thinking changed over the years on:
   - The gifts, ministries, and leadership of women
   - Same-sex marriage
   - Care and support for those who are transgender
3. How might controversies over issues of gender and sexuality be better managed into the future, and what might be the role of love?

---

53. After my initially having been employed as chaplaincy coordinator by Uniting Care, the Anglican Diocese of Newcastle through its welfare arm, Samaritans, employed me.

For a New Beginning
by John O'Donohue

In out-of-the-way places of the heart,
When your thoughts never think to wonder,
The beginning has been quietly forming,
Waiting until you were ready to emerge.

For a long time it has watched your desire,
Feeling the emptiness growing inside you,
Noticing how you willed yourself on,
Still unable to leave what you had outgrown.

I watched you play with the seduction of safety
And the gray promises that sameness whispered,
Heard the waves of turmoil rise and relent,
Wondered would you always live like this.

Then the delight when your courage kindled,
And out you stepped onto new ground,
Your eyes young again with energy and dream,
A path of plenitude opening before you.

Though your destination is not yet clear,
You can trust the promise of this opening;
Unfurl yourself into the grace of beginning
That is at one with your life's desire.

Awaken your spirit to adventure;
Hold nothing back, learn to find ease in risk;
Soon you will be home in a new rhythm,
For your soul senses the world that awaits you.

Chapter 8

Liberating Faith

THERE IS SOMETHING ABOUT a quest for truth that delivers feelings of exhilaration when you arrive at a place of discovery, like a gold prospector chancing upon a rich seam or an archaeologist unearthing a previously undisturbed tomb. I thought about using exhilaration in the title of this chapter. It would have worked, I think. But I decided on liberating instead because many of the beliefs I have shed over a lifetime were in fact burdensome, the lightening of which has been liberating.

In thinking about the liberation I've experienced, I couldn't help but think of Plato's allegory of the cave. Although imagined for slightly different purposes,[1] some of the psychology involved resonates. All humans are captive to some degree to the beliefs and presuppositions they bring with them to any and all acts of perception. We are inescapably influenced by these preformed beliefs. It is nevertheless possible to revise, reject, and/or replace them. This can be liberating, which is often the case when there is a paradigm shift; when one's whole way of seeing things changes.

That is what Plato attempts to illustrate in his allegory of the cave. As he often does, Plato has Socrates engaged in dialogue, in this case with Plato's brother, Glaucon. Socrates asks Glaucon to imagine an underground cave. The cave has access to the outside world, with light from outside reaching into the cave. Within the cave are humans who have been there all their lives. Unfortunately for them, their ankles and necks are chained so they are unable to release themselves or move their heads. They are forced to look

---

1. Plato's allegory of the cave was concerned with illustrating the problem of epistemic access to the Forms or Ideas, which in Plato's philosophy were fundamental to all experienced reality.

straight ahead. Behind and above them is a blazing fire, which throws their shadows onto a wall in front of them.

Socrates asks Glaucon to imagine that some additional shadows are created by unfettered people who walk and talk behind the wall, while also carrying various artifacts including carvings of humans and other animals made of stone, wood, and other materials.

Socrates asserts that the chained humans are like ourselves in being able to see only shadows and not any of the real things. There is more to Plato's story than we can pursue here, but the allegory has relevance beyond its original intent.

Socrates conjectures that humans living in such circumstances are likely to believe that all there is to reality is these shadows and the sounds apparently made by them. He asks Glaucon to imagine what might happen if some of the humans were released from their bondage and allowed to turn around, and to exit the cave. He suggests it wouldn't initially be easy, that they would struggle with the bright glare of the light from the fire and from sunbeams entering the cave. They'd also be faced with the challenge of adjusting their thinking to countenance, for the very first time, the thought that it was not the shadows but the objects themselves that were more truly real.

Socrates surmised, and Glaucon agreed, that the adjustment of thinking would be large and daunting. There would therefore be a temptation to retain their original belief that it was the shadows that were real. The cave dwellers would certainly need some time to fully adjust to this new way of seeing and understanding.

Socrates then speculates that those who take the time to adjust their perceptions and beliefs are likely to then feel sorry for their fellow humans still enslaved in the cave. He continues his analogy:

> SOCRATES: What if some honors, praise, and gifts were bestowed on them by other cave dwellers, while they still were in the cave, for their superior ability to detect the passing shadows; to remember best in which sequence those shadows usually moved (which of them went before, and which followed after, and which moved together); and to predict how the shadows would move in the future based on their past observations? Do you think they would care for such honors or even envy the ones who were honored and considered powerful among the cave dwellers? Or do you think they would rather choose "to become servants of a poor man," to quote Homer (Odyssey 11.489–490),

> and to endure anything, rather than admire such things and live in that way?
>
> GLAUCON: Yes, I think that they would rather suffer anything than accept this sort of life.
>
> SOCRATES: Now imagine this. If such a person goes back down into the cave and ends up back in the same boat as the other prisoners, would [his] eyes not be filled with darkness after [he] suddenly comes out of the sun?
>
> GLAUCON: To be sure.
>
> SOCRATES: And what would happen if such a person were once again to compete against the permanent cave dwellers in judging those shadows? Remember that his sight would still be weak before his eyes once again got used to the darkness, and the recovery time could be considerable. Would he not, then, become the butt of jokes, and would they not say about him that up he went and down he came with his eyes totally destroyed, and that it is not advisable even to think of climbing up? And if someone attempted to free another prisoner and then lead him upwards, would they not kill that leader if they could only lay their hands on him?[2]

Plato's allegory certainly resonates with my experience, though not in every respect. I grew up in a quite conservative Christian family. I saw the world through the lens of a literalistic, plain-sense understanding of the Bible. It was easy enough until at least high school and university to believe in a literal Adam and Eve, a worldwide flood, the confusing of human languages at Babel, and also to accept a biblical storyline where descriptions of the exodus and conquest were factual. I believed that the Bible, in this and all matters, was reliable and trustworthy, even inerrant. That was how I saw things, and it informed my worldview.

A difference for me was that I wasn't quite captive to these views. I went to university wanting to subject them to critical analysis. You might say, I was given permission to get out of my seat. The shackles were only loosely attached. A big part of the reason for that was that I had imbibed a large dose of the spirit of Socrates. I grew up with a respect for the sciences and for scholarship.

What initially attracted me to Sydney Anglicanism was its apparent willingness to engage the academy. This was very appealing. Having studied philosophy and history at university, and having benefitted from the ministry

2. Plato, "Allegory of Cave," 3.

of its Anglican chaplains, three of whom had trained at Moore College,[3] I decided that that was where I would go to study. I did so with great benefit. After some years in pastoral ministry, I was invited onto the faculty and entrusted with the privileged task of teaching philosophy, apologetics, and pastoral ministry. This further loosened the shackles and enabled me to look around in search of light wherever it might shine.

Moore Theological College

I am forever grateful to the then principal of Moore College, retired Archbishop Peter Jensen, for giving me this responsibility and the associated freedom to explore. I guess one could now say it was a dangerous appointment because I soon began to have doubts about the form of Christianity I was entrusted to understand and defend. These doubts emerged slowly and in an initially cautious and step-by-step process, with moments of realization and associated cognitive dissonance. One key step was to find that the propositional evidence for the truth of theism and Christianity is not as strong as I had thought. It isn't without strength, but the evidence is not strong enough to compel belief or to render unbelief irrational or immoral. That was, and still is, a watershed realization.

There were many other moments of realization or worldview-denting puzzlement along the way. What surprised me was that fellow faculty members sometimes seemed oblivious to the sorts of challenges this book and the previous two describe. Or they were aware but believed the challenges had been or could be met. Following are a few examples, not mentioning names and in no particular chronological order.

I was surprised one day when one of our Old Testament lecturers surmised that the long ages of the Bible's early humans made sense, he thought, given that these early humans were living not long after the fall, before the ravages of our sinful natures were fully felt. I was startled and didn't know what to say. Even before I had come to teach at Moore, I had concluded that these early biblical verses cannot sensibly be taken literally. This lecturer (and a fine one at that) wasn't the only one to think otherwise.

Another, at a graduation event, mentioned Noah's flood as if it were factual. I remember being embarrassed. Other faculty members, whom I discussed the flood story with, either avoided the question or suggested it may have

---

3. Michael Hill, Tony Doran, and Kevin Giles were the three (very fine) chaplains who had studied at Moore. Maurice Betteridge, who went on to be principal of Ridley College in Melbourne, was chaplain in my first year and was also a very fine chaplain.

been a local flood (which is how it is *not* described). One suggested that if we were to get into a time machine and go back to see for ourselves what had happened with respect to this and other biblical stories, they might be very different than how they are described in the Bible. I couldn't get my mind around that possibility. If the flood and other biblical stories did not happen more or less as described, how are we to know what happened? And how can the theological conclusions drawn from these events (as described) be trusted?[4]

Another fellow faculty member balked at the idea (which I had raised as a possibility) that Adam and Eve were not two actual human beings, let alone the first two. His reason: Paul appeared to believe in a literal Adam. More seriously still, Jesus appeared to have believed this. And, as one faculty member put it to me recently, "Jesus never lied." There are any number of complications associated with this response, including reasonable doubt about what Jesus did or didn't say, as well as uncertainty about how exactly Jesus might have understood these stories.

For many years, a simple and credible alternative has suggested itself to me, and no doubt to others, and that is that a robust doctrine of the incarnation doesn't require that Jesus knew everything, including that ancient cosmologies and associated stories are not factual. He was, after all, fully human.[5]

This suggestion has not generally been taken up by Evangelicals, as far as I know. My suspicion is that the reason for this is that any concession to ignorance or lack of relevant knowledge on the part of Jesus runs the serious risk of the domino effect. Concede this, and how can we know that anything that Jesus or the Bible asserts is true.

Another faculty member decided to study the authorship of the Pastoral Epistles[6] for his doctoral dissertation. An influential fellow faculty member urged him to go instead for something a little safer such as the authorship of Daniel or Isaiah. The advice wasn't accepted, and when, in his studies, this faculty member concluded that Paul was unlikely to have written the Pastorals, his short career as a Moore College lecturer ended abruptly. He was told that powerful people in the diocese would not tolerate any movement whatsoever in a liberal direction and that the inerrancy of the Bible must be

---

4. For example, one expressed purpose of the ten plagues with which God afflicted the Egyptians was that the Egyptians would know that Yahweh was God (Exod 7:5, for example).

5. And there are instances where Jesus is depicted as not knowing everything. For example: "But about that day or hour no one knows, neither the angels in heaven nor the Son, but only the Father" (Mark 13:32).

6. 1 and 2 Timothy and Titus.

maintained, especially on a matter so important to Sydney Anglicans, which was preventing women from having pastoral leadership in the church.

There are less scandalous reasons for resistance to any concessions about Jesus's and the Bible's humanity. As mentioned in *Faith Without Fear*, another faculty member said to me that if the exodus did not happen, in some form, if not exactly as described,[7] then his Christian faith would collapse. I think I understand where he was coming from. If one of the two great redemptive events of the Bible, the exodus, did not happen, and (to add to the problem) if the second of these events (the death and resurrection of Jesus) cannot be verified beyond reasonable doubt, then how can people retain confidence in their Christian faith?[8]

What I think has happened as a result of this disturbing uncertainty is that uncertainty is denied or minimized. Events considered doubtfully historical by critical scholars are reaffirmed as true, factual, and historical. There may be no evidence for Adam and Eve, a worldwide flood, the exodus and subsequent conquest. This is readily acknowledged by current faculty members. There could well be hyperbole and embellishment in the way the events are described, but because they are (apparently) presented as factual in God's word, they can be accepted as true.[9] It seems to me that this tendency to go with the Bible, and to let the Bible have the final or decisive say on matters of scholarly contention, has resulted in an unstable and hybrid form of Evangelicalism. It is hybrid in that it appears on the one hand to be sensitive to and accommodating of scholarly conclusions while simultaneously trying hard to stick with what the Bible appears to be affirming. It is unstable in having to always find innovative ways to reconcile often well-established critical conclusions with older approaches to reading the Bible, including inerrancy.[10]

---

7. Another faculty member more recently responded to a question about the exodus by saying, "Something happened, but we don't know what." It was an honest answer, but it has all sorts of hermeneutical implications seldom explored adequately.

8. I am aware that Evangelicals are currently struggling to negotiate a way forward on this issue. See, for example, Hoffmeier and Magary, *Do Historical Matters Matter*.

9. I've heard it argued that because the early chapters of the Bible contain genealogies, however inaccurate or contradictory, those who wrote Genesis intended the stories to be accepted as historical. That is possibly so, but it doesn't follow that *we* must consider them factual or historical. The Greek historian Herodotus (c. 484–424 BCE), described by Cicero as the father of history, included genealogies in his history along with mythical and clearly nonfactual figures. The Bible appears to mirror that pattern.

10. Inerrancy inevitably prejudices interpreters against conclusions that appear to contradict the Bible, but which would otherwise be considered reasonable, even probable, given all relevant evidence. Stephen L. Young describes this tendency as a "protective strategy" because it serves to inhibit critical historical and scientific analysis of the

To illustrate, Peter Jensen broke ranks with his predecessors in acknowledging biological evolution, including the evolution of humankind. His immediate successor, John Woodhouse, and Peter himself, were therefore accused of being liberal. They were even called upon to repent. But this liberalizing step only went so far, and neither Peter nor John nor other members of the faculty (myself included) did the necessary work to think through the implications for theology of evolutionary theory. Mark Thompson, the current principal of Moore College, has embraced a creationist and literalistic reading of the early chapters of Genesis and of the Bible as a whole.

My hunch is that Mark, and perhaps others on faculty, simply found it too hard to follow Peter or John. It is nigh impossible to locate an actual Adam and Eve, and a fall into sin and death, along an evolutionary timeline. It is equally impossible to insist that it was God's intention to create just two genders, male and female, without any of the many variations evolution has delivered. It is far easier to accept the authority of Jesus and of the Bible (read in its plain sense, with a nod to genre) on these and other matters.

I happily grant that good scholarship is happening at Moore, as has always been the case. I also acknowledge the efforts of the faculty to make best sense of what we find in the Bible, but I judge that this scholarship continues to be impeded by the albatross of inerrancy and literalism, however nuanced.

Nevertheless, there are positive signs of possible change. As said, faculty members are aware that the exodus and conquest probably did not happen as described. Not all current or past faculty members subscribe to inerrancy or infallibility. There is a willingness, perhaps a growing willingness, to employ the word "myth" to describe Gen 1–11. Not all are creationists, and possibly only a handful.

In recent correspondence with Mark Thompson and a number of other faculty members, I was assured that Moore College is actively committed to academic freedom and to providing the necessary space for diverse points of view. I found that encouraging. I hope it is true. I do wonder, however, if someone was to again come to the conclusion that Paul was not the author of the Pastoral Epistles, or that women can and should be accepted into the priesthood and episcopacy, or that same-sex marriage or the blessing of same-sex unions is good for both Christians and Australians in general, whether they would be allowed to remain on faculty. I don't believe they would be. Nor would anyone with these views be appointed to faculty. On the Moore College website is a values statement that includes scholarship,

---

Bible, especially when these studies threaten to deny the truth of biblical stories and affirmations ("Protective Strategies").

gender complementarity, and freedom of inquiry. Those three simply do not mix.

Of greater concern to me is that the leadership of Moore College is deeply committed to, and influential within, the GAFCON movement.[11] Not all faculty members, present or past, are happy about this, nor should they be.

GAFCON

GAFCON, which stands for the Global Anglican Future Conference, has become a movement known by that acronym. As its website explains:

> The Gafcon journey began in 2008 when moral compromise, doctrinal error and the collapse of biblical witness in parts of the Anglican Communion had reached such a level that the leaders of the majority of the world's Anglicans felt it was necessary to take a united stand for truth. A crowd of more than one thousand witnesses, including Primates, Archbishops, Bishops, clergy and lay leaders gathered in Jerusalem for the first Gafcon Conference.[12]

At this inaugural conference, a declaration, the Jerusalem Declaration, was forged and signed by attendees. Those joining the movement subsequently are encouraged to sign it as well. Following are some of its relevant contents, all of which are described as "tenets of orthodoxy":

> The Jerusalem Declaration
>> In the name of God the Father, God the Son and God the Holy Spirit . . . we agree to chart a way forward together that promotes and protects the biblical gospel and mission to the world, solemnly declaring the following tenets of orthodoxy which underpin our Anglican identity.
>
> Declaration 1, on the gospel and its impact:
>> We rejoice in the gospel of God through which we have been saved by grace through faith in Jesus Christ by the power of the Holy Spirit. Because God first loved us, we love him and as believers bring forth fruits of love, ongoing repentance, lively hope and thanksgiving to God in all things.

---

11. Included among current Moore College faculty are Bishops Peter Jensen and Glenn Davies, both emeritus.
12. See https://www.gafcon.org/about, s.vv. "The birth of Gafcon."

Declaration 2, on the authority of the Scriptures:
> We believe the Holy Scriptures of the Old and New Testaments to be the Word of God written and to contain all things necessary for salvation. The Bible is to be translated, read, preached, taught and obeyed in its plain and canonical sense, respectful of the church's historic and consensual reading.

Declaration 3, on the historic creeds:
> We uphold the four Ecumenical Councils and the three historic Creeds as expressing the rule of faith of the one holy catholic and apostolic Church.

Declaration 4, on the Thirty-Nine Articles:
> We uphold the Thirty-nine Articles as containing the true doctrine of the Church agreeing with God's Word and as authoritative for Anglicans today.

Declaration 8, on the creation of males and females in the image of God:
> We acknowledge God's creation of humankind as male and female and the unchangeable standard of Christian marriage between one man and one woman as the proper place for sexual intimacy and the basis of the family. We repent of our failures to maintain this standard and call for a renewed commitment to lifelong fidelity in marriage and abstinence for those who are not married.

Declaration 12, on acceptable disagreements:
> We celebrate the God-given diversity among us which enriches our global fellowship, and we acknowledge freedom in secondary matters. We pledge to work together to seek the mind of Christ on issues that divide us.

Declaration 13, on churches that have deviated from orthodoxy:
> We reject the authority of those churches and leaders who have denied the orthodox faith in word or deed. We pray for them and call on them to repent and return to the Lord.[13]

As one reads through these declarations, they present the movement well. First impressions are likely to be good. Here is a movement dedicated to upholding the historic faith, grounded in its ancient creeds. GAFCON thereby presents itself as nothing more than a return to long-standing orthodoxy. At a time of uncertainty, when people are exiting the church in large numbers, in the West at least, a call back to the safety of earlier forms of the faith is

---

13. GAFCON, "Jerusalem Statement," s.vv. "The Jerusalem Declaration."

likely to be attractive, even comforting. This is especially so since among the founders of this movement are leaders from the Global South, whose churches are thriving.

First impressions are not always reliable, however, and in this case certainly not. There are all sorts of problems with these declarations, some of which are worth mentioning.

Orthodoxy: The use of the word "orthodoxy" is problematic. The declaration describes itself as upholding orthodoxy as expressed at the first four Ecumenical Councils (Nicaea 325 CE, Constantinople 381 CE, Ephesus 431 CE, and Chalcedon 451 CE) and as articulated in the Apostles', Nicene, and Athanasian Creeds, and within the Thirty-Nine Articles. The first thing to note is that these are ancient or very old creeds and articles, many elements of which have come under reasonable challenge, for example the Virgin Birth. More relevant though is that none of these creeds/articles specifically mentions matters of gender and sexuality, and most make no declaration about biblical authority, the two major issues that have given birth to GAFCON. Appeal to the historic creeds is therefore misleading.

Biblical authority: A statement on biblical authority is included in the Thirty-Nine Articles. It is worth quoting the relevant article, Article 6:

> VI: Of the Sufficiency of the Holy Scriptures for salvation
>
> Holy Scripture containeth all things necessary to salvation: so that whatsoever is not read therein, nor may be proved thereby, is not to be required of any man, that it should be believed as an article of the Faith, or be thought requisite or necessary to salvation.[14]

It is interesting that Thomas Cranmer and those who helped finalize the Thirty-Nine Articles restricted the authority of Scripture to "all things necessary to salvation" and to things that could be proved to be necessary to salvation. That has not been done by the GAFCON movement, and I can't see how it possibly could be. First, they would need to "prove" (a strong word) that their hermeneutic as well as their exegesis of relevant texts (about gender and sexuality) were correct beyond reasonable doubt. That certainly has not happened. And, second, they would need to "prove" that their beliefs about marriage, sexuality, and gender must also be believed by others "as necessary for salvation." Those are gargantuan tasks, made all the more difficult by doubts about the authorship and dating of the Pentateuch.

The gospel: The preamble to the Jerusalem Declaration indicates that the GAFCON movement is designed to "chart a way forward together that

---

14. Standing Committee, *Australian Prayer Book*, 627–28.

promotes and protects the biblical gospel."[15] The linking of the gender, sexuality and marriage cause with the gospel is also problematic. The final statement of the 2008 GAFCON Conference asserts that the "acceptance and promotion . . . of a different 'gospel' (cf. Galatians 1:6–8), contrary to the apostolic gospel" was a major reason for the formation of GAFCON. It goes on to say, "This false gospel undermines the authority of God's Word written and the uniqueness of Jesus Christ as the author of salvation from sin, death and judgement."[16] I am not sure what this "false gospel" is, but it is significant and revealing that there are any number of evangelical Anglicans, who accept biblical authority and have an evangelical understanding of the gospel, who have also come to believe that Christian marriage can and should be extended to those of diverse sexualities and genders, and that it is the gospel itself which provides the impetus for this.

For example, on November 15, 2023, the Synod of the Church of England, including Evangelicals, approved a proposal to encourage its bishops to continue their work in creating and implementing liturgical prayers of blessing for same-sex unions. The synod also voted to approve an amendment that will allow clergy to conduct stand-alone services of blessing on a trial basis. The GAFCON reaction, a day later, was as expected. A statement was released by the GAFCON primates, which begins:

> This week marks a tragic moment in the history of the Church of England. . . . This [decision] means that, beginning next month, Anglican clergy in Church of England churches will be able to do what the prophet Balaam could not and would not do by going against the Word of God and blessing that which God has condemned (Num. 24:12–14).
>
> Holy Scripture is clear and unequivocal in its affirmation that the only proper context for sexual intimacy is the relationship of a man and woman who have been joined together in marriage. All forms of sexual intimacy outside of this context are condemned as immorality and are behaviors from which the people of God are regularly called to repent.[17]

The sentiments expressed are understandable, but the statement is disturbingly misleading. Scripture is not at all clear and unequivocal that the "only proper context for sexual intimacy is the relationship of a man and a woman

---

15. GAFCON, "Jerusalem Statement," s.vv. "The Jerusalem Declaration."

16. GAFCON, "Jerusalem Statement," s.vv. "The Global Anglican Context."

17. Mbanda, "Statement," paras. 1–2. The statement was penned by the Most Rev. Dr. Laurent Mbanda, archbishop and primate of the Anglican Church of Rwanda, chairman, Gafcon Primates Council.

joined together in marriage." If that was true, then Abraham, Isaac, Jacob, David, and many other of the Bible's heroes of faith would have been immoral and in need of repentance for having more than one wife and, in some cases, having sex with servants. Also there were others engaged in biblically warranted levirate marriages, which often necessitated taking an additional wife (one's widowed sister-in-law). The Bible is extraordinarily tolerant, if not encouraging, of marital variations.

Considerations such as these have been influential among Evangelicals. Just prior to the general synod's decision to cautiously introduce blessings for same-sex couples, a group of over six hundred evangelical Church of England clergy (in England) signed an open letter on behalf of inclusive evangelical Anglicans. The letter notes that a majority of general synod members "want to see affirmation of same-sex relationships through the prayers for God's blessing of same-sex couples," and that this desire cuts across "all traditions and perspectives" including their own evangelical perspective. Here are a few snippets from the letter:

> As evangelicals whose prayerful reading of scripture has led us to an inclusive position on same-sex relationships, we urge that there be no further changes to the proposals of the House of Bishops (GS2289). . . . We look forward to being able to give thanks in prayer before God for faithful, loving same-sex relationships. We also believe that pastoral guidance should be issued by the House of Bishops, as a matter of urgency, which will permit clergy to enter same-sex civil marriage, in accordance with Article 32, which states that clergy may marry at their own discretion.[18]

> As evangelical Christians we celebrate the diversity of the Church of England, and are committed to joyfully working, worshipping and ministering alongside Anglicans of different theological traditions and views on this issue. . . . We do not feel the need for any structural differentiation to accommodate different opinions. We oppose any approach which would divide the church, including alternative episcopal structures. We are one church, with a breadth of convictions, united in Christ. We recognize that same sex relationships is an area of disagreement, but we believe it is not one over which Christians should divide.[19]

---

18. Inclusive Evangelicals, "Open Letter," para. 3.
19. Inclusive Evangelicals, "Open Letter," para. 4.

Hermeneutics: Declaration 2 of the Jerusalem Declaration asserts: "The Bible is to be translated, read, preached, taught and obeyed in its plain and canonical sense, respectful of the church's historic and consensual reading."[20] This is quite a revealing statement. It was Martin Luther who pioneered the plain-sense (sensus literalis) approach to reading the Scriptures, in the belief that God would surely make the Bible accessible to every reader, including the most uneducated. As argued in a chapter of my previous book,[21] the plain-sense-meaning approach has been a disaster ever since Luther suggested it, leading countless Christians astray. Moreover, this was not the Bible's hermeneutic, nor is the grammatical-historical approach, which is favored by many Evangelicals.

If "canonical sense" refers to letting individual biblical passages be interpreted through the lens of the Bible as a canonical whole, there is certainly value in that, although there was no canon, of either the Old nor the New Testament, when the Bible was being written. There is value in taking account of the church's consensual (or agreed-upon) readings, but, once again, this approach, necessarily, wasn't how the biblical authors approached their Scriptures. They employed interpretative techniques current at the time, as already explained in chapter 6. Moreover, historic understandings (which do need to be respected) have often been anything but consensual, with contrary understandings proliferating over time. Even where agreement has been long lasting,[22] this is no guarantee of truth, as we are increasingly finding.

Love: Someone guided by a more biblical hermeneutic will also be guided by the two great commandments, as argued in the previous chapter. GAFCON's whole approach to homosexuality continues to damage, hurt, and destroy lives. This has been sadly illustrated by Archbishop of Uganda Dr. Stephen Kaziimba's support for his government's anti-homosexuality legislation, which in May 2023 introduced new offences (to add to the illegality of homosexuality), including the promotion of homosexuality (up to twenty years in prison), and harsher penalties, including (up to) life imprisonment for consensual sex and the death penalty for "aggravated homosexuality."[23] What is disturbing is that Archbishop Kaziimba is a member of GAFCON and was apparently unmoved by worldwide negative reactions, including from Christian leaders, but not, it seems, from GAFCON. He stood by

---

20. GAFCON, "Jerusalem Statement," s.vv. "The Jerusalem Declaration."
21. Entitled "The Lure of Literalism," in Mascord, *Faith Without Fear*.
22. Such as on the subservience of women.
23. Defined to include repeat offences, gay sex that transmits terminal illness, and same-sex intercourse with minors and disabled persons.

his comments, which were made in a statement released by the Church of Uganda, in which he writes,

> The Church welcomes the diligent work of Parliament and His Excellency, the President, in crafting the Anti-Homosexuality Act 2023 . . . offering greater protection of children through strong anti-grooming measures, strong restrictions on promotion, and protection of children by not allowing those convicted under the act to be employed in organizations that work directly with children.[24]
>
> Homosexuality is currently a challenge in Uganda because it is being forced on us by outside, foreign actors against our will, against our culture, and against our religious beliefs.[25]
>
> There is no moral equivalence between LGBTQ relationships (which cannot procreate) and lifelong, heterosexual, monogamous marriage.[26]

Both he and GAFCON appear oblivious to the damage, hurt, and grief these laws will occasion, including hatred and violence directed against LGBTIQ+ people, including fearfulness about seeking help from medical professionals, including the inevitable retreat back into the closet of self-hatred, despair, and soul-destroying loneliness. The archbishop's ignorance on relevant issues is breathtaking; his linking of homosexuality to child abuse is inexcusable.

Arrogance: It is ironic that members of GAFCON consider themselves to be more faithfully biblical than those Christians who disagree with them. The Scriptures display an adaptability, flexibility, and willingness to countenance new understandings, which is in direct contrast with the legalistic and inflexible approach of GAFCON. A truly Bible-believing Christian would be following the Bible's example. There is a dynamism about the Bible that is lost by Pharisaic-like movements such as GAFCON.

What is most galling is the expressed sense of superiority and self-righteousness. Declaration 13 asserts: "We reject the authority of those churches and leaders who have denied the orthodox faith in word or deed. We pray for them and call on them to repent and return to the Lord."[27] In actual fact, those Christians who have come to different conclusions about marriage, sexuality,

24. Kaziimba, "Church of Uganda Grateful," paras. 1–2.
25. Kaziimba, "Church of Uganda Grateful," para. 5.
26. Kaziimba, "Church of Uganda Grateful," para. 7.
27. GAFCON, "Jerusalem Statement," s.vv. "The Jerusalem Declaration."

and gender have mostly done so with a clear conscience, often after a long and taxing process, involving hermeneutics, exegesis, scientific investigation, compassionate listening, and a strong conviction that their conclusions are true to the Scriptures in their spirit and direction. The profound disrespect involved in calling fellow Christians to repent is itself grounds for repentance.

Returning to Plato and his cave, it seems to me that it is the members of GAFCON who, "in word or deed," have retreated into the shadowy safety of profoundly erroneous ways of seeing both the Scriptures and the world around them. They have effectively blinded themselves. The intellectual leaders of the movement know better. They know that their conclusions are not certain. They are well enough aware of the scholarship that delves behind the pages of the Bible to when it was written, by whom, and why. The partial light from these discoveries and research has been beaming into their cave for long enough, but they have chosen to look away, and are thus culpable in their chosen ignorance.

To further aggravate matters, they have acted just like Plato's cave dwellers in disrespectfully attacking and sidelining those who don't see things the same way they do, though not quite to the point of execution (as happened to Socrates and Jesus).

In conclusion, it is no exaggeration to say that the declarations above are an exceedingly fragile house of cards, built on morally and intellectually doubtful foundations.[28]

Liberation

Speaking personally, I am really glad to be mostly out of the above-described scene. Judy and I have retired to the outer reaches of the gentler and more epistemically humble Diocese of Newcastle. Retirement is liberating. It has given me time to write this book. Being away from toxic forms of the faith is wonderful. In terms of Plato's allegory, movement out of the cave has been an almost lifelong process. For some, I am sure, liberation happens more quickly, and the associated emotions are therefore stronger.

Peter Enns, in his helpful book *The Sin of Certainty*, taught for years in a theological seminary until some changes to the faculty altered the atmosphere of the college from being, in his words, "collegial and generous to

---

28. For a contrastingly honest and historically revealing approach to the complex subject of gender and sexuality as understood and appropriated by Christians over the last two thousand–plus years, I'd recommend MacCulloch, *Lower Than the Angels*.

tense and adversarial." The college's board was intent on safeguarding its long-standing conservative identity. Enns elaborates:

> Our teaching and writing began to be closely monitored. It seemed that the slightest perceived deviation in thinking led to very serious meetings about "the future of the school" and "maintaining our heritage."[29]

Enns resigned with immediate feelings of a great freedom:

> I recall those first few months of sweet freedom. I hadn't felt that light and joyful in probably a decade. Pick your cliché: I felt alive, born again, as if I had been liberated from a prison camp, released from a dungeon, and had seen the sunshine and felt the cool breeze for the first time in ages. And I had boundless energy. I was bursting at the seams with fresh and exciting ideas. I felt free to put them out there without threats of a scolding.[30]

In chapter 2, I included a graph of responses to an online survey of people who had abandoned Christian faith or an earlier form of that faith. The author, Brandon Flanery, asked participants to describe what their current existential framework offered them that their earlier framework perhaps hadn't. Some had become agnostic, others atheist, still others had embraced an alternative religion, denomination, or spiritual framework. Following is a summary of their responses.

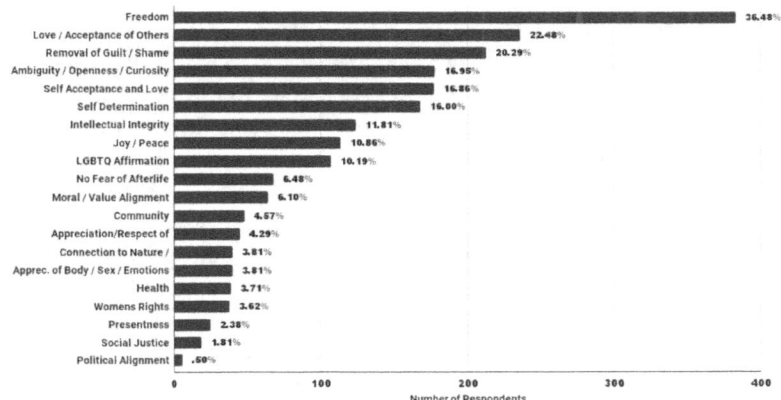

29. Enns, *Sin of Certainty*, 12.
30. Enns, *Sin of Certainty*, 12.

From what limited reading I have done, these responses are typical. Steph Lentz, in her book *In/Out*, describes some grief resulting from her loss of faith. As she puts it:

> I missed having a strong sense of identity as a child of God. I missed deferring to someone else's authority, following men's instructions and believing they were correct, in my best interests. I missed regularly playing music and singing in a group. I missed being a Christian.[31]

Steph realized she couldn't turn back the clock to her earlier faith nor its false certainties, but she also felt liberated by leaving behind a harmful and misleading form of the faith. She found that she'd become more compassionate, forgiving, humbler, and blessed with a new freedom.

> Closer to the chaos at the heart of living, I felt freer. It was not a freedom like the one that had been sold to me, squashed into a small box of constrained choices and limited options. It was freedom to feel it all. It was freedom to be patient with mystery.[32]

Not everyone who goes through a process of faith deconstruction leaves the faith entirely or permanently. For many, this new sense of freedom creates the necessary room for a constructive rethink of their faith. That was certainly the case for Fr. Richard Rohr, who in a podcast dedicated to the theme of deconstruction, describes his own journey in this way:

> Picture three boxes. The first is order, the second is disorder; the third is reorder.
>
> We're all raised in the first box of order. We were given our explanation of what reality means and what God means. It gives you so much comfort that most people want to stay in the first box forever. But what has to happen between your 30s and 50s is the glib certitudes of the first box have to fall apart. Who's right, who's wrong, who's holy and who's a sinner—I know these beliefs gave your ego great comfort—but if you stay inside the first box, it creates angry people, rigid people and unhappy people. When you leave the first box it feels like dying. When I had to leave my early Catholic certitudes it felt like a loss of faith.
>
> But that wonderful early evangelical gospel holds you strong enough to endure the second box and not throw the baby out with the bathwater. In the second box you realize "it wasn't as simplistic as I was told, but it's not all wrong either." If you can

---

31. Lentz, *In/Out*, 274.
32. Lentz, *In/Out*, 277.

let God lead you through the second box while hanging onto order, God can lead you to the third box, reorder.

People want the first box at all costs but it doesn't make them love Jesus. The crucified one who identifies with the poor and tells *the outsider* "never have I found such faith inside Israel"—you see why they killed him! He was so comfortable with disorder inside of his own highly ordered religion. But he never throws it out—he still respects the temple. But he doesn't waste much time there. That's the position we're in. I live with that same tension—figuring out what was good about the tradition I was given and what was accidental and arbitrary.[33]

Rohr's words draw upon Paul Ricoeur's arc (first naïveté, critical engagement, second naïveté). Doubtless Rohr's journey has been the journey of many, with many more likely to follow. I am certainly willing to be a fellow traveler with any who would like assistance in taking what some will find to be scary steps.

By nature, I am an advocate and a helper. It's why I have written *A Restless Faith*, *Faith Without Fear*, and *An Honest Faith*. The books are meant to be an encouragement to step out. I have walked away from a form of the faith but not from the faith itself. And so, I am happy to enter into dialogue with readers who may have walked a similar journey. The journey itself hasn't always been plain sailing, and there have been some repercussions from being so public in detailing my story, but they have not been harsh nor have they silenced me. That too has been liberating. I am grateful. I would love to see others having that same freedom.

I would like to finish with some stanzas from a beautiful poem by Irish philosopher, theologian, and poet John O'Donohue. They represent a rebuke to those peddling false certainty and an encouragement to recognize the many shades of certitude that, if we recognize them, can have us living with integrity, humility and grace.

For Light
by John O'Donohue

In the glare of neon times,
Let our eyes not be worn

---

33. Richard Rohr, in Hailes, "Deconstructing Faith," s.v. "Defining Deconstruction" (callout). See further, for an elaboration of these thoughts, Rohr, "Order, Disorder, Reorder."

By the surfaces that shine
With hunger made attractive.

That our thoughts may be true light,
Finding their way into words
Which have the weight of shadow
To hold the layers of truth.

That we never place our trust
In minds claimed by empty light,
Where one-sided certainties
Are driven by false desire.

Questions for Reflection and Discussion

1. How have you experienced constriction or liberation in your faith journey?
2. What have been some of the more significant "light bulb" moments in your life, and what have been their impact?
3. Do you think that Christian churches, organizations, and denominations can change for the better, and if so, how and how quickly?

"I Am Willing. Lead Thou Me On."
by Noel Davis

It is the willingness to be where we are now called to be
to be what we are being called to become.
There is a path opening up before us.
We know not its destination
yet it is known to our hearts
calling on our trust, openness, courage
self-confidence and willingness to move forward
regardless of fear, doubt, hesitancy
or what we might anticipate to be the outcomes.

There is a peace, freedom and empowerment
in our willingness to take the path
and a deep sense of the Presence
and companionship of Spirit
Can our response be "Lead Thou me on
Do with me as you will"
as You love us into life
to choose the way of life and love.

Chapter 9

Hopeful Faith

THE HEADING OF THIS chapter may surprise readers. One might be tempted to think that all hope has been dashed in the preceding chapters of this book, that there is no longer room for hope but only doubt, and serious doubt at that. But not so.

It is worth taking a step back to some of the themes previously explored, this time from the vantage point of hope. I have come to see the Bible as an essentially hopeful book or collection of books. Some are perhaps more hopeful than others, with Ecclesiastes at the more cautious end of the spectrum. But hope is plentiful throughout the Bible.

At its very beginnings, a foundation for hope is laid with an extraordinarily positive view of God and of humankind. Throughout the seven days of creation, God's consistent verdict is that what God saw was good, and, after day six, "very good," including its dignified depiction of humankind as created in the very image and likeness of God. So good are things, and so lacking in any mention of violence or death, that humans and all animals are depicted as vegetarian. In Gen 2–3, Adam and Eve are gifted with the possibility of immortality, which they subsequently squander.

This aetiological myth[1] was devised, it seems, to explain the inevitability of death, which is sheeted home to human disobedience. But even in this our world of frustration, toil, and death, God's continual graciousness is repeatedly emphasized as the biblical story unfolds. It is God's graciousness that makes hope always possible. For most of the biblical authors up

---

1. Aetiology (or etiology) in religion and mythology refers to an explanation, often in narrative form, of a practice, epithet, monument, or place name, typically drawn from the mythical past.

until the New Testament, this hopefulness was not for a life (or much of a life) after death. Humans were instead destined for the shadowy half-life of Sheol. Hope was limited to this-worldly blessings, which the author or authors of Deuteronomy spell out in terms of a fruitful and prosperous life in the promised land for those who obey God (Deut 28:1–14). To disobey was unwise, in fact disastrous, as the following curses make clear:

> The LORD will cause you to be defeated before your enemies; you shall go out against them one way and flee before them seven ways. You shall become an object of horror to all the kingdoms of the earth. 26 Your corpses shall be food for every bird of the air and animal of the earth, and there shall be no one to frighten them away. 27 The LORD will afflict you with the boils of Egypt, with tumors, scurvy, and itch, of which you cannot be healed. 28 The LORD will afflict you with madness, blindness, and confusion of mind; 29 you shall grope about at noon as blind people grope in darkness, but you shall be unable to find your way, and you shall be continually abused and robbed, without anyone to help. (Deut 28:25–29)

It doesn't make for happy reading, and this is but a sample. Nevertheless, even in this, and in the chapters and books that follow, hope remains, with frequent reminders of God's mercy, even to those who have gone astray, even to a city as wicked as Nineveh, even to a widowed Moabite. On Mount Sinai, during the fabled exodus, God describes God's self as:

> The LORD, the LORD, the compassionate and gracious God, slow to anger, abounding in love and faithfulness, maintaining love to thousands, and forgiving wickedness, rebellion and sin. (Exod 34:6)

This description of God is quoted nine times in the Old Testament[2] and in all likelihood was used in worship. Jonah quotes it disapprovingly! The Israelite and Judean prophets continuously called upon their peoples to turn back to God as the hopeful key to redemption, reminding them of God's gracious nature, as in these verses from Micah:

> Who is a God like you, pardoning iniquity
>   and passing over the transgression
>   of the remnant of his possession?
> He does not retain his anger forever
>   because he delights in showing steadfast love.

---

2. For example, Pss 86:15; 103:8; 145:8.

> 19 He will again have compassion upon us;
>   he will tread our iniquities under foot.
> You will cast all our sins
>   into the depths of the sea.
> 20 You will show faithfulness to Jacob
>   and steadfast love to Abraham,
> as you have sworn to our ancestors
>   from the days of old. (Mic 7:18–20)

In the New Testament, hope rises to a new level. The relatively new idea of bodily resurrection to an even better world emerged in the intertestamental period, and was embraced by Jesus and his followers. It was this hope that propelled the formerly tribal or ethnic religion of Judaism into the transnational Christian movement, with the firstfruits resurrection of Jesus at the core of this new faith. The New Testament ends with another glorious picture of what God will provide for those who believe in Jesus and faithfully follow him and his ways:

> Then the angel showed me the river of the water of life, bright as crystal, flowing from the throne of God and of the Lamb 2 through the middle of the street of the city. On either side of the river, is the tree of life with its twelve kinds of fruit, producing its fruit each month, and the leaves of the tree are for the healing of the nations. 3 Nothing accursed will be found there anymore. But the throne of God and of the Lamb will be in it, and his servants will worship him; 4 they will see his face, and his name will be on their foreheads. 5 And there will be no more night; they need no light of lamp or sun, for the Lord God will be their light, and they will reign forever and ever. (Rev 22:1–5)

The promise of immortality, dashed in Genesis, is finally realized at the end of time. The Bible's early mythological themes are combined with apocalyptic imagery to envisage a most glorious (for some, though not all) future.

What are we to make of this hopeful biblical tale? The first thing to notice is that it is imaginative. As mentioned previously, it needed to be. As the Bible's "largely mythical epic"[3] was being created, its authors could only conjecture about first things (protology) or last things (eschatology). And although they could draw upon various historical and other resources to help them in telling the in-between stories, even these required the creative use of imagination. The biblical authors were not doing history as we understand that discipline. They were doing theology. It is for that reason

---

3. My own description at the beginning of ch. 6.

that the so-called historical books of the Hebrew Bible are included under the category of prophecy. The major divisions of the Hebrew Bible are Torah, Prophets, and Writings. God is the Bible's major player and speaker throughout. This is no ordinary history. It was the revolutionary conviction that God, just one God, the only God, was essentially good and kind, and therefore also just, which inspired the employment of myths, legends, and other likely stories. Historicized myths and mythologized history are common, not only at the beginning and end of the Bible but all the way through.

A second thing to notice about this largely mythical epic is that it quickly became, and still is, very precious to those who embraced it. The very idea that there is only one God, and that this one God is essentially good, kind, and just, was unprecedented. The idea that life in this world can be redeemed and transformed, *and* that there is full-bodied, beautiful, and everlasting life to come, was music to so many who heard it. It certainly helps to explain the rapid rise and continuing strength of the Christian movement. It has been important in my life and in the life of my family of origin.

I refer often in this and previous books to my dad and to his influence on my life, but my mum, Audrey Mascord (née Furseth), was equally influential in complementary ways. She was a beautiful person in every way and was much loved by those who knew her. For Mum, belief in the resurrection, Jesus's and her own, was central to her life and faith. I remember visiting her not long before she died and noticing her looking out the window into a more distant space as she told me her time on earth would soon be coming to an end. She was content, even happy, for this. It meant, for her, "going home."

On the order of service at her funeral on March 30, 2010, were the words "Called home on the 23rd of March, 2010." Inside was this poem:

> I am standing upon the seashore. A ship at my side spreads her white sails to the morning breeze and starts for the blue ocean. I stand and watch her till she disappears where sea and sky meet.
>
> Then someone at my side says, "She's gone!"
>
> Gone? Gone from my sight. That is all.
>
> The diminished size is in me, not in her, and just at the moment when someone at my side says, "She is gone," there are other eyes watching her coming and many other voices ready to take up the glad shout, "Here she comes!"[4]

---

4. Truncated version of Van Dyke, "I Am Standing."

The poem was there at Mum's request. She had also asked that the following hymn be sung.

Because He Lives
 —William J. Gaither and Gloria Gaither

God sent his Son—they called him Jesus
He came to love, heal and forgive
He lived and died to buy our pardon
An empty grave is there to prove my Savior lives.

Because he lives, I can face tomorrow
Because he lives, all fear is gone
Because I know he holds the future
And life is worth the living—just because he lives.

And then one day, I'll cross the river,
I'll fight life's final war with pain
And then, as death gives way to victory,
I'll see the lights of glory—and I'll know he lives.

It is hard to write about this without choking up. Family members and so many friends talk about the joy of one day being reunited with loved ones, including our parents, including children who have preceded us. It is indeed a precious belief.

So how does one deal with the challenges to resurrection belief that this book has sought to detail? As pointed out, there is reasonable uncertainty about whether there is life after death. What should we do about this? How do we make sense of the apparent (I would say actual) presence of legend, myth, and fable in the Bible? What about all those beliefs we just do not know are true, though they may be? I'd suggest there are three broad approaches.

The Bible as Factually Accurate

One way to deal with the above-mentioned questions is to deny that there are myths, legends, and fables in the Bible and to follow something like the hermeneutical approach of Martin Luther. Luther counseled acceptance of the literal and plain-sense meaning of biblical texts. One might also agree with Luther that human reason is an "enemy of God," a "source of mischief," and the "devil's whore" when it comes to matters of saving faith, and that the only sure way to know what is true in such matters is to go to the Bible and believe what one finds there. It is to be trusted above all other sources of knowledge (*sola scriptura*—Scripture alone).

This is a very common approach among Christian conservatives,[5] Evangelicals, and fundamentalists. I recently came across the website of a Bible college in Canada, Millar College of the Bible, which seemed to exemplify this approach very well. Its doctrinal statement is partially reproduced below. What struck me was that nothing is asserted that is not supported by a relevant biblical reference. One could reasonably call into question the interpretation of these verses, but the hermeneutical approach is clear.

> The Old and New Testaments are God's written revelation to man, fully inspired by the Spirit of God to the very words penned by the human authors (2 Pet. 1:20–21; 3:14–16). Therefore all 66 books are inerrant and foundational as the final authority in matters of doctrine, practice, and lifestyle (2 Tim. 3:14–17)....
>
> The Heavens and the Earth and all that are within them were created by the power and wisdom of God for His pleasure and glory (Rev. 4:11). The creation of the heavens and earth was accomplished in six literal days (evening and morning) and was very good in its original form without the presence of sin and death (Gen 1:31; 2:1–3; Exod. 20:11). The church is to hold to God's promise and look forward to a new heaven and a new earth where righteousness dwells (2 Pet. 3:13).
>
> Man was created in the image and likeness of God (Gen. 1:25–27; James 3:9). Man was created from the dust of the ground on the sixth day of creation apart from any process of death (Gen. 1:27, 31; 2:7). On the same day woman was taken from the side of man to become fellow-heir of life (Gen. 2:21–23). Through Adam's disobedience, man became dead in trespasses and sins, born with a corrupt nature and is incapable of turning to God for salvation apart from God's grace (Gen. 3:19; Jn. 6:65; Rom 3:10–11; 5:12–21; Eph 2:1–2). Holy matrimony consists of one man and one woman, reflecting strengths and roles of each gender (Gen. 2:24; Matt. 19:4–6; 1 Cor 11:7–10; Eph 5:22–33)....
>
> The Resurrection of Christ is bodily and gives witness to the future resurrection (Matt. 28:1–10; 1 Cor 15:1–11). The first resurrection is unto life eternal for all those who believe in Him (Job 19:26; 1 Cor 15:12–23; Rev. 20:4–6). The second resurrection,

---

5. Scott Cowdell helpfully notes that this first approach, in modified form, is also characteristic of conservative forms of Roman Catholicism. These take a similarly deductive approach of drawing their beliefs and guiding convictions from Scripture or church tradition while resisting well-founded contemporary understandings (Cowdell, *Church Matters*, 217).

> one thousand years later, is for all who died in their sins unto condemnation (Rev. 20:4-6). . . .
>
> The Second Coming of Christ will be personal, bodily, visible, and triumphant (Matt. 24:30-31; Acts 1:8-11; 1 Thess. 4:13-18; Tit. 2:13). No one but the Father knows the time of His Coming (Mk. 13:32). Christ will establish the throne of David upon the earth and reign in righteousness for one thousand years (2 Sam. 7:16; Isa. 9:6-7; 61:1-5; 63:1-6; 65:1-25; Zech. 14:3-9; Lk. 1:32-33; Acts 3:17-23; Rev. 20:1-6).
>
> The Destiny of the Wicked, the devil and his angels, and of all who are unbelievers is eternal punishment called Hell (Matt. 25:41-43; Mk. 9:48). The devil is the enemy of God and His saints (Eph 2:2; James 4:7; 1 Jn. 3:7-10). He and his angels were defeated at the cross (Jn. 12:31; Col. 2:15), yet he roams to and fro now seeking whom he may devour (Job 1:7; 1 Pet. 5:8). Believers overcome his schemes through faith in Christ and the sword of the Spirit, the word of God (Eph 6:10-18). At the Second Coming, the devil will be cast into the abyss. After one thousand years, he will be released for a short time to deceive the nations and finally he will be sent to the lake of fire, also known as Hell (Rev. 20:1-3, 7-10). All unbelievers will be judged at the Great White Throne from where they will be consigned to eternal conscious torment (Lk. 16:19-31; Rev. 20:11-15).[6]

This is a very stark presentation of the Christian message, but to be fair, it is by far the easiest and least complicated approach to the Scriptures. Every word in the Bible's sixty-six books is important. Everything asserted as divine truth is true. Every story that presents as factual is factual. As for there being myths, there aren't any. And because the Bible is God's inspired word, it is without error. It can therefore be trusted "as the final authority in matters of doctrine, practice, and lifestyle."

An advantage of this approach is that all or many of the most hopeful and historically appealing aspects of the Christian epic are retained: the initial high valuation of humankind, an originally good creation marred by sin, God's gracious intervention to redeem, the prospect of divine justice at the end of human history and beyond, life eternal for those who put their faith in Jesus. All of this is retained, which is a big part of this approach's continuing appeal.

Millar College of the Bible exists towards one end of the theological spectrum, but there are any number of similar iterations among contemporary

---

6. See https://www.millarcollege.ca/about/doctrinal-statement.

fundamentalists, Evangelicals, and conservatives. Millar College has many siblings, or perhaps cousins.[7] Among those close relatives are Christians who insist on an inerrant Bible and on a plain-sense or literalistic reading of the Scriptures. I would guess that this is the majority approach among Evangelicals, and certainly among fundamentalists, worldwide.

As said, this approach has certain advantages, but there are also significant downsides. Parts of the Bible that many would judge ought to be taken as metaphor, myth, or apocalyptic exaggeration are accepted as literal truth. This then inevitably runs counter to the increasingly well-evidenced contrary conclusions of scientific, historical, and biblical scholarship. Inerrant literalism also generates significant moral and ethical problems. I've recently reread the book of Revelation, which includes the wonderfully hopeful passage from Rev 22 quoted above. What isn't quoted so often is what comes before it, which is chapter after chapter, wave after wave, of divine retribution against those who don't believe in God or in Jesus. Peace is removed; famine, pestilence, and wild animals are unleashed; the sun is darkened; stars fall from the sky; human habitats are destroyed; oceans and waterways are turned to blood; earthquakes obliterate; huge hailstones crush; locusts torture; and large swathes of unrepentant human beings are slaughtered. It is a grim picture of an angry God and, if taken literally, a frightening description of what is in store for the world. And, as if this wasn't disturbing enough, we are also informed that those who succumb to satanic deception will be made to "drink the wine of God's wrath." They will be "tormented with fire and sulphur," with the "smoke of their torment" rising "forever and ever . . . with no rest day or night" (Rev 14:10–11), a description consistent with the abhorrent (to me, certainly) notion of "eternal conscious torment."

I can understand Luther (and others) arguing against including the book of Revelation in the biblical canon. But even if it were to be removed, there are problems, big problems, with biblical literalism. One of those problems is that those who take this approach find themselves having to defend the indefensible, largely because they have mistaken the genre of what they are commending.[8] They have also needlessly put themselves out of step with the academy, which is then viewed with suspicion. The very best of scholarship

---

7. After coming across Millar College, I looked around here in Australia for something similar. Though not identical, the following colleges have similar statements of belief: the Bible College of South Australia, the Eastern College of Australia, Charis Bible College, and the Australian Christian College, International.

8. In the case of the book of Revelation, there are enough indications within and beyond it that its multiple violent descriptions are not to be taken literally but understood and appropriated as apocalyptic and/or as a form of myth as I now understand that term.

(Christian or otherwise) is ignored or subverted if it runs counter to a plain-sense reading of the Bible.

Combine this with a very negative (Revelation-like) evaluation of corrupt humankind, along with fearfulness about end-times turmoil and the ubiquitous sensed presence of deceiving spirits, and people can quickly become prey to conspiracy theories and authoritarian demagogues and snake-oil salesmen like Donald Trump.[9] The consequent othering, blaming, and victimizing of those considered responsible for society's ills, including people from other lands and faiths and LGBTIQ+ peoples, is simply awful, and one further reason why people are rejecting and/or leaving Christian faith.

The Bible as Misleading

A second and completely contrasting approach to the multiple challenges to traditional Christian belief is to conclude that the Bible is a poor guide on almost all matters and is not to be trusted. While the Bible may provide a historically interesting window into ancient ways of thinking, beyond that we don't need to take much notice. Its account of beginnings is interesting but nonfactual. Its account of endings is far fetched and scary. Its anthropology is limited, especially on matters of sexuality and gender. Taken literally, it simply misleads all who accept the carrot of forgiveness and eternal life without realizing the terrible prospect facing those who don't. The largely mythical Christian epic is without doubt mythical, according to this second approach, and it has well and truly had its day.

What is needed is for us to grow up as a race and to stop trying to wish reality away. We are alone in the universe. There is no God to rescue us. If there is to be any rescuing, we will need to do it ourselves. There is no life after death. There will be no just and happy (for some) climax to human history. What is required is the sort of reality check that Macbeth supplies in the wake of his wife's suicide:

---

9. It may seem harsh to describe Donald Trump in these terms, but I simply cannot find a better way to account for conservative Christian support for someone who is so manifestly dishonest, narcissistic, revengeful, predatory, xenophobic, misogynistic, and criminal. It is for me profoundly disappointing that disciples of Jesus could think it acceptable (even on balance) to support someone who orchestrated a deadly attack on the US capitol, who openly admires dictators, who denies the increasingly dangerous impact of climate change, and who disparages immigrants and the disabled. That as many as 82 percent of white evangelical Christians voted for Trump in 2024 (NBC News, "Exit Polls") does, however, suggest the widespread and lingering presence of racism, sexism, homophobia, transphobia, and anti-intellectualism within American Evangelicalism.

> Tomorrow, and tomorrow, and tomorrow
> Creeps in this petty pace from day to day
> To the last syllable of recorded time.
> And all our yesterdays have lighted fools
> The way to dusty death. Out, out, brief candle.
> Life's but a walking shadow, a poor player
> That struts and frets his hour upon the stage,
> And then is heard no more. It is a tale
> Told by an idiot, full of sound and fury,
> Signifying nothing.[10]

The Bible as Continuingly Inspirational

There is a third possible way to deal with the various challenges to traditional Christian beliefs, and that is to argue that even if the biblical epic is predominantly mythical, it still retains its ability to inspire and to guide. The popular historian Tom Holland, in his book *Dominion: How the Christian Revolution Remade the World*, lays out the nature and reach of this abiding impact, particularly in the Western world. Critical to the early success of Christianity was its unprecedentedly high view of humankind, along with its countercultural celebration of suffering and servanthood. As Holland points out, this not only upended Greco-Roman culture, it continues to permeate our Western understanding of life and value. Holland is aware of the limitations and evolutionary nature of the Christian story.[11] For example, he describes Paul as a "product of his schooling" in his understandings of sexuality and gender.[12] He happily employs the notion of myth with respect to Moses[13] and to the Christian gospel, but Holland also leaves his readers in no doubt about the transformative power of myth, as in the final paragraph of his book:

> For two thousand years, Christians have themselves become agents of terror. They have put the weak in their shadow; they have brought suffering, and persecution, and slavery in their wake. Yet the standards by which they stand condemned for this are themselves Christian; not, even if churches across the West continue to empty, does it seem likely that these standards

---

10. Shakespeare, *Tragedy of Macbeth*, act 5, scene 5, 103.

11. For example, he draws attention to remnants of polytheism within the Jewish Scriptures and in the New Testament to expectations of Jesus's imminent return (Holland, *Dominion*, 62–63).

12. Holland, *Dominion*, 94.

13. Holland, *Dominion*, 73.

will quickly change. "God chose the weak things of the world to shame the strong." This is the myth that we in the West still persist in clinging to. Christendom, in that sense, remains Christendom still.[14]

There is no doubt that Christianity, along with Judaism, has had a profound impact for good, and that this impact can and will continue through those who embrace the Christian story. It is what I choose to do.

This third approach is one that is willing to acknowledge the role, the limitations, and the power of myth. Of the three approaches, it is the most complicated and will involve the most work. It isn't easy, as one reads the Scriptures and endeavors to take best account of our growing knowledge of the Bible's history and cultural background, to decide whether what we are reading is myth, legend, fable, fact, or a mixture thereof. Genre studies are helping, but it is not always easy to tell which exact genre we are dealing with.[15] More complicated still is the task of deciding the contemporary relevance of what we are reading. My wife, Judy, and I attempt this in our mostly daily morning devotions. Complicated it might be, but it is possible. We've found it so. We've also been happy to conclude that we simply don't know what to make of various texts. We are often reminded of our lack of understanding and knowledge.

Over the years and increasingly so, I have been content with not knowing. I align more and more with Christian and other religious traditions that emphasize the incomprehensible otherness or mystery of God. There is within Christianity and the other monotheistic religions, Judaism and Islam, and also within Hinduism and Buddhism, an apophatic tradition, or *via negativa*,[16] which holds that all positive statements about God will be false and that the best we can do is to say what God is not. Even that can get us into trouble. God, from our point of view, is essentially mystery.

This is not to say, however, that the reality of this mystery is inaccessible. Iain McGilchrist, in his magisterial two-volume *The Matter with Things*, has a chapter on "The Sense of the Sacred." In it, he suggests that it is not knowing that precipitates the quest to find answers to life's big questions.

---

14. Holland, *Dominion*, 542.

15. Andrew Judd, a graduate of Moore College, currently teaching at Ridley College in Melbourne, has recently published a helpful book on genre, entitled *Modern Genre Theory*. In it, Judd notes that genres evolve, have fuzzy edges, and often coexist with other forms. I've noted some evolution in the concept of myth, which, somewhat surprisingly, Judd avoids any discussion of.

16. Also described as "negative theology."

> For me, and for many philosophers historically, the deepest question in all philosophy—both the most important, and the hardest to answer—is why there should be something rather than nothing.
>
> And close on its heels comes the question why that "something" turns out to be complex and orderly, beautiful and creative, capable of life, feeling and consciousness, rather than merely chaotic, sterile, and dead. It is not a matter of opinion, but a fact, if ever there was one, that, somehow or other, this "something" has within it the capacity to give rise to Bach's *St Matthew Passion*. Any attempt at understanding the cosmos needs to take that fact into account.[17]

I am well aware that arguments for and against the existence of God are fairly evenly balanced, and therefore by no means conclusive either way. However, what has consistently tipped the balance for me has been these facts: music, art, consciousness, intelligence, morality, and awe. I simply cannot get past the wonder of life itself, even with the acknowledged facts of suffering, evil, injustice, and death.

McGilchrist, though not himself a Christian, comes to similar conclusions:

> Neither of my parents, and none of my grandparents, was at all religious—rather the opposite. They did not take me to church, and, nearing the end of my life, I still don't attend one. Am I a religious person? Not in a conventional sense, then. Yet in a sense that is as important to me as it is hard to express, I surely am. I didn't get there by believing propositions, but from experience . . . No visions or voices. It has all been entirely quintessentially natural—starting indeed from Nature herself.
>
> It struck me from an early age that there was more going on than my senses were able to encompass: that nothing "super" needed to be added to the "natural" for it to invoke wonder. I suspect that if you rigorously disattend to that intuition, it will sooner or later go away. However, I did not, and it didn't. It seemed to me that there was something "beyond" in some sense that drew me forward; something I had intuitive acquaintance with but could say almost nothing about, except that it seemed both real and beautiful.
>
> Intellectual debate in the culture in which I grew up seemed dominated by what all my life has seemed to me a terribly impoverished philosophy, that of reductive materialism—just one model among many, an outlier in the history of humanity; and

---

17. McGilchrist, *Matter with Things*, 2:1193.

> this formed the sharpest possible contrast with the world I encountered, not just in Nature, but in music, poetry and painting; and friendship and, later, in love.
>
> From every side I saw how clearly the edifice of Western civilization—its literature, its poetry, its architecture, its painting, its music—at all times and in all ages was to a large extent an expression of a spiritual impulse. And one we have largely lost.
>
> What underlies and unites all these aspects of experience for me is the conviction of a direct and reciprocal engagement with whatever-it-is that is the ground of Being; and which we call God.[18]

When I first read this passage, it struck me just how similar has been my own experience, though coming from an entirely different background of strong Christian belief. Perhaps Alvin Plantinga is right that belief in God typically arrives in a nonpropositional or experiential way. Whether that is so or not, experiences and reflections like McGilchrist's remain influential in my continuing belief in God. Moreover, it is thoughts like these and the intuition that is activated by them that nicely explain the origins of all religions and of philosophy as well.[19]

From what we know and can piece together, religious ideas began to emerge among early humans as far back as two hundred thousand years or more, with archaeological finds identifying the early emergence of symbolic behavior and complex imagery, which is a prerequisite for the development of religious ideas, including belief in an afterlife, ancestor worship, and the worship of gods. It seems that various forms of animism were common among our hunter-gatherer ancestors, with polytheism and monotheism emerging later.

We understand that modern humans evolved initially in Africa, before a migration out of Africa around sixty-five thousand years ago. Humans arrived in Australia not long afterwards, bringing with them religious beliefs that developed over time. Today there are nine hundred distinct Aboriginal tribal groups across Australia, and so it is impossible to generalize about their mythical and religious beliefs, except to say that they vary, with some common themes. All or most have origin myths. The Council for Aboriginal Reconciliation's booklet *Understanding Country* generalizes to this extent:

---

18. McGilchrist, *Matter with Things*, 2:1215–17.

19. I've always thought that intuition involves forms of inference and can be considered an often unconscious, though still rational, form of inference to the best explanation. Theism remains the best explanation of my own life and experiences, and of reality as a whole.

> [Aboriginal myths] generally describe the journeys of ancestral beings, often giant animals or people, over what began as a featureless domain. Mountains, rivers, waterholes, animal and plant species, and other natural and cultural resources came into being as a result of events which took place during these Dreamtime journeys.
>
> The routes taken by the Creator Beings in their Dreamtime journeys across land and sea . . . link many sacred sites together in a web of Dreamtime tracks crisscrossing the country. Dreaming tracks can run for hundreds, even thousands of kilometres, from desert to the coast [and] may be shared by peoples in countries through which the tracks pass.[20]

Common within many tribal groups was a belief in spirit beings understood in godlike terms.[21] In a cave in the Hunter Valley in New South Wales, not far from where we live, is a painting of one such being, called Baiame, known among the local Wanarua people as the creator of all things. With long, outstretched arms, Baiame embraces creation. With large, bulbous eyes, he appears to be all seeing, similar to how the Christian God is described. The cave painting is estimated to be about three thousand years old. Aboriginal spirituality reaches back much further.

In the aftermath of the agricultural revolution, and in other locations around the world, various religious ideas and ideologies emerged. In their distinctive and imaginative ways, the big questions of life were wrestled with and addressed. Hinduism, for example, often touted as the world's oldest religion, emerged by degrees and over time on the Indian subcontinent in the second millennium BCE. In its earlier incarnations, associated with its sacred writings, the Vedas, this multifaceted religious movement was polytheistic, with a thousand or more gods or devas, all very humanlike, as were the Greek and Roman gods. In its efforts to understand the universe, a complementary idea emerged that in the background to all of reality, as its ultimate explanation, was a universal, unifying, and ultimately mysterious principle named Brahman.

At about the same time and in different parts of the world, other still-influential religious belief systems were being created, always in response

---

20. Smyth, *Understanding Country*, 3.

21. Graham Poulson, in his helpful essay, "Towards an Aboriginal Theology," elaborates: "Hidden in the sky, in the sea and under the surface of the earth are dreamtime heroes who are part human, in terms of their emotions and intellect, part animal bird or reptile, in terms of their physical shape, and part super-human in terms of their power and their creative ability" (313).

to experienced reality and always designed to create life pathways. One of those religions was Zoroastrianism, which emerged in Persia under the influence of Zarathustra (c. 1500–1000 BCE). Zarathustra trod a similar path to the Hindus in moving beyond polytheism to posit the existence of the high god, Ahura Mazdā, who was engaged in a primal and eternal struggle with the evil, destructive spirit, Angra Mainyu. Zarathustra also introduced ideas of heaven and hell, which were possibly borrowed by Judaism.

At the other side of the world, and again at about the same time, though possibly unknown to Judaism, lived the Chinese philosopher Confucius (551–479 BCE). Confucius considered himself a transmitter of cultural values inherited from the Xia Dynasty (c. 2070–1600 BCE). There is some debate about whether Confucianism is a religion or a philosophy, which is interesting given our exploration of their differences and agreements. Nevertheless, as with the others we have discussed thus far, Confucius was certainly attempting to discover a wise way of living in a world he also sought to understand. Confucius believed in the abiding influence and importance of ancestors. He also believed that living well and living ethically affected the way the world was, creating or disrupting cosmic harmony depending on how well one lived.

At about the same time, and certainly influential within Judaism and Christianity, was Greek philosophy. Without going into detail, the Greek philosophers were similarly animated by a desire to make sense of their experience of the universe. They also tended to move beyond polytheism towards more comprehensive and unifying understandings of the cosmos. Heraclitus (who was active around 500 BCE) suggested the logos as the underlying principle of rationality, which he tentatively identified with Zeus, the supreme god. Plato posited the existence of eternal forms or archetypes that God used to fashion the universe. He wasn't committed to monotheism, but was looking to discover principles of order by which the universe could be understood. Aristotle's god was the impassive originator of order, change, and purpose. As the highest of all beings, towards which all things aspire, God engages in eternal contemplation of the most worthy object, God's self, and is unaware and uncaring of the universe beyond God's self.

When Judaism emerged as a world religion, and its sacred texts approached their final form, a large volume of religious and philosophical water had already gone under the bridge, as we have just seen. In ways not often acknowledged, Judaism is undoubtedly influenced by those running waters, which they drew upon and contributed to.[22] Judaism's own journey is similar to the religious and philosophical journeys mentioned above.

As noted previously, Jewish monotheism emerged out of polytheism, with evidence of that journey dotted throughout the Hebrew Scriptures. James Alison, in his excellent book *God, Not One of the Gods*, details this perhaps surprising fact:

> I hope it will not come as a shock to you to hear that the Hebrew Scriptures are not, strictly speaking, monotheistic. An absolutely clear, unadulterated monotheism finally emerges in the Scriptures as late as the texts of Second Isaiah, from the postexilic period. In earlier texts we have plenty of reminiscences of a polytheistic past in which the basic Canaanite word for God (El) has number (Elohim is a plural word), there are references to God among the gods (who later became angels); and there are hints of varied gender: there are traces of a mother goddess figure as recently as just prior to the Babylonian exile.
>
> What the texts do bear witness to is a movement from polytheism to what is called "monolatry" or "henotheism," meaning "Plenty of gods exist, but you are to worship only one of them." It is worth noticing that the first of the Ten Commandments, "Thou shalt have no other gods before me," is a monolatrous, or henotheistic commandment, not a monotheistic one. It takes for granted the existence of other gods.[23]

Alison here mentions references to God among the gods who are later described as angels. In Deuteronomy, written or finalized just prior to the exile, is this intriguing verse:

> When the Most High [Elyon] apportioned the nations,
>   when he divided humankind [the sons of man],
> he fixed the boundaries of the peoples
>   according to the number of the gods [the sons of God];
> 9 the LORD's [Yahweh's] own portion was his people,
>   Jacob his allotted share. (Deut 32:8–9)

In Canaanite mythology, Elyon was the supreme god, like Zeus in the Greek pantheon. In these verses, Elyon apportions various places of oversight to

---

22. For example, the Israelite scribes who composed the second creation account in Gen 2–3 are likely to have drawn upon earlier Sumerian, Babylonian, and Ugaritic myths such as the Ugaritic myth of Athtar, a version of which appears to be alluded to in Ezek 28:11–19.

23. Alison, *God*, 143.

his sons, the lesser gods. Yahweh, who appears to have been initially adopted by the northern tribes as their tribal god, was here allocated Jacob (or Israel).[24] Psalm 82 is a similar and similarly intriguing passage. It too begins with Elyon (v. 1) who, in the following verses, removes immortality (v. 6) and therefore divinity from various gods of the heavenly assembly because they have been unjust and have failed to care for the orphan, the lowly, and the destitute (vv. 2–4).

Here again are examples of an ever-evolving understanding; a constant fine-tweaking of earlier answers to the big questions of life. We can add this to many other examples of such tweaking, including belief in life after death, notions of heaven and hell, the shedding of purificatory rituals and practices, and the gradual dismantling of patriarchy.

You might ask or be thinking, "What about the Bible being inspired, being God's inspired word?" If by that one means that almost everything in the Bible, especially those things depicted as God's speech, is true, reliable, and God's very word, then there are obvious problems. Some of the things God is reported as saying are not terribly godlike, such as instructing "his people" to wipe out other nations and tribes; or dictating laws that now appear archaic, discriminatory, and/or immoral;[25] or allowing sacrifice in every place where God's name is remembered, while almost simultaneously[26] restricting sacrifice to just one chosen place;[27] or revealing future events that don't eventuate;[28] or implying that there are gods other than Yahweh before insisting there is just one God; or revealing that there isn't much of a life after death before revealing there is.

If the Bible is divinely inspired, such inspiration is better thought of as the gentle encouragement of a dynamic, warts-and-all process of ongoing

---

24. The authors of the LXX, doubtless uncomfortable with this verse, translated the "sons of God" as "angels of God."

25. The laws of Deut 22 on proving the virginity of women accused of adultery are particularly troubling, but there are many such passages embedded in Old Testament law. One often hears that these are "more enlightened" than the laws of surrounding nations, which simply confirms their absolute inadequacy. It also suggests what is being argued in this book, which is that biblical communities were on a journey, which we need to continue.

26. According to the Bible's chronology.

27. Exod 20:24 and Deut 12:13–14, with this latter instruction likely to (anachronistically) have Jerusalem in mind.

28. For example, the prophet Ezekiel being specifically told by God that Tyre would be permanently destroyed (Ezek 26–28) before the prophecy is amended somewhat embarrassingly in 19:17–21. Similarly Ezekiel is told by God that Egypt will be plundered by Nebuchadnezzar and left as a wasteland for forty years (Ezek 29:11–12), with its peoples scattered, none of which occurred (Ezek 29–32).

wrestling with the mysteries, the wonders, and the often painful and perplexing experiences of life. That way of seeing things makes sense to me. Seeing things that way means that God can be seen as active within all religions and within philosophy as well. This divine activity didn't just suddenly begin two to three thousand years ago. The spirit of God, which in Gen 1 is depicted as moving over the dark waters of creation, has always been at work.

I've entitled this chapter "A Hopeful Faith." This way of understanding the Bible's inspiration gives me hope, or it keeps me hopeful that God is involved in processes of discovery and learning, that there is hope for real progress over time, that my own life and unfolding journey have meaning and purpose. This insight also helps us to honor the lives and spirituality of others, including that of our nation's first peoples.

Panentheism

What has helped me in my lifelong process of thinking and rethinking has been the deepening conviction that if there is a God (which I believe there is), God is best understood as both separate from and inherent within the created order. God and nature are not identical (pantheism), nor are they essentially separate (classical theism).[29] God is both other and within (panentheism).[30] This way of thinking, which many would consider orthodox or original Christianity,[31] increasingly makes sense to me. It has made a large difference to my life and spirituality.

On our post-retirement trip in early 2023, Judy and I had the privilege of visiting the island of Iona on the southwest coast of Scotland. It was to Iona that St. Columba and twelve companions arrived in 563 CE to establish a monastery from which to evangelize Scotland. Iona has been described as the birthplace of Christianity in Scotland. In recent years, it has become a

---

29. Classical theism is noted for its emphasis on the transcendence or otherness of God, though it also acknowledged God's imminence within an essentially different and dependent created order.

30. Modern process theologians, including Charles Hartshorne (1897–2000) and John B. Cobb (b. 1925), suggest that God and the universe are in a relationship of mutual interdependence, with both in a process of growing and becoming; God influencing the created order (drawing it to God's self) and being influenced by it.

31. Catholic mystic Richard Rohr, who identifies as a panentheist, argues that panentheism is the original view of Christianity, exemplified in teaching about Christ being "all and in all" (Col 3:11). One could add the Johannine emphasis on mutual indwelling. Eastern Orthodoxy, Celtic spirituality, and process theology are also often identified as panentheistic.

center of worship for the still-active (and worldwide) Iona community. We enjoyed their hospitality and shared in worship during our two days there. It was indeed special for us both. For me, it was also a watershed. This is what I wrote in my diary a few days after being there:

> I came to the tiny island of Iona not knowing quite what to expect. I hoped but didn't expect that I'd have an experience I could describe as "spiritual." I wasn't sure or very clear about what is meant by "spiritual" or a "spiritual experience."
>
> While on the island, someone shared with Judy, Chris (a good friend who accompanied us) and me her experience of finding Iona the most spiritual place she had encountered. She'd been to many a spiritual retreat over the years, and in many locations, but Iona topped them all. It was where she felt the most spiritually inspired and rejuvenated.
>
> I too found the two days we spent on Iona inspiring and rejuvenating. This was partly because of the island's natural beauty. The island was not more beautiful than so much of what we'd experienced elsewhere on our wonderful, post-retirement trip—in Hong Kong, Greece, France, England and Ireland. We were nevertheless again filled with wonder and delight as we observed the island's natural beauty. This, I suspected, was a form or aspect of spirituality—marveling at God's creative genius.
>
> But there was more. The visit to Iona was a turning point, a long-time-coming watershed in my understanding of spirituality, and, in particular, my own spirituality. On a late afternoon walk with Judy, on our final day at Iona, I lamented my poor understanding of spirituality. I surmised that my spirituality was something like the spirit of enquiry or of inquisitiveness which I have had my whole lifelong, inherited somewhat from my father, but made my own from adolescence to eventual grave.
>
> I wondered out loud whether this might this be an authentic spirituality. A bit later that day I asked our travel companion, Chris, what she thought, and she reminded me that as finite creatures made in the image of God our inbuilt creativity impels us, and ever draws us towards knowledgeable mastery of our lived environments. Inquisitiveness is a function of our finiteness and inevitable limitation. As Augustine suggested, the quest for knowledge is ultimately a quest for God.

That was rather comforting and inspiring. While at Iona and subsequently, we've come to better appreciate the sort of Celtic spirituality that Iona is famous for. We'd earlier discovered one of its skillful apologists and practitioners in the Irish philosopher, poet, and theologian John O'Donohue. At the top of my pre-Christmas wish list in 2023 was a request for one of his books. I was given two! Judy and I worked our way through them in our morning quiet times, along with a reading from the Scriptures and prayer.

Celtic spirituality is panentheistic. We can experience God both in nature and within our Scriptures, as we can within each other. The mystery of God is always mystery, not something we can prove or domesticate, but it is something we can live in awe of and worship.

There are passages of Scripture that are suggestive of panentheism. These include Ps 139:7-8, "Where can I go from your spirit? . . . If I ascend to heaven you are there; if I make my bed in Sheol, you are there," and Acts 17:28: a quote, possibly from the Greek poet Epimenides, "In him we live and move and have our being." The idea that God is everywhere present (omnipresent) is hardly new. Nor is it revolutionary to see the created order as in some sense existing within God and animated by God.

It is not an idea unique to Christianity, yet it has been revolutionary for me. If God is intimately involved in all creation, including in the lives of all humans, God is not a parachuting-in God, a God up there who comes down here, but a God who works through and in normal human and natural processes. God can, of course, intervene in unusual ways, but that doesn't appear to be God's normal way of acting. In terms of the world's suffering and evil, God isn't entirely let off the hook, but it could just be, as atheists must say, that we are the ones who need to address, overcome, and move beyond violence, greed, and injustice. The impulses towards this are both human and divine. It could just be that Martin Luther King Jr.'s oft-quoted conviction that the arc of the moral universe, though long, bends towards justice, is true to reality. I sure hope so.

What this also means is that God's active presence in the world has been a constant throughout all of time. God can be understood as the skillful architect of the whole universe (of all universes, if there are more), as overseeing (or brooding over) the evolutionary process, and gently coaxing the inquisitiveness (my own included) that gave birth to both religion and philosophy. God was always near to early humans, indigenous populations, philosophers, theologians, mystics, and artists. We mustn't think that God was mostly inactive until Judaism became monotheistic or until Jesus arrived. As the Bible makes clear enough, the logos of God and/or the spirit of God have been around always.[32]

---

32. For example, John's Gospel: "In the beginning was the Word, and the Word was with God, and the Word was God. He was in the beginning with God. All things came

This panentheistic view of God has implications for our understanding of Jesus. It means that Jesus wasn't a last-minute thought of God's, God finally rousing God's self to do something. It also fits comfortably with the idea of the incarnation or divine indwelling. However exactly one understands Jesus, God can be understood as being "in" Jesus, as Jesus was "in" God.

One further thought: panentheism therefore also enables me to see God in others, to varying degrees of similitude. God is not simply "up there" looking down. God is everywhere present, and perhaps most obviously seen in our fellow humans, and most clearly in Jesus.

To draw this discussion to a close, panentheism, and its implication for my understanding of God and Jesus, gives me hope. It is a humbled hope. Much of what I once considered sure or certain simply isn't. I don't even know whether these insights are true, but I am living as if they are. In terms of some of those earlier hopes and expectations, I am not sure if there is a life after death. I hope there is—in the ordinary sense of that word. I hope because I don't know. I'd love to have the certitude of my mum as she faced death. I don't believe there was the slightest doubt in her mind that she was about to be reunited with Dad. I'd like to have that certitude as well. I'd love to see Mum again. I'd like to tell Dad he was right about Calvinism. He didn't like it much, nor do I. I'd like to thank him and Mum for trusting me with my decision to study philosophy and keep asking questions. My parents were my inspiration.

It could be that there isn't life after death. Hans Kung (1928–2021), the ever-provocative and exploratory Roman Catholic theologian, was a lifelong believer in life after death, but in his early eighties he asked himself, "But what if I am wrong, and I do not enter God's eternal life, but nothingness?" He too countenanced that possibility, but he also concluded that not knowing would make no difference to how he lived his life and that "I will have lived a better life than I would have done without this hope."[33]

I resonate. I am similarly hopeful. It is not hard to see the appeal of resurrection hope. To believe in an even better life than this one is certainly to be preferred to the shadowy deathlike existence envisaged by the earlier biblical authors. The idea that there will be both justice and mercy post-death is attractive for theists such as myself. I can certainly understand the strength

---

into being through him, and without him not one thing came into being" (John 1:1–3). And Gen 1:1–2: "When God began to create the heavens and the earth, the earth was complete chaos, and darkness covered the face of the deep, while a wind (or spirit) from God swept over the face of the waters."

33. Kung, *What I Believe*, 181.

and resilience of belief in an afterlife, especially for those facing death. I won't be at all surprised if when I breathe my last breath, I too will awaken to that life. The God who can create this amazing universe is more than capable of extending human consciousness beyond the grave.

The fact that there is within us all an insatiable thirst for transcendence suggests that there just might be more story to tell when our life on earth is over. Maybe the meaning of this is restricted to life in this world. If so, there is certainly much to do. Our lives can still have meaning and purpose. Either way, I am thankful to God for the impulse to keep searching, to remain in the quest to better understand the world and our place in it.

Questions for Reflection and Discussion

1. What do you think is the best possible understanding of biblical inspiration?
2. What are your thoughts about panentheism as a way of understanding God's relationship to yourself and to the world?
3. How would you describe your own spirituality?
4. What are your hopes or expectations with respect to life after death?

Poetry and Religion
by Les Murray

Religions are poems. They concert
our daylight and dreaming mind, our
emotions, instinct, breath and native gesture

into the only whole thinking: poetry.
Nothing's said till it's dreamed out in words
and nothing's true that figures in words only.

A poem, compared with an arrayed religion,
may be like a soldier's one short marriage night
to die and live by. But that is a small religion.

Full religion is the large poem in loving repetition;
like any poem, it must be inexhaustible and complete
with turns where we ask Now why did the poet do that?

You can't pray a lie, said Huckleberry Finn;
you can't poe one either. It is the same mirror:
mobile, glancing, we call it poetry,

fixed centrally, we call it a religion,
and God is the poetry caught in any religion,
caught, not imprisoned. Caught as in a mirror

that he attracted, being in the world as poetry
is in the poem, a law against its closure.
There'll always be religion around while there is poetry

or a lack of it. Both are given, and intermittent,
as the action of those birds—crested pigeon, rosella parrot—
who fly with wings shut, then beating, and again shut.

Chapter 10

Being a Dual Citizen of Athens and Jerusalem

WE HAVE AT LAST arrived at this book's final chapter. I can now answer the question posed at its beginning, "What does Athens have to do with Jerusalem?" Or, more exactly, "Can Athens and Jerusalem be friends?" They can, and certainly have been. Over the years, theologians, including the biblical authors, have extensively drawn upon philosophical ideas, categories, and methodologies. The contention of this book is that Jerusalem needs Athens. It benefits from these borrowings, but it also needs the inquisitive and exploratory impulse of philosophy and science. Without these, Jerusalem will crumble and become an irrelevant ruin. With them, it can revive and thrive.

For me, a key reason for thinking that Jerusalem and Athens can be friends is that they share an originating impulse. They each came to birth as efforts to understand the universe and our place within it. At the very core of both was the still-unfinished quest to make best sense of experienced reality. We might not be persuaded by many of the evolving understandings of philosophy or theology, but the quest to understand is one we are all invited into, ultimately by God in my understanding. Steph Lentz, in her autobiographical account of her movement out of Sydney Anglican fundamentalism, comes to a similar conclusion. In her words,

> [It is my belief] that the Bible—indeed all of Christian tradition—is a very human attempt to wrap arms around the concept of the divine and the human experiences of the spiritual. Instead of aligning myself with a set of truth claims and concomitant traditions (that is, religion), I find myself both motivated and calmed by the idea that all of life is a wrestling with the nature of

relations between our human existence and what many intuit to be a divine source behind all of this. All the words we utter, all the art we make, all the love we create is just as valid an expression of religious exploration as any traditional religion might be.[1]

Steph is certainly right about the humanity of the Christian Scriptures. As has already been observed, the Bible shares with the philosophical and scientific enterprises that very same humanity. Biblical theology, philosophy, and science are progressively and endlessly correctable. None is static nor finalized. Jerusalem and Athens in this respect are similar. One could almost say that Jerusalem *is* Athens. The Bible taken as a whole is at least akin to philosophy, philosophy in story form. It seeks to understand the world and its authors' experiences in the world from a theistic point of view, more specifically, from an evolving Jewish and then Christian point of view. Christian faith and philosophy are thus closer to each other than a surface reading of the Bible might suggest.

On that surface reading, God is a frequent speaker, and the biblical authors, especially the prophets and apostles, often claim to be speaking for God. Moreover, the Old Testament laws in their totality are depicted as coming directly or indirectly from God. This would appear to torpedo any notion that theology and inquisitive philosophy are similar. But it really isn't that simple.

If we were to gather up all the things God is depicted as saying or revealing, mandating or predicting in the Bible, we would very quickly come to grief. What God says at one point is contradicted at other points. God appears to have changes of mind or takes issue with earlier utterances, or predicts events that do not occur. There appears to be progress in God's thinking, which doesn't sit comfortably with most people's understanding of God.[2]

For me, the most credible approach is one that sees the biblical authors as operating a little like the ancient Greek and Roman poets such as Homer, who liberally included the gods in his poetry and storytelling.[3] The biblical authors were, likewise, bringing God into their stories as an active and vocal

1. Lentz, *In/Out*, 286–87.
2. There are notable exceptions, including process theology.
3. The key involvement of God in the biblical storyline is similar to the involvement of the gods in Greco-Roman storytelling. It is also one reason for me describing the biblical epic as mythical. According to the *Oxford Reference Dictionary*, a myth is a traditional story, especially one concerning the early history of a people or explaining some natural or social phenomenon, and typically involving supernatural beings or events.

participant and as lawgiver, thereby illustrating and authorizing their evolving beliefs. And, inasmuch as their theology and understandings developed over time, they were being philosophical. They too were questing towards an improved grasp of reality. Their life and faith experiences, which were often painful and puzzling but also joyful and hopeful, were fed into their theology and storytelling, creating a dynamic, imaginative, and inspired storyline, a blockbuster freighted with meaning that we can still draw upon millennia later.

One further and crucial potential similarity between Athens and Jerusalem is epistemic humility. As Christians, if we are willing to be honest, we can rightly conclude as Socrates did that we know very little. We don't know for certain whether the basic tenets of the Christian faith, as summarized and brought together in our historic creeds, are true. We may believe them. We may have conviction, even strong conviction, that the things many of us affirm or are taught in church are true. It may be that they are true, in the sense of being an accurate representation of reality. We may also think that they make best sense of other things we believe or know in a belief system that coheres well. But we cannot be sure, and our beliefs will have varying degrees of warrant.

If I am honest, as I seek to be, a great number of my beliefs as a continuing Christian are uncertain. If I choose to also be a philosopher, someone willing to scrutinize beliefs, I must acknowledge this uncertainty. Dale Allison, in his lengthy investigation of the claimed resurrection of Jesus, comments at the outset of his book that he too is uncertain about much, and especially so from the vantage point of the historical-critical method that he employs in his meticulous work as a historian. He describes himself as multifaceted and complex, "not consistently 'liberal' or 'conservative,' but sometimes the one, sometimes the other, and just as often neither."[4] But one of the places he does occupy is the place of humility when it comes to knowledge.

> [Another of my inner voices] belongs to the I Don't Know Club. He [that is this voice of mine] is relentlessly skeptical about almost everything, including know-it-all skepticism. [Insisting] on epistemic humility, he loathes all species of dogmatism. He refuses to cash anyone's ideological check. He scoffs at the notion that all problems are conveniently mind-sized. He knows that people are always more often in error than they are in doubt, and that he cannot be an exception. He idolizes the wise Socrates, who knew that he knew nothing. . . . The cloud of unknowing hangs low over the whole world. *Neti Neti*. Our

---

4. Allison, *Resurrection of Jesus*, 4.

prefrontal cortex may be oversized, and our scientific triumphs may be breathtaking, yet we remain mammals, which means that we own mammalian brains, and all such brains are severely bounded. This voice regularly recites . . . the words of William James: "We may be in the universe as dogs and cats are in our libraries, seeing the books and hearing the conversation, but having no inkling of the meaning of it all."[5]

Allison is acutely aware, as I have become over the years, of the severe limitations of human thinking. Not that we don't try. Not that we don't follow the example of Socrates in seeking to be knowledgeable about as much as we can, but that journey must always be walked with humility. We are not God.

On What Might Happen if Philosophy Is Muzzled

If an ongoing process of questioning and consequential adjustment is not allowed, Christianity will descend into sectarianism and cult. Healthy self-questioning, which is the way of philosophy, keeps movements honest and accountable.

Dale Allison explains his understanding of the complementary roles of theology and the historical-critical method:

> I adopt a historical-critical approach not because I have pledged my troth to pure immanence or care nothing for theology. I am, quite the contrary, vitally interested in theological matters, and I want to do much more than stumble around in the darkness of history. My historical orientation also does not stem from a conviction that theology and history are non-overlapping magisteria; that theology is theology while history is history and never the twain shall meet. There is no safe space where theology can go about its business while ignoring historical criticism.[6]

One can expand Allison's final sentence to include philosophy and science generally, all the many disciplines that have been generated by the questing spirit of philosophy. Efforts to find "safe space" away from the healthy accountability of unfettered questioning will result only in fearful and authoritarian forms of the faith. The dead-set giveaway for churches that have become sectarian or cultish is that searching questions are discouraged and only some questions (and answers) are allowed. It is a giveaway because

---

5. Allison, *Resurrection of Jesus*, 4–5.
6. Allison, *Resurrection of Jesus*, 6.

it means only one thing really. The gatekeepers know that there aren't any good answers or that there are good answers, but those good answers will demolish or undercut the truth claims of their church.

A sign put up outside a church (literally or metaphorically) saying, "Not too many questions please!" is an implicit acknowledgment of error, ignorance, or both. It would be far better to have a sign that reads, "Questions welcome. They help us towards better understandings." It is a good thing to acknowledge ignorance. Errors in understanding have happened and still are happening. Questions, even the most searching of questions, are good because they facilitate growth in understanding. They also expose our ignorance, our finiteness, our lack of knowledge and mistakes, which is essential to a humble approach to truth and God.

The role of philosophy is to assist in the task theology must engage in as well, of understanding and then skillfully appropriating the biblical stories and teachings, while scraping off some of the accumulated barnacles slowing down the big ship *Christianity*. John Locke (1632–1704) famously said, "It is ambition enough to be employed as an under-laborer in clearing the ground a little, and removing some of the rubbish that lies in the way of knowledge."[7] That is what Athens can bring to its friendship with Jerusalem.

Jerusalem, for its part, can keep reminding Athens of transcendent possibilities, and of the essential limits to human understanding, which the early philosophers including Socrates were aware of.

Forms of the Faith Dismissive of Athens

Despite all that has been asserted above, there is something to be said for churches having settled statements of belief. Every human organization has rules and/or assumed values and beliefs. Churches and denominations are no different. An advantage is that churches are voluntary organizations. People can choose not to join. They can walk away. There will be no inquisition pursuing them, hopefully. The fact that there are so many churches and denominations, along with a wide spectrum of ideological and theological positions, is evidence of the impact of Athens, as churches and individuals wrestle with the deep questions constantly being asked of them. Whether one identifies as a fundamentalist or a liberal or somewhere in between, one is sure to be able to find a faith community to suit one's particular orientation and beliefs.

7. Quoted in Allison, *Resurrection of Jesus*, 4.

Moreover, unlike philosophers, most people do not have the time nor the inclination to just sit around endlessly conjecturing. Churches aren't set up to do that either. They have a job to do in creating communities of faith, maintaining social bonds, devising rituals and faith practices, while also trying to make a positive impact in the world. Some degree of settled belief is important to this sociological process.

The problem is that people are exiting all forms of the faith; none is immune. Something is new here. Something has changed. My suggestion is that information such as I have shared in this book is getting through to people like never before. Questions that have been posed through all of Christian history, which were then sharpened and made more acute during the European Enlightenment, are coming home to roost at a time when the Christian belief system is no longer dominant. The plausibility structures have shifted away from Christianity, which is increasingly struggling to win adherents.

In the midst of this tumultuous time for Christianity, an appeal to historic or traditional or orthodox Christianity is unlikely to be a remedy for the problem of diminishing churches. The thing about historic orthodoxy is that so much of the biblical narrative was accepted at face value when those earlier orthodoxies were established. Pretty much all the biblical stories, reaching all the way back into Gen 1–11 and all the way forward to the gospels, were accepted as broadly factual, as were the designations of authorship, as were the moral laws, as was all that Jesus was reported as saying and doing. Those earlier times have gone.

There is no way of returning to a pristine or better past, not even into the Bible itself, nor even to just a generation or so ago. As William Dever puts it, "There can be no turning back to the innocence of our parents or our youth; we know too much."[8] What was possible or plausible when I was growing up is no longer so possible or plausible. And so, although it is understandable that churches will create and then adhere to statements of belief, this in no way excuses them from the need to keep thinking and to change when there is good reason to. This brings us back to the question of whether and to what extent contemporary churches and denominations are willing to promote a friendship with Athens. Some are not. Too many are not.

Without attempting a comprehensive list, the following churches or types of church are not friends with Athens, to their impoverishment:

---

8. Dever, *Has Archaeology Buried the Bible*, 25.

- Churches that discourage questions; particularly the more searching ones
- Churches that insulate from criticism beliefs considered core or nonnegotiable
- Churches that punish questioners, especially if they arrive at "unacceptable" conclusions[9]
- Churches that value uniformity over diversity
- Churches that privilege their own reading of the Scriptures, while not respectfully giving room for alternative readings
- Churches that are not only Bible first but Bible only
- Churches that are dominated by strong leaders and/or by controlling factions who determine which are acceptable beliefs and who should be considered in or out

There are some clear cases of churches and organizations that fit all or most of these descriptions. Many of the evangelical churches I have encountered over the years are poor when it comes to accommodating the questioning and questing spirit of Athens. Evangelical academics and thought leaders have tended to be inconsistent in their scholarship, creating unstable fundamentalist/liberal hybrids. They often value scholarship and *say* that they encourage questions, but such questioning always appears to have limits.

For the Anglican Diocese of Sydney, scholarship that calls into question sacred-cow beliefs, such as the permanent subservience of women or the impossibility of same-sex marriage or the supreme authority of the Bible, is resisted or buried. More concerning still is the diocese's leadership within and strong commitment to GAFCON. This unfortunate worldwide grouping is another prime example of a movement that has sought to immunize itself from philosophical and scientific critique, while also being apparently blind to the intellectual, social, and moral damage it continues to wreak around the world.

---

9. This can happen in a multitude of ways, including being quietly sidelined and removed from any positions of influence, often without explanation.

On a Way Forward

Discerning God in Nature

Theologians and philosophers are likely to come close to agreement that the emergence of life on this planet, in all of its amazing, intricate, and beautiful forms, is at least suggestive of purposeful intent, that there could well be a divine being who is the ground of all being. They would agree, I think, that humans are special; that love, generosity, humility, and integrity bring about flourishing; and that our lives therefore have meaning. Socrates and Paul both believed in the gods or God, that life is purposeful, and that morality is paramount.

I know that there is contrary evidence, examples of waste, false starts, along with violence and predation. There are reasons to think there is no God, but I choose to believe. I opt for belief in God, just as the atheist opts for disbelief, not irrationally, but still involving a leap. They cannot know that God does not exist, and the existence of God does help to make sense of a great deal of those things we value most.

Philosophy and faith can coexist, as they have done down through the centuries, and still to this day. The scientific enterprise, in all of its many fields of discovery, can coexist with theology. I've had on my shelf for a few years now Chet Raymo's book *Skeptics and True Believers: The Exhilarating Connection Between Science and Religion*. Raymo is Professor Emeritus of Physics at Stonehill College in North Easton, Massachusetts. He was raised in a traditional Christian faith, but, while taking academic degrees in science, came to the conclusion that various tenets of his faith were "based on long-discredited views of the world."[10] These he believes must be jettisoned. However, he also believes that the now deep and wide chasm that has opened up between traditional theology and science can be bridged. Perhaps surprisingly, this can happen by way of the scientific method, which Raymo suggests is uniquely able to reveal the profound and wonder-evoking mysteries of nature. Raymo believes that science and religion can happily and with integrity coexist. He explains:

> If the prodigious energy of the new scientific story of creation is to flow into religion, the story will need to be translated from the language of scientific discovery into the language of celebration. This is the work of theologians, homilists, liturgists, poets, artists, and, yes, science writers. Only when we are emotionally at home in the universe of the galaxies and the DNA will the

---

10. Raymo, *Skeptics and True Believers*, 5.

new story invigorate our spiritual lives and be the cause of authentic celebration. Knowing and believing will come together again at last.[11]

Van Harvey's contention (mentioned in ch. 1) that believing tentatively as a historian is not compatible with believing passionately as a Christian is not quite right, so long as one's belief is tempered by humility and an acknowledgment of uncertainty. Somewhat artificially, Raymo divides people into skeptics and true believers:

> Sceptics are children of the Scientific Revolution and the Enlightenment. They are always a little lost in the vastness of the cosmos, but they trust the ability of the human mind to make sense of the world. They accept the evolving nature of truth and are willing to live with a measure of uncertainty. Their world is colored in shades of grey. Since they hold their beliefs tentatively, Sceptics are tolerant of cultural and religious diversity. If they are theists, they wrestle with their God in a continuing struggle of faith. They are often plagued by personal doubts....
>
> True believers . . . look for help from outside—from God, spirits or extra-terrestrials. Their world is black and white. They seek simple and certain truths, provided by a source that is more reliable than the human mind. They are repulsed by diversity, comforted by dogma, and respectful of authority.[12]

These are caricatures of what, in reality, is likely to be a spectrum along which people will locate themselves. But they more or less conform to distinctions I have been making. Those who have imbibed the spirit of Socrates are likely to be more careful in their believing, more humble, and thus more accepting of differences. And yet they can be, contra Van Harvey, believing skeptics.

Spirituality

Raymo suggests that knowledge gained by scientific endeavor enhances our wonder and awe as we encounter the world in all of its wild grandeur, and as we encounter in each other whole new dimensions of beauty, truth, and goodness. As already mentioned, I've increasingly been attracted to Celtic spirituality, with its emphasis upon nature and our embeddedness within nature, of our worship of God being informed by what we encounter

---

11. Raymo, *Skeptics and True Believers*, 157.
12. Raymo, *Skeptics and True Believers*, 2.

within nature, understood as God's creation. This I have found liberating and inspiring.

The panentheistic nature of Celtic spirituality was especially appealing because it envisages God as both the transcendent ground of all being and also as imminent in the created order and within our lives. God is mostly invisible and inscrutable in both cases, but also as close as our breathing or heartbeat.

The aforementioned John O'Donohue expounds this ancient idea and its implications.

> God is omnipresent, and life itself is the primal sacrament, namely *the* visible sign of invisible grace. The structures of our experience are the windows into the divine. When we are true to the call of experience, we are true to God.[13]

Panentheism makes all of life sacred. It sanctifies the quest for truth, beauty, and goodness. It therefore sanctifies philosophy. It also sanctifies the wisdom tradition, which within the Bible is the philosophical corrective to dogmatism. It sanctifies human history and prehistory, as it sanctifies all of nature.

Discerning God in Jesus

Panentheism contains a key to understanding and appropriating the notion of incarnation, of God becoming human. Iain McGilchrist argues that the doctrine of the Trinity provides something of a rationale for a panentheistic view of God. Not that the doctrine is without problems, including its use by churches to identify acceptable and unacceptable ideas,[14] splitting the Eastern and Western Churches, for example.[15] However, an important function of Trinitarian belief was its ability to account for the incarnation, as here explained by theologian Jürgen Moltmann in his 1984 Gifford Lectures:

> The Trinitarian concept of creation binds together God's transcendence and his immanence. The one-sided stress on God's transcendence in relation to the world led to deism, as with

---

13. O'Donohue, *To Bless the Space*, xvi; emphasis in original.

14. It most certainly had that function, right from its initial acceptance. The Emperor Constantine wanted a unifying document that would assist his efforts to unify the empire. The two bishops who refused to sign the final statement (one of whom was Arius) were excommunicated. Arius's and others' earlier expressed views were declared heretical.

15. As a result of the famed *filioque* clause.

> Newton. The one-sided stress on God's immanence in the world led to pantheism, as with Spinoza. The Trinitarian concept of creation integrates the elements of truth in monotheism and pantheism. In the pan*en*theistic view . . . God, having created the world, also dwells in it, and, conversely, the world which he has created exists in him. . . . [The] de-divinization of the world has progressed so far that the prevailing view is totally godless, and the relationship of human beings to nature is a disastrous one. This means that today we have to find an integrating view of God and nature which will draw them both into the same vista. It is only this that can exert a liberating influence on nature and human beings alike.[16]

The idea that God can be in Jesus, as Jesus is in God, makes sense on a panentheistic view. Whether and to what extent one follows the trajectory of the New Testament, and then all the way to Nicaea to the idea that Jesus is the only and eternally existing Son of God, the second person of the Trinity, is a matter of some uncertainty, but it is without doubt a possibility, with promising implications, as Moltmann has observed.

Speaking personally, I simply don't know whether the doctrine of the Trinity, as articulated in our creeds, is an accurate description of reality. I certainly don't have the relevant expertise to decide whether this doctrine provides us with the best or most coherent understanding of what is said about Jesus, his Father, and God's Spirit in the New Testament. I also wonder whether drawing from disparate biblical passages is a reliable method of deciding the issue. As we have come to see, the New Testament is a complex document containing contrasting views and developing understandings. It is also an ancient document populated with assumptions now alien to us, about what divinity entails, for example. We are definitely looking through a glass darkly. Complicating matters even further is the almost universal recognition that the doctrine of the Trinity is incomprehensibly mysterious.

Nevertheless, I am happy to remain agnostic and even happier to consider myself a lifelong disciple of Jesus. On any understanding, Jesus is worthy of a following.

Discipleship

Somewhat unexpectedly, in the process of writing this book, I've encountered the tantalizing suggestion that the gospel authors may have been

---

16. Moltmann, *God in Creation*, quoted in McGilchrist, *Matter with Things*, 2:1166–67.

influenced in their depictions of Jesus by the example of Socrates. Robyn Faith Walsh, an assistant professor of New Testament and early Christianity at the University of Miami, suggests that the obviously well-educated gospel authors were likely to have been schooled in Greco-Roman forms of writing, including biography. They were therefore likely to be aware of biographical accounts of Socrates, largely found in the writings of Plato and Xenophon.

Walsh identifies a number of biographical traditions still current at the time the gospels were written. Among them is one she describes as a subversive tradition within which the hero takes on the dominant culture, thus representing a threat to establishment ideology. Walsh identifies the writings of Xenophon in particular as exemplifying this tradition in his mostly positive portrayal of Socrates. Unlike the normal heroes of Greco-Roman biography, Socrates is portrayed as:

> at the margins of society, puckish and nonconformist. In relation to the powers that be, he is the underdog despite his sharp wits; indeed, it is precisely because he is politically weak that he must rely on clever ripostes and arguments to defend himself. In doing so, he tends to upset inherited beliefs and thereby threatens the establishment ideology.[17]

We can certainly recognize an outline of the story of Jesus in the story of Socrates. Of course there are differences, many, but the similarities stand out, as described by Walsh:

> Like Socrates . . . Jesus is at the margins of society, a Judean peasant powerless in relation to the state. In his encounters with Pharisees or other interlocutors, he wins his victories by means of his wits and his ability to turn the words of his opponents against them.
> . . . Although we are not given a description of his physical appearance, he is depicted as an underdog from a lower class of society and of few means. He is followed by fishermen and teaches and interacts with other marginalized persons. He is baptized by John, who lives as a Cynic-like recluse in the desert, eating nothing but locusts and honey (e.g. Matt. 3:4). And he comes to an untimely end, accused of impiety, and publicly executed.[18]

---

17. Walsh, *Early Christian Literature*, 179.
18. Walsh, *Early Christian Literature*, 192.

As described in the gospels, Jesus is much more than a subversive, but he is certainly that. As already noted, there are additional similarities. Both were brave in their criticism of current orthodoxies. Both were on a mission. Both believed in the essential goodness of God (or the gods). Both prioritized piety over knowledge. Both were teachers. Both paid for their subversive teachings with their lives. Both died willingly.

I am, for those sorts of reasons and more, a disciple of Jesus and of Socrates as well. Thinking historically, there is much we don't know about the historical Jesus and about the historical Socrates. Neither wrote anything, as far as we know. Recollections from those who knew them, or knew about them, are varied and sometimes contradictory. Nevertheless, enough is known, and the stories themselves are inspirational.

The stories about Jesus fuel, inform, and inspire my Christian discipleship. It is my daily desire to be Christlike and therefore godlike, and this not simply by imitating Christ. A profound insight of the New Testament, and of the Johannine writings in particular, is that heeding the call of Jesus ushers us into the very life of God. This provides me with added incentive to want to be like Jesus in being gentle, kind, courageous, humble, and loving. The stories about Socrates are similarly inspirational. They have been built into the DNA of my life. They are a valued aspect of my spirituality, which I've come to believe is God created and God encouraged. I do want to keep questioning and questing towards the truth.

Moreover, I would love to see Christians in general, and their churches certainly, becoming more Socratic in the sense of being willing to question, to investigate, and to change where necessary. Being willing to be subversive, as Jesus was, can also be an aspect of their discipleship.

Doctrinal Review

Somewhat consequentially, being a twenty-first-century follower of Jesus will require a process of doctrinal revision. Our understanding of the Bible has grown. It has always been growing, but the pace and potential impact of that growth has increased. It is not just a matter of integrating contemporary cosmology and evolutionary theory, though that is needed. There is much more to do. Our growing understanding of Israelite, Judean, and Christian history is massive in its implications, as is the associated growing awareness of the role of mythology and imaginative storytelling.

All Christian doctrines need to come under the microscope of careful reexamination. As a sampling, this would include doctrines associated with protology, soteriology, eschatology, and ethics. Included under these broader categories are doctrines of biblical authority, the kingdom of God, the divinity of Christ, the Trinity, the atonement, life after death, heaven and hell, original sin, marriage, and other religions. It may be that for some of these, it will turn out that there is very little need for significant revision. Doctrines that have been hammered out over many generations, and even centuries, often with high degrees of sophistication, may in fact pass the test of time. But that will be discovered only in the context of careful reconsideration. There remains a massive amount of work to be done. An honest faith will acknowledge this, roll up its sleeves, and get on with the task.

More work is required in the area of hermeneutics. In chatting to some current and former faculty of Moore Theological College, I was heartened to hear that alternative approaches to hermeneutics are being explored. Trustworthiness was proposed as an alternative to inerrancy. It is a promising suggestion, which, of course, could be elaborated on in multiple of ways. I could use the term myself to describe the divine inspiration undergirding the creative, self-correcting, and evolutionary nature of the Jewish and Christian Scriptures. Older ways of understanding the Bible have misled Christians, and this has contributed to the conclusion that the Scriptures are not trustworthy.[19]

Without doubt, we are at a moment of required deconstruction. The task of re-formation will depend for its success on the results of this deconstruction. We need to move on both fronts, deconstruction and re-formation, and will for some time to come. As we do, opportunities will open up for "homilists, liturgists, poets, and artists" to devise contemporary creeds, liturgies, music, and art. Too much of what we currently have is tired, doubtful, and alienating. It won't be enough to revamp our church services so they appear up to date and chic. We will need to bring them actually up to date in contemporizing not just the wrappings but the content of our faith. We need to bring all that we've been learning (about the Bible and the world) to our theology and practice.

Thankfully, there are hopeful signs of this happening. Theologians of all persuasions and backgrounds are striving, as always, to make best sense of all relevant knowledge, and to plot imaginative and integrative ways forward. Fr. Richard Rohr is one such theologian, relatively new to me but attractive in his embrace of panentheism.[20] Rohr is fully apprised of contemporary

---

19. Clearly there is more work to be done. What I have found over the years is that scholars have struggled to come up with a view of biblical authority that makes good sense of what we find in Scripture, while also successfully aligning this with extra-biblical knowledge.

20. Rohr self-identifies as a panentheist, for example, in *Universal Christ*, 43.

biblical and secular scholarship, and he integrates this information into his thinking and writing. He also looks backwards to the widely neglected treasures of the perennial tradition and of Orthodox theology. This he does in an effort to expand the vision of Christ to lovingly include all of creation, all of human history, and all of time. Whether and to what extent Rohr's vision of *The Universal Christ* meets the challenges laid out in this book has yet to be seen. Whether and to what extent it can precipitate, as Rohr believes it can,[21] a fruitful reformation of Christian theology and philosophy, only time will tell. But the project he has embarked upon is admirable. I'm hopeful it will inspire many more such efforts.

There are other less monumental efforts at theological and ethical reform. At the time of writing, news came through of a new book by Richard B. Hays, coauthored by his son, Christopher Hays. Back in 1996, Richard had released *The Moral Vision of the New Testament*, a text that was, and still is, widely influential among Evangelicals. In April 2000, it was included in a list of the ninety most influential religious books of the twentieth century by *Christianity Today*.[22] Chapter 16 of Hay's book carefully argues from relevant New Testament passages that homosexuality is a sign of human brokenness and that churches should not sanction or bless homosexual unions. Almost thirty years later, Richard Hays has changed his mind, perhaps under the influence of his son. Father and son chronicle and explain that change of mind in *The Widening of God's Mercy: Sexuality Within the Biblical Story* (2024). The title is revealing. According to prepublication information, father and son point out that the Bible is not static in its views, and that there exists within the Bible ongoing conversations in which traditional rules, customs, and theologies are rethought.[23] That is how I understand things as well.

Richard Hays is not the first to have changed his mind. Others, including Evangelicals, have preceded him, including David Gushee,[24] James

---

21. Rohr believes that the universalizing impact of panentheism can supply "the deep and universal meaning that Western civilization seems to lack and long for today. It has the potential to reground Christianity as a natural religion and not one simply based on a special revelation, available only to a few lucky enlightened people" (*Universal Christ*, 6).

22. As judged by contributors to *Christianity Today*.

23. Yale University Press, the book's publisher, includes a useful summary of the book's thesis at https://yalebooks.yale.edu/book/9780300273427/the-widening-of-gods-mercy/.

24. David P. Gushee has been influential in my and many others' developing understandings. His own evolving perspectives are highlighted in books included in this book's bibliography.

Brownson,[25] Tony Campolo, Jim Wallis, Glennon Doyle, Rachel Held Evans, and Eugene Peterson.[26] There are countless others who are less well known.[27] Younger Evangelicals, or the children of Evangelicals, and growing numbers of ex-Evangelicals have similarly changed their minds. Doctrinal review is definitely under way, some of it now being led by queer theologians and biblical scholars.[28]

Uncertainty and Diversity

If what I have argued in this book is correct, an atheist or an agnostic or a believer who concludes differently about even creedal aspects of the faith is not thereby irrational. This has implications. It means, I think, that we will need to be more accepting of difference, more humble with respect to our own believing. It will have implications for our churches and for their witness in the world.

When we lived in Sydney, before our welcome retirement to country NSW, Judy and I were members of Holy Trinity Anglican Church, Dulwich Hill. We loved the church. One thing we especially treasured about this faith community was that it valued and honored diversity. All were welcome, truly welcome, and no pressure was applied to convert people to a particular point of view, though we did seek to commend the Christian faith as variously understood. There were people from other religions and denominations who occasionally attended and were warmly welcomed. This was especially true during the tenure of Fr. Dave Smith, who forged close links with a nearby Islamic community.

At one point when we were between rectors, a fellow parishioner, Graeme Sanders, decided to have a go at describing the church's ethos, including

---

25. James V. Brownson has been similarly influential. This book's bibliography includes two of his valuable books.

26. This widely respected pastor and author was so fiercely criticized, mocked, and threatened after changing his mind that he retracted a statement he had made about him being willing to marry a gay couple. A shameful episode, too often repeated.

27. Including Daniel Kirk, formerly from Fuller Theological Seminary, and Daniel Neff, a retired editor of *Christianity Today*. Here in Australia, Rowland Croucher, a retired pastor and author; Matt Glover and Mike Hercock, two former Baptist pastors; and Rob Buckingham are four prominent examples. Buckingham was the first Pentecostal megachurch pastor in the world (at Bayside in Melbourne) to welcome LGBTIQ+ people into his church. Glover and Hercock paid high prices for their changes of mind, as have countless others lesser known.

28. Emerging queer theologians whom I've been made aware of are Patrick Cheng, Elizabeth Edman, Linn Marie Tonstad, and Austen Hartke. I'd also include Jo Inkpin and Steff Fenton, whom I've mentioned in this book.

its guiding convictions. This appealed to me, and I joined him in the early stages of composing a Holy Trinity Charter. This was then tweaked, and it ended up being used to inform prospective ministers about the church they might be joining. The charter definitely did not appeal to some of them, but it was influential in Rev. Simon Keith's decision to apply. And he was successful.

What was so special about this charter was that the whole congregation had a say in its composition. We had two congregational meetings and some smaller gatherings. We modified the charter as we went until we had more or less unanimous support for it. I know of no one who objected or felt it wasn't us. Here is some of what we came up with:

Holy Trinity Dulwich Hill Charter

The congregation at Holy Trinity Dulwich Hill is an Anglican Christian community located in the inner west of Sydney. We are diverse in our thinking and backgrounds and welcome the exploration of different points of view. We are somewhat traditional in our corporate worship, but enjoy contemporary elements including music. We are an outward-looking congregation with a shared commitment to social justice. We highly value prayer and support for each other in the pursuit of our callings, ministries, life and work in the world and church.

We are:

1. Christian in being committed followers of Jesus Christ. Inspired by his life and teachings, and enabled by his Spirit, we endeavour to worship God in all we do, say and are. We endeavour to love, support and be patient with each other in the many challenges and opportunities of life and faith, and in our on-going determination to keep working at what it means to be Christian in a 21st century world.
2. Anglican in our liturgical practices, including use of a Prayer Book and regular celebration of Holy Communion, whilst remaining open to new expressions of faith and worship.
3. Open in that we welcome interaction and cooperation with other Christian traditions and with people of other religions, while being true to our own beliefs.
4. Inclusive in that we aim to offer acceptance and refuge to all who are hurting or who, for whatever reason, don't feel welcome in other communities. We recognise the intrinsic worth

of all people who both image God and are loved by God in all of their uniqueness and difference. We welcome people from different cultures, with different occupations, interests, levels of education, theological persuasions, and from all walks of life. We aim for a humility which allows relationships to be maintained among a community of faith with people of differing perspectives and convictions, including those who strongly support the leadership and full participation of women and LGBTIAQ+ people within the life and ministries of the church.

5. Socially active in that we aim to work with others to help bring about a society in which all can thrive and prosper, including refugees, Aboriginal and Torres Strait Islanders, those who are sexually and gender diverse, people of other religions, and all who are disadvantaged, marginalised, or who have a disability. We aim to do this by extending practical care, and by offering support, advocacy and expert assistance in so far as we are equipped to do so.

I found it inspirational to reread this charter. The process was special that brought it to birth. It is also worth noting that this charter very deliberately gave room to a range of different opinions, including doubts about the Trinity, the virgin birth, and bodily resurrection.

Community

What you may have noticed from the above charter is that the congregation has both an inward and an outward focus. It is first, a community of faith, a learning, thoughtful, prayerful, loving, and worshipping community. And second, even within its inward focus is an outward focus. Holy Trinity, Dulwich Hill, has sought to be a welcoming and safe place for any who attend but, more than that, has aimed to contribute to the wider world via social justice initiatives, so that all can "thrive and prosper." At the core of this vision is faith and discipleship. The congregation is decidedly Christian in being "committed followers of Jesus Christ . . . inspired by his life and teachings, and enabled by his Spirit."

It struck me as I again read this charter that this is or can be the future for Christianity. Here is a congregation willing to wrestle with its own and others' understandings of the faith, to allow and even encourage diversity, which is a key to both deconstruction and re-formation. Here is a congregation committed to love both within and beyond its community.

What has happened here in microcosm can happen in all our churches and denominations.

Inspirational in all of this is the founding example of Jesus. For Christianity to have a thriving future it will need to be Jesus-like. The life of its communities will need to be thoroughly shaped by Jesus, by his courage, integrity, honesty, and gentle kindness; by his willingness to speak and act against injustice and against any demeaning behavior or ideologies that diminish, harm, or degrade people.

Humility

As *An Honest Faith* is brought towards its conclusion, another nod to humility seems appropriate. One person well placed to provide this is Bono, the Irish lead vocalist of U2. When Judy and I were in Dublin, we walked past the studio where U2 first began recording as they launched their illustrious career. Bono's 2022 book, *Surrender: 40 Songs, One Story*, contains some of his reflections on life and religion, including these:

> Somewhere at the heart of "I Still Haven't Found What I'm Looking For"—an Edge song title—is John Bunyan's idea of the pilgrim's progress. Or in my case, the lack of it. If I mostly find religiosity annoying, right up the top of annoying is the pigheaded certainty of the devout without the doubt. Not just no room for doubt in the God they follow, but no doubt in their ability to decipher the holy tracts. No doubt their version of events is the right one.
>
> What's the point of a conversation with someone who's already made up their mind?[29]
>
> But if my faith is a crutch, I want to throw it away. I'd rather fall over. I remain more suspicious of religion than most people who'd never darken the door of a church. I've never quite found a church I could call home, and I tell the kids to be wary of religion, that what the human spirit longs for may not be corralled by any sect or denomination, contained in a building. Its more likely a daily discipline, a daily surrender and rebirth. It's more likely that church is not a place but a practice, the practice becomes the place. There is no promised land. Only the promised journey, the pilgrimage. We search through the noise for signal, and we learn to ask better questions of ourselves and each other.
>
> I call the signal "God" and search my life for clues that betray the location of the eternal presence. For starters we look to who is standing beside us or down the road, the ones whose

---

29. Bono, *Surrender*, 507.

roof we share or the ones around the corner who have no roof. The mystics tell us God is present in the present, what Dr. King described as "the fierce urgency of now."

> God is present in the love between us. In a crowd. In a band. In marriage.
>
> In the way we meet the world.
>
> God is present in love expressed as action.

I sang the statement "I still haven't found what I'm looking for" as a question when I was twenty-seven. But in trying to make peace with my own uncertainty, I grew to be certain in one regard. That whatever our instincts or ideas about what the great mysterious He or She or They, whatever the differences of the great faith traditions, they find common ground in one place: among the poor and vulnerable is where the signal is strongest.[30]

Honesty

What I have wanted to emphasize most throughout this book is the indispensable importance of honesty. We just do need to acknowledge that there is much we don't know. We must also be willing and brave enough to admit that things we thought we knew, we don't. Honesty must also involve being open to new information that comes across our paths. That will include beliefs that can now be classified as knowledge. Our knowledge of the Bible, of its historical setting, and of its development over time is growing. It is growing so rapidly it is hard to keep up. Our knowledge of the universe and of the development of life, including human life, is constantly growing. We need to be honest and open about all of this. Our churches, denominations, and theological institutions certainly need to be. Moreover, it is their responsibility to assist us in integrating these new learnings into our intellectual and spiritual life as communities of faith.

By doing this, they will thereby allow Athens to be a friend (even a friendly critic) of Jerusalem, as Jerusalem can be of Athens. The quest for truth has the same requirements of honesty and humility whether you are a philosopher, a scientist, a historian, or a theologian. Dale Allison, in a coda at the end of his book, acknowledges the inherent limitations of his discipline, while also leaving room for faith:

> When Christians, on Easter Sunday, greet each other with the acclamation, "Christ is risen," the expected answer "Christ is risen indeed!" is not a statement about investigative results.

---

30. Bono, *Surrender*, 530–31.

People do not go to church because they have been thinking like Hercule Poirot.

Harvey Cox once rightly protested against a "detective-novel approach" to an understanding of the resurrection. Although ignorance should not be the mother of devotion, religious life and experience are not the products of a rational solution to a whodunit. They rather involve realms of human experience and conviction that cannot depend on or be undone by the sorts of historical doubts, probabilities, and conjectures with which the previous pages have concerned themselves. There is no religion within the limits of history alone, just as there is no religion within the limits of reason alone. For myself, all I have to do is look up at the night sky or look into the face of my neighbor, and then I know that is there more to life and faith than this.[31]

Hopefulness

Allison hasn't lost his Christian faith despite his ready acknowledgment of the limitations of historical method. Despite our own limitations of knowledge, we still need to opt for a way of living that, for us, makes best sense of our humanity and of the almost universal human sense of transcendence. Speaking personally, I choose to stay with the faith I was born into, a faith which has many riches still to be mined; and which, because of its dynamic and open character, can continue to bless and enrich. In the remaining days or years of my life, however many or few, I want to live them with integrity, grace, love, and compassion.

For the world, I hope and pray that God will indeed animate and inspire all efforts to peace, justice, love, and understanding. However exactly God acts in the world, if something of the spirit that animated the morally sensitive, exploratory, and trustful small nation of Judah is drawn upon by contemporary Jews, Christians, and all peoples, the world will be a better place. If the spirit of the early Christian movement, of Jesus and his disciples, is allowed to impact not just the West, as it has, but all nations, then there really will be hope for the world. If the high value placed on each and every human life is honored, and priority is given to integrity, service, love, forgiveness, and grace, then we will be better able to forge a pathway through the confusion, anger, hatred, and violence that currently blight our world. God will do this in and through us.

---

31. Allison, *Resurrection of Jesus*, 265.

If indeed God is quietly at work within every human being, throughout all of human history, prehistory, and now, then Christian efforts to evangelize will necessarily involve listening, learning, and surprise, along with some confidence that the truth of what we share will resonate and find a receptive landing. We might again climb the slopes of contemporary Areopagus's to humbly and honestly commend the Christian gospel as we best understand it.

Dual Citizenship

There has probably never been a more important time to be a dual citizen of Jerusalem and Athens. Dishonesty, misinformation, and cruel misunderstanding are rife. It is therefore not only possible but imperative that Christians work to become joint citizens or, at the very least, to be friends. This is especially needful for those who want to lead Christianity through a process of reformation into an honest and sustainable future.

Questions for Reflection and Discussion

1. What sorts of things have been influential in your own faith journey?
2. What are some of the things you have learned or come to appreciate better after reading *An Honest Faith*?
3. Where would you locate your faith journey at the moment?

Coda

PJ: Well, that was quite some read!

Socrates: You are right. Have you just finished the book as well?

PJ: Yep. Just finished. I didn't mind it. I liked the title, *An Honest Faith*. I thought the book was pretty honest. Confronting though as well. I'll need to spend a bit of time digesting it—as I have had to do with our conversations, Socrates!

Socrates: Me likewise, PJ. What I found a bit startling, although also encouraging about *An Honest Faith*, was the author's conclusion that a truly biblical faith is (or at least it can be) philosophical and that the Bible itself is philosophical to some degree.

PJ: I am sure not everyone is going to agree. A bit cheeky too to describe his hermeneutic as closer to the biblical hermeneutic than what is typically employed by those who describe themselves as "biblical" or "Bible believing."

Socrates: Ha. Probably so. Though, I wouldn't be surprised if he persuades a few people. Or at least gets them thinking. What do you think of his idea that Christianity itself might need to change to take better account of new knowledge?

PJ: I'm not sure, but I guess history tells us that our faith has taken many different shapes over time. My dad sometimes speaks about the church needing to be "always reforming," an idea that came out of the Protestant Reformation.

Socrates: Do you think your dad would like this book?

PJ: I'm pretty sure he wouldn't. His first instinct would be to label it liberal hogwash. And perhaps even as dangerous in encouraging doubt, and not just about *some* things, but almost everything!! The book was challenging enough for me. Still, I might offer it to him to have a read.

Socrates: I had the opposite reaction. Funny. It opened the door for faith a little bit for me. I haven't and hadn't ruled out a transcendent dimension to life, and I was encouraged by the idea that no question should be off limits . . . and that it is possible to be a "skeptical believer."

PJ: I think I was somewhere in between. I was both confronted and engaged. I especially do not want to keep believing things that aren't true, or believing with more certitude than the evidence warrants. That's a word he used a few times. I think I know what it means.

And, I've just loved chatting with you, Socrates. There is a quote I came across the other day on Facebook—attributed to your namesake. No idea if it was his. It read, "Education is the kindling of a flame, not the filling of a vessel." You've kindled a flame for me, Socrates. Thank you.

Socrates: You've done the same for me, PJ. You've convinced me to have a closer look at your religion and others . . . with my many questions. And I am leaning towards the author's conclusion that Athens and Jerusalem can, and in fact should, be friends.

PJ: I am as well. Let's keep these conversations going.

Socrates: I'd like that.

Bibliography

Alison, James. *God, Not One of the Gods*. Vol. 2 of *Jesus the Forgiving Victim: Listening for the Unheard Voice*. Glenview, IL: Doers, 2013.

Allison, Dale C., Jr. *The Resurrection of Jesus: Apologetics, Polemics, History*. London: T&T Clark, 2021.

Alter, Robert, trans. *Strong as Death Is Love: The Song of Songs, Ruth, Esther, Jonah, and Daniel; A Translation with Commentary*. Berkeley: University of California Press, 2015.

Aquinas, Thomas. *Summa Theologiae*. Translated by E. Hill. 5 vols. New York: McGraw-Hill, 1964.

———. *Super Epistolas S. Pauli Lectura, t. 1: Super Epistolam ad Romanos Lectura*. Edited by R. Cai. 8th ed. Marietti, It.: Taurini-Romae, 1953.

Audi, Robert, ed. *Cambridge Dictionary of Philosophy*. Cambridge: Cambridge University Press, 1995.

Augustine, Saint. *Confessions*. Translated by R. S. Pine-Coffin. Penguin Classics. New York: Penguin, 1961.

———. *The City of God*. Translated by Marcus Dods. Modern Library. New York: Modern Library, 2000.

Australian Bureau of Statistics. "2021 Census Shows Changes in Australia's Religious Diversity." Australian Bureau of Statistics, June 28, 2022. https://www.abs.gov.au/media-centre/media-releases/2021-census-shows-changes-australias-religious-diversity#.

Bainton, R. H. *Here I Stand: A Life of Martin Luther*. New York: Lion Hudson, 2013.

Bartlett, Anthony. *Signs of Change: The Bible's Evolution of Divine Nonviolence*. Eugene, OR: Cascade, 2022.

Barton, John. *A History of the Bible: The Book and Its Faiths*. N.p.: Penguin, 2019.

Bauer, Greta R., et al. "Do Clinical Data from Transgender Adolescents Support the Phenomenon of 'Rapid Onset Gender Dysphoria'?" *Journal of Pediatrics* 243 (2022) P224–27. https://www.jpeds.com/article/S0022-3476(21)01085-4/.

Bettenson, Henry, and Chris Maunder, eds. *Documents of the Christian Church*. Oxford: Oxford University Press, 1999.

Bono. *Surrender: 40 Songs, One Story*. London: Hutchinson Heinemann, 2022.

Bregman, Rutger. *Humankind: A Hopeful History*. London: Bloomsbury, 2020.

Bretherton, Ingrid, et al. "The Health and Well-Being of Transgender Australians: A National Community Survey." *LGBT Health* 8 (2021). https://doi.org/10.1089/lgbt.2020.0178.

Brettler, Marc Zvi. *How to Read the Bible*. Philadelphia: Jewish Publication Society, 2005.

Brockhaus, Hannah. "Pope Francis on Women Deacons: 'Holy Orders Is Reserved for Men.'" Catholic News Agency, Oct. 25, 2023. https://www.catholicnewsagency.com/news/255804/pope-francis-on-women-deacons-holy-orders-is-reserved-for-men.

Brownson, James V. *Bible, Gender, Sexuality: Reframing the Church's Debate on Same-Sex Relationships*. Grand Rapids: Eerdmans, 2013.

———. *Questions Christians Aren't Supposed to Ask*. Grand Rapids: Eerdmans, 2021.

Brown University. "Updated: Brown Statements on Gender Dysphoria Study." News from Brown, Mar. 19, 2019. https://www.brown.edu/news/2019-03-19/gender.

Calvin, John. *The Second Epistle of Paul to the Corinthians and the Epistles of Timothy, Titus and Philemon*. Translated by T. Smail. New Testament Commentaries. Grand Rapids: Eerdmans, 1964.

Caputo, John D. *What Would Jesus Deconstruct? The Good News of Postmodernism for the Church*. Grand Rapids: Baker Academic, 2007.

Cheung, Ada, and Sav Zwickl. *Pursuit*, Mar. 23, 2021. "Why Have Nearly Half of Transgender Australians Attempted Suicide?" https://pursuit.unimelb.edu.au/articles/why-have-nearly-half-of-transgender-australians-attempted-suicide.

Childers, Alisa. *Another Gospel? A Lifetime Christian Seeks Truth in Response to Progressive Christianity*. Carol Stream, IL: Tyndale, 2000.

Clarke, Stephen R. L. *From Athens to Jerusalem: The Love of Wisdom & the Love of God*. Brooklyn, NY: Angelico, 1984.

Cross, Frank Moore. *Canaanite Myth and Hebrew Epic: Essays in the History of the Religion of Israel*. Cambridge, MA: Harvard University Press, 1973.

Cowdell, Scott. *Church Matters: Essays and Addresses on Ecclesial Belonging*. Bayswater, Aus.: Coventry, 2022.

Dans, Paul, and Steven Groves, eds. *Mandate for Conservative Leadership: The Conservative Promise*. Washington, DC: Heritage Foundation, 2023. https://static.project2025.org/2025_MandateForLeadership_FULL.pdf.

Davies, Paul. *The Mind of God: Science and the Search for Meaning*. London: Simon & Schuster, 1992.

Dever, William G. *Has Archaeology Buried the Bible?* Grand Rapids: Eerdmans, 2020.

Diocese of Sydney. "Proceedings of the 2002 Ordinary Session of the 46th Synod." Sydney Anglicans, Oct. 14–22, 2002. https://www.sds.asn.au/sites/default/files/2002%20Synod%20Proceedings%20%281st%20Session%20of%20the%2046th%20Synod%29.pdf?doc_id=NjE1MjM=.

Dunn, James D. G. *Christology in the Making: A New Testament Inquiry into the Origins of the Incarnation*. 2nd ed. London: SCM, 1989.

Ehrman, Bart D. *How Jesus Became God: The Exaltation of a Jewish Preacher from Galilee*. San Francisco: Harper, 2014.

Ehrman, Bart D., et al. *When Did Jesus Become God? A Christological Debate*. Louisville: Westminster John Knox, 2022.

Ellis, E. Earle. *The Old Testament in Early Christianity: Canon and Interpretation in the Light of Modern Research*. Wissenschaftliche Untersuchungen zum Neuen Testament 54. Tübingen: Mohr Siebeck, 1991.

Enns, Peter. *Inspiration and Incarnation: Evangelicals and the Problem of the Old Testament*. Grand Rapids: Baker Academic, 2005.

———. *The Sin of Certainty: Why God Desires Our Trust More Than Our "Correct" Beliefs*. New York: Harper One, 2016.

Fenton, Steff. "Gender Expansive Faith: The Transgender Sacred Superpower Healing Christian Patriarchy." Unpublished manuscript, last modified Dec. 20, 2024. Microsoft Word document.

Flanery, Brandon. "I Asked People Why They're Leaving Christianity, and Here's What I Heard." *Baptist News Global*, Dec. 13, 2022. https://baptistnews.com/article/i-asked-people-why-theyre-leaving-christianity-and-heres-what-i-heard/.

GAFCON. "The Jerusalem Statement." GAFCON, June 2008. https://www.gafcon.org/about/the-jerusalem-statement/.

Giles, Kevin. *The Headship of Men and the Abuse of Women: Are They Related in Any Way?* Eugene, OR: Cascade, 2020.

———. *What the Bible Actually Teaches on Women*. Eugene, OR: Cascade, 2018.

Glesson, Kate, and Luke Ashton. *Trust in Religion Among Women in Australia: A Qualitative Analysis*. Analysis and Policy Observatory, May 4, 2024. https://apo.org.au/sites/default/files/resource-files/2024-05/apo-nid326466_0.pdf.

Grayling, A. C. *The God Argument: The Case Against Religion and for Humanism*. London: Bloomsbury, 2013.

Gushee, David P. *After Evangelicalism: The Path to a New Christianity*. Louisville: Westminster John Knox, 2020.

———. *Changing Our Mind: A Call from America's Leading Evangelical Ethics Scholar for Full Acceptance of LGBT Christians in the Church*. 2nd ed. Canton, MI: Crumm, 2015.

———. *Introducing Christian Ethics: Core Convictions for Christians Today*. N.p.: Front Edge, 2022.

Hailes, Sam. "Deconstructing Faith: Meet the Evangelicals Who Are Questioning Everything." *Premier Christianity*, Mar. 17, 2019. https://www.premierchristianity.com/features/deconstructing-faith-meet-the-evangelicals-who-are-questioning-everything/267.article.

Hartke, Austen. *Transforming: The Bible and the Lives of Transgender Christians*. Louisville: Westminster John Knox, 2018.

Harvey, Van A. *The Historian and the Believer: The Morality of Historical Knowledge and Christian Belief*. Urbana: University of Illinois Press, 1996.

Hays, Christopher B., and Richard B. Hays. *The Widening of God's Mercy: Sexuality Within the Biblical Story*. New Haven, CT: Yale University Press, 2024.

Hays, Richard B. *The Moral Vision of the New Testament: Community, Cross, New Creation; A Contemporary Introduction to the New Testament*. N.p.: HarperOne, 1996.

Hays, Richard B., and Joel B. Green. "The Use of the Old Testament by New Testament Writers." In *Hearing the New Testament: Strategies of Interpretation*, edited by Joel B. Green, 222–38. Grand Rapids: Eerdmans, 1995.

Held Evans, Rachel. *Searching for Sunday: Loving, Leaving, and Finding the Church*. Nashville: Nelson, 2015.

Hill, Graham Joseph. *Holding Up Half the Sky: A Biblical Case for Women Leading and Teaching in the Church*. Eugene, OR: Cascade, 2020.

Hoffmeier, James K., and Dennis R. Magary, eds. *Do Historical Matters Matter to Faith? A Critical Appraisal of Modern and Postmodern Approaches to Scripture*. Wheaton, IL: Crossway, 2012.

Holland, Tom. *Dominion: How the Christian Revolution Remade the World*. New York: Basic, 2019.

Inclusive Evangelicals. "An Open Letter on Behalf of Inclusive Evangelicals in the Church of England." Inclusive Evangelicals, Nov. 2023. https://www.inclusiveevangelicals.com/post/an-open-letter#viewer-170q0.

Jones, Jeffrey M. "Belief in God in U.S. Dips to 81%, a New Low." Gallup, June 17, 2022. https://news.gallup.com/poll/393737/belief-god-dips-new-low.aspx.

Judd, Andrew. *Modern Genre Theory: An Introduction for Biblical Studies*. Studies in Method. Grand Rapids: Zondervan Academic, 2024.

Kaziimba, Stephen. "Church of Uganda Grateful for Anti-Homosexuality Act 2023." Anglican Ink, May 29, 2023. https://anglican.ink/2023/05/29/27921/#google_vignette.

Keener, Craig S. *Paul, Women and Wives: Marriage and Women's Ministry in the Letters of Paul*. Grand Rapids: Hendrickson, 1992.

Kempis, Thomas à. *The Imitation of Christ*. Translated by Leo Sherley-Price. Penguin Classics. Baltimore: Penguin, 1952.

Kant, Immanuel. *Practical Philosophy*. Edited by Mary J. Gregor. Cambridge Edition of the Works of Immanuel Kant. Cambridge: Cambridge University Press, 1999.

Kesslen, Ben. "How the Idea of a 'Transgender Contagion' Went Viral—and Caused Untold Harm." *MIT Technology Review*, Aug. 18, 2022. https://www.technologyreview.com/2022/08/18/1057135/transgender-contagion-gender-dysphoria/.

Kimbell, John. *The Atonement in Lukan Theology*. Newcastle upon Tyne, Eng.: Cambridge Scholars, 2014.

Kuefler, Mathew. *The Manly Eunuch: Masculinity, Gender Ambiguity, and Christian Ideology in Late Antiquity*. Chicago Series on Sexuality, History, and Society. Chicago: University of Chicago Press, 2001.

Küng, Hans. *What I Believe*. Translated by John Bowden. London: Continuum, 2010.

LaCocque, André, and Paul Ricoeur. *Thinking Biblically: Exegetical and Hermeneutical Studies*. Translated by David Pellauer. Chicago: University of Chicago Press, 1998.

Lentz, Steph. *In/Out: A Scandalous Story of Falling Into Love and Out of the Church*. Sydney: ABC, 2023.

Levinson, Bernard M. *"The Right Chorale": Studies in Biblical Law and Interpretation*. Classical and Near Eastern Studies. Winona Lake, IN: Eisenbrauns, 2011.

———. "You Must Not Add Anything to What I Command You: Paradoxes of Canon and Authorship in Ancient Israel." *Numen* 50 (2003) 1–51. https://doi.org/10.1163/156852703321103238.

Luther, Martin. *Commentaries on 1 Corinthians 7, 1 Corinthians 15, Lectures on Timothy*. Edited by Hilton C. Oswald. Translated by E. Sittler and M. Bertram. Vol. 28 of *Luther's Works*. St. Louis: Concordia, 1958.

———. *Luther's Commentary on Genesis*. Translated by J. Theodore Mueller. 2 vols. Grand Rapids: Zondervan, 1958.

———. *What Luther Says: An Anthology*. Edited by Edwin M. Plass. 3 vols. St. Louis: Concordia, 1959.

MacCulloch, Diarmaid. *Lower Than the Angels: A History of Sex and Christianity*. N.p.: Allen and Lane, 2024.

MacDonald, Dennis R. *The Gospels and Homer: Imitations of Greek Epic in Mark and Luke-Acts*. 2 vols. New Testament and Greek Literature. Lanham, MD: Rowman & Littlefield, 2014.

———. *The Homeric Epics and the Gospel of Mark*. New Haven, CT: Yale University Press, 2000.

Manne, Anne. *Crimes of the Cross: The Anglican Paedophile Network of Newcastle, Its Protectors and the Man Who Fought for Justice*. Collingwood, Aus.: Black, 2024.

Mascord, Keith A. *Alvin Plantinga and Christian Apologetics*. Paternoster Theological Monographs. Eugene, OR: Wipf and Stock, 2007.

———. "The Bible Is the True Prejudice in Christian Opposition to Marriage Equality." *Guardian*, Mar. 22, 2016. https://www.theguardian.com/commentisfree/2016/mar/22/the-bible-is-the-true-prejudice-in-christian-opposition-to-marriage-equality.

———. "The Ever Shrinking Case Against Same-Sex Marriage." ABC, Oct. 7, 2016. https://www.abc.net.au/religion/the-ever-shrinking-case-against-same-sex-marriage/10096458.

———. *Faith Without Fear: Risky Choices Facing Contemporary Christians*. Melbourne: Morning Star, 2016.

———. "The Interview: Rev Keith Mascord on Faith Withour [sic] Fear." ABC, June 12, 2016. Interview by Noel Debien. https://www.abc.net.au/sundaynights/stories/s4480492.htm.

———. *A Restless Faith: Leaving Fundamentalism in a Quest for God*. N.p.: Xlibris, 2012.

———. *A Restless Faith: Leaving Fundamentalism in a Quest for God*. Eugene, OR: Wipf and Stock, 2016.

———. "Video: *The Drum* Wednesday September 27." ABC, Sept. 28, 2016. Interview by Julia Baird. https://www.abc.net.au/news/2016-09-28/the-drum-wednesday-september-27/7886618.

Mbanda, Lauren. "Statement from the Gafcon Primates on Church of England General Synod." GAFCON, Nov. 16, 2023. https://www.gafcon.org/communique-updates/statement-from-the-gafcon-primates-on-church-of-england-general-synod/.

McGilchrist, Iain. *The Matter with Things: Our Brains, Our Delusions, and the Unmasking of the World*. 2 vols. London: Perspectiva, 2021.

McNeill, John J. *The Church and the Homosexual*. 4th ed. Boston: Beacon, 1993.

Merrell, Judith, ed. *Celtic Blessings*. N.p.: TLM, 2020.

Mesa, Ivan, ed. *Before You Lose Your Faith: Deconstructing Doubt in the Church*. Wheaton, IL: Gospel Coalition, 2021.

Miller, Richard C. *Resurrection and Reception in Early Christianity*. Routledge Studies in Religion. New York: Routledge Taylor & Francis, 2015.

NBC News. "Exit Polls." NBC, last updated Nov. 25, 2024 https://www.nbcnews.com/politics/2024-elections/exit-polls.

O'Donohue, John. *To Bless the Space Between Us: A Book of Blessing*. New York: Convergent, 2008.

Office for National Statistics. "Religion, England and Wales: Census 2021." Office for National Statistics, 2021. https://www.ons.gov.uk/peoplepopulationandcommunity/culturalidentity/religion/bulletins/religionenglandandwales/census2021.

Pew Research. "Modeling the Future of Religion in America." Pew Research, Sept. 13, 2022. https://www.pewresearch.org/religion/2022/09/13/modeling-the-future-of-religion-in-america/.

Phelps-Roper, Megan. "The Witch Trials of J. K. Rowling." Free Press, Feb. 14, 2023. https://www.thefp.com/p/the-witch-trials-of-jk-rowling.

———, host. *The Witch Trials of J. K. Rowling*. Free Press, 2023. https://www.thefp.com/witchtrials#about__the-show.

Pierce, Ronald W., et al., eds. *Discovering Biblical Equality: Biblical, Theological, Cultural, and Practical Perspectives*. 3rd ed. Downers Grove, IL: IVP Academic, 2021.

Plantinga, Alvin. "Christian Philosophy at the End of the 20th Century." In *Christian Philosophy at the Close of the Twentieth Century*, edited by Sander Griffioen and Bert M. Balk, 29–54. Kampen, Neth.: Kok, 1995.

———. *Warranted Christian Belief*. Oxford: Oxford University Press, 2000.

Plato. "The Allegory of the Cave (*Republic*, Book Seven)." St. Bonaventure University, n.d. Translated by Oleg Bychkov. https://web.sbu.edu/theology/bychkov/plato%20republic%207.pdf.

———. "The Apology of Socrates, 28–36." Lexundria, n.d. Translated by Benjamin Jowett. https://lexundria.com/plat_apol/28-36/j.

———. "The Apology of Socrates, 37–42." Lexundria, n.d. Translated by Benjamin Jowett. https://lexundria.com/plat_apol/37-42/j.

Poletti, Jonathan. "The #1 Female Evangelical Scholar Says She's Leaving the Religion." Medium, Nov. 21, 2023. https://medium.com/belover/the-1-female-evangelical-scholar-says-i-give-up-on-the-religion-293aab184d1f.

Poulson, Graham. "Towards an Aboriginal Theology." *Pacifica* 19 (2006) 310–20.

Powell, Russell. "PM, Premier Attend Orlando Commemoration Service." Sydney Anglicans, June 16, 2016. https://sydneyanglicans.net/news/pm-premier-attend-orlando-commemoration-service.

Prior, Karen Swallow. "Don't Go Into a Relationship—or Institution—Thinking You Can Change Them." RNS, Nov. 20, 2023. https://religionnews.com/2023/11/20/dont-go-into-a-relationship-or-institution-thinking-you-can-change-them/.

Pusey, Edward Bouverie, et al., eds. *A Library of Fathers of the Holy Catholic Church: Anterior to the Division of the East and West*. 51 vols. Oxford: Parker, 1838–81.

Raymo, Chet. *Skeptics and True Believers: The Exhilarating Connection Between Science and Religion*. New York: Walker, 1998.

Ricoeur, Paul. "The Critique of Religion." In *The Philosophy of Paul Ricoeur: An Anthology of His Work*, edited by Charles E. Reagan and David Stewart, translated by R. B. DeFord, 213–22. Boston: Beacon, 1978.

———. "Existence and Hermeneutics." In *The Conflict of Interpretations: Essays in Hermeneutics*, edited by Don Ihde, translated by Kathleen McLaughlin, 16–17. Evanston, IL: Northwestern University Press, 1974.

———. *Freud and Philosophy: An Essay on Interpretation*. Translated by Denis Savage. Terry Lectures. New Haven, CT: Yale University Press, 1970.

———. *The Symbolism of Evil*. Boston: Beacon, 1967.

Roberts, Alexander, and James Donaldson, eds. *The Ante-Nicene Fathers*. 1885–87. 10 vols. Repr., Grand Rapids: Eerdmans, 1968.

Rohr, Richard. "Order, Disorder, Reorder (The Stage of Initiation)." YouTube, Apr. 21, 2018. https://www.youtube.com/watch?v=QfI2bw653wc.

———. *The Universal Christ: How a Forgotten Reality Can Change Everything We See, Hope For and Believe*. London: SPCK, 2019.

Russell, Bertrand. *"Why I Am Not a Christian": And Other Essays on Religion and Related Subjects*. New York: Simon & Schuster, 1927.

Shakespeare, William. *The Tragedy of Macbeth, with Related Readings.* Global Shakespeare. Albany: International Thomson, 1997.

Smyth, Dermot. *Understanding Country: The Importance of Land and Sea in Aboriginal and Torres Strait Islander Societies.* Council for Aboriginal Reconciliation Key Issue Paper 1. Canberra: Australian Government, 1994. https://www.dermotsmyth.com.au/wp-content/uploads/2019/01/Understanding-Country.pdf.

Standing Committee of the General Synod of the Church of England in Australia Sydney, The. *An Australian Prayer Book: For Use Together with the Book of Common Prayer, 1662.* Sydney: Anglican Information Office, 1978.

Statistics Canada. "The Canadian Census: A Rich Portrait of the Country's Religious and Ethnocultural Diversity." Statistics Canada, Oct. 26, 2022. https://www150.statcan.gc.ca/n1/daily-quotidien/221026/dq221026b-eng.htm.

Stewart, Al. "The Social Contagion Targeting Girls, and What Parents Can Do to Protect Their Children." Eternal Perspective Ministries, Sept. 18, 2023. https://www.epm.org/resources/2023/Sep/18/social-contagion-targeting-girls/.

Stumpf, Samuel Enoch. *Socrates to Sartre: A History of Philosophy.* New York: McGraw-Hill, 1966.

Sydney Anglicans. *Synod 2024: Attendance Patterns Report Appendices.* Sydney Anglicans, 2024. https://www.sds.asn.au/sites/default/files/Attendance%20Patterns%20Report%20-%20Appendices%20A%20to%20G.pdf?doc_id=NjkwNTE=.

Tennyson, Alfred, Lord. "In Memoriam A. H. H." Poets, n.d. https://poets.org/poem/memoriam-h-h.

Tobolowsky, Andrew. "History, Myth and the Shrinking of Genre Borders." *Eidolon,* May 16, 2016. https://eidolon.pub/history-myth-and-the-shrinking-of-genre-borders-e7ad46ca745.

Tordoff, Diana M., et al. "Mental Health Outcomes in Transgender and Nonbinary Youths Receiving Gender-Affirming Care." *JAMA Network Open* 5 (2022) e220978. https://www.doi.org/10.1001/jamanetworkopen.2022.0978.

Trans Justice Project. *The Anti-Discrimination Handbook.* New York: Trans Justice Project, 2020.

Van Dyke, Henry. "I Am Standing upon the Seashore." All Poetry, n.d. https://allpoetry.com/I-Am-Standing-Upon-The-Seashore.

Walsh, Robyn Faith. *The Origins of Early Christian Literature: Contextualizing the New Testament Within Greco-Roman Literary Culture.* Cambridge: Cambridge University Press, 2021.

Wesley, Margaret. "Her Hour Has Come: Birth and Breastfeeding Imagery in the Gospel of John." Rev Dr Margaret Wesley, Apr. 5, 2024. https://open.substack.com/pub/revdrmargaretwesley/p/her-hour-has-come.

Wright, G. Ernest. *God Who Acts: Biblical Theology as Recital.* Studies in Biblical Theology 8. Chicago: Regnery, 1952.

Wright, Jacob L. *Why the Bible Began: An Alternative History of Scripture and Its Origins* Cambridge: Cambridge University Press, 2023.

Wright, N. T. *The Resurrection of the Son of God.* Vol. 3 of *Christian Origins and the Question of God.* Minneapolis: Fortress, 2003.

Wright, N. T., and Michael F. Bird. *The New Testament in Its World: An Introduction to the History, Literature, and Theology of the First Christians.* London: SPCK, 2019.

Xenophon. *Memorabilia.* Translated by Amy L. Bonnette. Ithaca: Cornell University Press, 1994.

Young, Stephen L. "Protective Strategies and the Prestige of the 'Academic': A Religious Studies and Practice Theory Redescription of Evangelical Inerrantist Scholarship." *Biblical Interpretation* 23 (2015) 1–35.

Index

A
Adam/Eve, 18–20, 22, 28, 51–52
Advocacy, 119–26
Allison, Dale, 40–41,173–75, 190–91
Appropriation, 96–99
Aquinas, 7, 106, 108
Augustine, 7, 102, 106, 108
Authorship, Biblical books, 45, 69, 71, 78–79, 82–83, 99, 105, 110, 132–34, 149

B
Barton, John., 69–70
Belief, 36–43
Biblical authority, 29, 43, 64, 83, 95–96, 110, 134, 136–38, 153–54, 177, 184
Bible as revelation, 11–12, 44–45
Brettler, Marc, 44–45, 99–100
Brownson, James, 185–86
Buckingham, Rob, 186

C
Calvin, John, 42, 52–54, 56, 107, 168
Celtic spirituality, 165–67, 179–80
Certainty, 39, 42–44, 186–87, 189–90
Cheng, Patrick, 186
Christianity in decline, 20–28
Christology, 38, 86–89
Campolo, Tony, 186
Cooper, Natalie, 121–22
Courage, 8, 12, Ch.5, 183, 189
Creation/evolution, 17–19, 134, 183
Creeds, 10, 38–39, 173, 181, 184, 186
Croucher, Rowland, 186

D
Davies, Glenn, 120–22, 124–25, 135
Davies, Paul, 50–51
Davis, Noel, 14, 33, 101, 147
Deconstruction, Faith, 27, 30, 63, 96, 144–45, 184–86, 188
Deuteronomy/Deuteronomistic history, 82–85
Dever, William., 65–66, 80–81, 176
Dickson, John., 29–30, 68
Discipleship, 181–83
Doyle, Glennon, 186
Dunn, James, 88–89
Dulwich Hill, Holy Trinity, 186–88

E
Edman, Elizabeth, 186
Ehrman, Bart, 86–89, 91–94
Enns, Peter., 43, 143
Equal Voices,122–23
Eschatology, 89–91
Evangelicalism, 9, 17, 20, 27–28, 30, 42, 53. 57, 62, 72, 88, 95, 98, 104, 107, 115, 132–33, 138–40, 144, 153, 155–56, 177, 185–86
Evolution, 17–19, 134 , 167, 183
Exodus, The, 21–22, 37, 39, 64–66, 70–71

F
Fables, 23–24, 84, 87, 149, 152, 158
Fall of humankind, 131, 134
Fenton, Steff, 68, 105, 111–13, 121–22, 186
Fundamentalism, 43, 48, 153, 171

INDEX

G
GAFCON, 121, 135-42, 177
Genesis chapters 1-11, 78, 99, 133-34, 150, 176
Glover, Matt, 186
Gospel, The, 20, 117, 135, 138, 144, 157, 192
Gospel Coalition, 62, 66, 71, 109
Grayling, A.C., 11-12, 43-44
Gushee, David, 185

H
Hartke, Austen, 186
Harvey, Van, 9-11, 179
Hays, Christopher, 185
Hays, Richard, 185
Held Evans, Rachel, 27, 186
Hercock, Mike, 186
Hermeneutics, 95-100, 118-19
Holland, Tom, 7, 80-81, 157-58
Hollier, Joel, 68
Homosexuality, 29-31, 69, 72, 107-11, 124, 135-42, 185
Honesty, 12, 15-16, 31, 42-43, 45, 48, 57, 64, 66-67, 77, 96, 117-18, 173-74, 184, 189-92
Hope, 51, 79, 85, 97-98, Ch.9, 173, 184-85, 191-92
Humility, Ch.3, 64, 73, 142, 144-45, 168, 173-74, 178-79, 183, 186, 188-90

I
Imagination, Ch.6, 150, 173, 183-84
Incarnation, 87-89, 132, 168, 180-81
Indigenous history, culture/religion, 20, 53, 79, 160-61, 167
Inerrancy, 95, 123, 130, 132-34, 153, 155, 184
Inkpin, Josephine, 117-18, 186
Inquisitiveness, Ch.2, 34, 57, 67, 77, 166, 171-72

J
Jensen, Peter, 25, 131, 134-35
Jensen, Philip, 119
Judd, Andrew, 79, 158
Justin Martyr, 6, 23

K
Kant, Immanuel, 8-9
Kirby, Michael, 120, 125
Kirk, Daniel, 186
Knowledge, 36-43
Kung, Hans, 168

L
Lentz, Steph, 66-69, 71-72, 144, 171-72
Leviticus, 29, 110-11
Liberation 107, Ch.8, 180
Literalism, 5, 20, 66, 77, 124, 130-31, 134, 140, 152-56
Love, 85, Ch.7, 140-42, 149-50, 178, 183, 185, 187-88, 190-91
Luther, Martin, 4-6, 70, 106, 108, 140, 152, 155

M
Miller, Richard, 23-24, 54, 77-78
Monotheism, 38, 55, 65, 81, 160, 162-64, 181
Montgomery, John, 9-10
Mowczko, Margaret, 107
Moore Theological College, 7, 9, 70-71, 119-20, 131-35
Moses, 22-23, 29, 37, 44-45, 64-66, 69, 78, 87-88, 102, 157
Murray, Les, 170
Mythology, 9-10, 12, 20-24, 71, 77-79, 97, 99, 109, 133-34, 148, 150-52, 154-64, 173, 183

N
Neff, Daniel, 186
Newcastle, Anglican Diocese of, 26, 126, 142
Noah, 20, 22, 54, 69, 131

O
O'Donohue, John, 76, 127, 145, 167, 180

P
Panentheism, 165-69, 180, 184-85
Pastoral Epistles, 28-29, 105, 132, 134
Persistence, Ch.4, 61, 68, 78
Peterson, Eugene, 186

Plantinga, Alvin, 36–42, 160
Polytheism, 38, 55, 80–81, 157, 160, 162–64

R
Religion, origins of, 16–17, 77, 160–64, 167
Resurrection, 39–42, 57, 66, 86, 88, 90, 94, 133, 150–53, 168–69
Ricoeur, Paul, 96–99, 104, 110, 145
Rohr, Richard, 53, 144–45, 165, 184–85

S
Same-sex marriage, 30, 67, 109–10, 120
Socrates, 3, 34–35, 46, 48–49f, 61–62, 173–75, 178–79, 181–83
Spinoza, Baruch, 69
Spirituality, 112, 161, 165, 179–80, 183
Stead, Michael, 123–24

Stewart, Al, 115–18
Swallow Prior, Karen, 62–63, 71–72
Sydney, Anglican Diocese of, 24–25, 44, 67–68, 119–26, 130, 133, 171, 177

T
Tertullian, 4–6, 106, 108
Thompson, Mark, 134
Tonstad, Linn Marie, 186
Trinity, 38, 86–89, 180–81, 184, 188
Theodicy, 54, 82–84
Transgender/gender diverse, 111–19

W
Wallis, Jim, 186
Warrant, 36–37
Wesley, Margaret, 94
Women in ministry, 28, 103–7
Wright, N.T., 57

www.ingramcontent.com/pod-product-compliance
Lightning Source LLC
Chambersburg PA
CBHW070322230426
43663CB00011B/2197